007

'He's what you would expect of an adolescent mind – which I happen to possess'

Ian Fleming

The name's... Do we really need to go on? Just those two words are enough to conjure up the most famous fictional character of the 20th century. In this ever-changing world in which we live, James Bond remains essentially the same. His appearance has changed (albeit not as often as his favoured vintage of champagne) but 007 is recognisably the same character **Ian Fleming** dreamt up in 1952, the man every boy wants to be. He is a superhero without superpowers; a St George fighting contemporary dragons with a handgun and a stream of one-liners; a secret agent as admired by men (even his enemies) as he is irresistible to women; a hero so indestructible his popularity has survived changing political and sexual mores, some formulaic films and (post-Fleming) some deeply average thrillers.

We might not all want to be Bond (or slip between the sheets with him) but a character who started out as one man's fantasy has become a fantasy enough of us share (or enjoy) to support a small industry, symbolised by the seemingly unstoppable movie franchise which has racked up more than $2 billion at the box office. His global appeal is, perhaps, Bond's most stupendous feat of all: invented by a middle-aged, upper-middle class Brit, he has become a nationless, classless, ageless icon, as recognisable as Elvis, JFK or Madonna (mother of Lourdes, not of Jesus).

He may not be able to fly but he has proved as indestructible a superhero as **Superman**. And, in an industrial sense, he has more staying power than winged wonders or men of steel. Although there have been some duff Bond movies, the quality control exercised, mainly by the **Broccolis** (Cubby and Barbara), has, by Hollywood standards, been exceptional. You only have to look at the various Tarzan movies to see the shambles Bond's celluloid career could have become in other hands.

His appeal may rest in the fact that we don't know much about him. At least little that matters. He is a hero who never bores us because after half a century (and 20 movies, 33 novels, various novelisations and short stories) we know less about what makes him tick than we'd discover if we asked him round for dinner.

While this book won't tell you what makes Bond tick, it hopes to tell you almost everything else you need to know about 007, his creator, the books and movies, the girls he's bedded, the villains he's bested and the gadgets he's tested. So mix yourself a vodka martini (you'll find the recipe on p109) and enjoy.

In the 1960s, 007 caused the kind of mayhem usually associated with the Beatles ▲

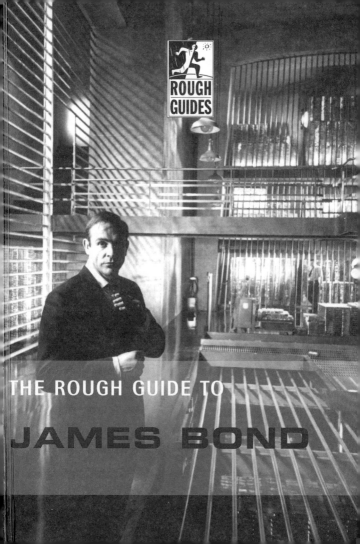

ROUGH
GUIDES

THE ROUGH GUIDE TO

JAMES BOND

Credits

Text editor: Paul Simpson
Contributors: Helen Rodiss, Richard Pendleton, Sean Campbell, Caroline Elliott,
Victoria Williams, Juliette Wills, Steve Morgan, David Cottrell, Derek Harbinson

Production: Michaela Dooley, Caroline Hunt, Sue Weekes
Picture editor: Dominique Campbell
Thanks to: Mark Ellingham, Simon Kanter, Michelle Draycott, Julia Bovis, Chas Chandler

Cover design by Jon Butterworth

Designed by Hazel Brown, Jon Butterworth
Printed in Spain by Graphy Cems
Dedicated to: Peter Fleming, Jack Simpson, Alex and Georgia Hunt,
Theo, Scott, the Rodisses, Dom Perignon and 007.

Pictures

Special thanks to Rex Features, Getty Images and Magnum Photos.
Cover: George Rodger/Magnum Photos
Rex Features; Getty Images; David Hurn, Martin Parr, George Rodger/Magnum Photos;
www.pictorialpress.com; Weiderfeld and Nicholson Publishing; Pan Books Ltd;
J.M. Dent & Sons Ltd; Jonathan Cape Ltd; jamesbond007.net; Coronet Books;
Hodder & Stoughton; Nead-An-Eoin Publishing; Warner Bros. Publication;
Warner Music; Switzerland Tourism/swiss-image.ch; www.islandoutpost.com;
Glidrose Publications Limited; John McLusky/Daily Express; Yaroslav Horak/
Daily Express; www.pcisys.net/~pak/ccg-movielists.html; Penguin Classics

Publishing Information

This edition published November 2002 was prepared by
Haymarket Customer Publishing for Rough Guides Ltd,
80 Strand, London WC2R 0RL

Distributed by the Penguin Group

Penguin Books Ltd, 80 Strand, London WC2R 0RL

No part of this book may be reproduced in any form without permission
from the publisher except for the quotation of brief passages in reviews.
© Rough Guides/Haymarket Customer Publishing 288pp

A catalogue record for this book is available from the British Library
ISBN 1-84353-142-9

CONTENTS

001
THE ORIGINS
The roots of the world's most
famous fictional character

007

'The scent and smoke and sweat of a casino are nauseating at three in the morning'

The opening line of Ian Fleming's first James Bond novel, Casino Royale

Let's be quite clear about this, **James Bond** is dead. Or to be precise, the ornithologist called James Bond (whose seminal book **Birds Of The West Indies** Ian Fleming was reading as he desperately searched for a name for his fictional secret agent) is dead. He died in 1989, having given his name to the 20th century's most famous fictional character and receiving, in slightly unfair exchange, a signed copy of *You Only Live Twice*. The two met briefly on Fleming's Jamaican estate Goldeneye and Fleming happily introduced the ornithologist to a Canadian TV crew saying: 'This is the real James Bond'.

Fleming liked the name immediately, saying later, 'I was determined my secret agent should be as anonymous as possible. This name, **brief, unromantic and yet very masculine**, was just what I needed.' If only everything about the creation of Bond

9

was as clear. In this chapter we look at the genesis of 007, the life of his creator, the immaculate timing of his conception, and cast a slide rule over all the various candidates who have been suggested as models for the real Bond.

The opening line about smoke and sweat in an early morning casino was a low-key entrance for a character who would found the world's most durable movie franchise. If you think of the major cultural icons of the last half of the 20th century – Elvis, the Beatles, Muhammed Ali, Madonna – James Bond is the only icon to be a figment of his creator's imagination. So the story of Bond should logically start with the story of Ian Lancaster Fleming, because only a man as complex as Fleming could have created such a character.

Fleming was born on 28 May 1908, the second son of snobbish, frivolous, wealthy socialite, **Evelyn Ste Croix Rose** (who claimed descent from John of Gaunt) and **Valentine Fleming**, Conservative MP, and friend to **Winston Churchill**. His father died in World War I when Ian was eight, and remained the dashing young hero in his son's loyal imagination, a role model who was almost impossible to live up to. As a child, Ian was encouraged to pray to be as good as his father – the prayers never worked. As if dad wasn't competition enough there was his elder brother **Peter Fleming**, a year older than Ian and ill with colitis as a young child. Sibling rivalry made a dramatic debut in the family when Ian became so incensed by the attention Peter was getting that he screamed down the dining room in a Swiss hotel.

Peter duplicated his father's success at both Eton and Oxford, whilst Ian refused to enter any kind of academic competition, preferring to spend his hours in such Bondian activities as chasing women from nearby Windsor. Sandhurst proved equally pointless, Ian discovering only that obeying orders wasn't his thing. A string of careers followed spells in journalism (the contacts would later prove useful when he was soliciting good reviews for his novels) and a period as 'the world's worst

As a commander of naval intelligence, Fleming was less heroic than 007 ▲

More than a spy novelist

If you're going to be typecast as anything, it might as well be as the creator of the most famous spy stories ever written. Amazing as it may sound, James Bond didn't occupy every waking hour of Ian Fleming's life. Once in a while he did leave the torrid world of villains, world domination and women, and offered the world a very different side to himself...

A desperate Truly Scrumptious pleads with Q to tell her where the 'Fly' button is ▲

Chitty Chitty Bang Bang

'You'll find a slight squeeze on the hooter an excellent safety precaution, Miss Scrumptious.' Not exactly what you'd expect to read in a 007 novel (although you can't help but notice the innuendo), but between *Thunderball* and *On Her Majesty's Secret Service*, Fleming wrote this children's story about a magical flying car. Inspired to write something for his young son Casper, after suffering a heart attack, Fleming's imagination went wild. His first foray into

children's books, Professor Caractacus Potts and friends were an instant success, with Fleming's friend Roald Dahl writing the screenplay for the 1968 film version (he also contributed to the screenplay for *You Only Live Twice*).

The Man From U.N.C.L.E.

Considering the reception which James Bond's first big-screen adventure, *Dr. No*, received, it wasn't a surprise that television producers scrambled onto the spy bandwagon. One such producer was Norman Felton, then better known as the producer of *Dr. Kildare*. Felton cheekily approached the man who started the phenomenon, Ian Fleming. From here, as is usual in Hollywood, everyone has their own story. Some say Fleming was forced to pull out due to pressure from Bond producers Harry Saltzman and Cubby Broccoli, who weren't keen on Fleming sharing his expertise. Others maintain Sam Rolfe, who was credited with creating the series, rejected most of Fleming's suggestions. In either case, Fleming's involvement with the spy series which was to become *The Man From U.N.C.L.E.* was brief – although he is credited with coming up with the name which would become synonymous with 1960s TV spies, Napoleon Solo, as well as that of *The Girl From U.N.C.L.E.* heroine, April Dancer. And THRUSH (as a sinister organisation of evildoers) pays obvious homage to SMERSH.

Poppies Are Also Flowers

Two years after working on what was to be his last James Bond film, veteran 007 director Terence Young joined forces with Fleming again on a vastly different project. In association with the UN, who were keen to bolster efforts to stop drug trafficking, Fleming came up with a story examining the progress of heroin from a simple flower to a drug on the streets of New York. Fleming died before his vision was brought to the screen, but Young, with the help of his wife

Jo Eisinger, produced a star-studded tale, with Omar Sharif, Trevor Howard and Rita Hayworth appearing, amongst others.

The Diamond Smugglers

Written in 1957, Fleming stuck to what he knew best, with another espionage thriller, this time based on actual events of diamond smuggling in Africa. Minus the imitable charm of 007, Rank originally bought the film rights, but the film still resides in development hell.

Thrilling Cities

Although Ian's wife Ann was confused how her husband managed to make cities 'thrilling', as he never stopped to have a proper look around, Fleming wrote a series of books in 1959 on places such as Berlin, Monte Carlo and Tokyo. These focused on areas which traditional travelogues steered clear of, such as brothels, massage parlours, casinos and mobsters. Although the series also included a mini Bond adventure (*007 in New York*) not everyone was enamoured by Fleming's unusual slant on travel writing, his editor complaining, 'We have to remember that for a great many of our readers, probably the majority, prostitution is not even a necessary evil, but something immoral and degrading. Again, striptease acts may be all right for callow youths and frustrated middle-aged men, but they are a vulgar and debased sort of entertainment for balanced people'.

stockbroker'. In 1939, with another world war imminent, Fleming found his niche in **Naval Intelligence**. Rapidly promoted to Commander, he acted as the right-hand man to one of Britain's top spymasters, **Admiral John Godfrey**. More of a Q than a Bond, Fleming took charge behind a desk, plotting.

Opinions vary about his effectiveness. Alexander Cockburn, in his essay *The Secret Agent*, denigrates Fleming's service, accusing him of indulging boyish fantasies, while simultaneously crediting him with being instrumental in the formation of the

The number 7

Ian Fleming may have thought that his spy hero needed a nondescript name, but he was careful to choose a suitably catchy codename, 007. He doubtless had specific reasons for choosing seven. For example, why not 006, who instead featured in both *Dr. No* and *GoldenEye*, played by Timothy Moxon and Sean Bean respectively? Or 009, who featured in *Octopussy*, played by Andy Bradford? Or 001, a number generally associated with the best? There's just something about the number seven.

7 = number of deadly sins
Pride, envy, wrath, sloth, avarice, gluttony, lust. If it's not Bond lusting after the ladies, it's his arch-enemies greedily trying to take over the world. Seven is also famously the number of years after which a married man is supposed to get the itch to play around; 007 has never wanted to wait that long.

7 = number of archangels
007 may not be as pure as an angel, but you can't deny his determination to watch over the world.

7 = number of Os of advent
There are seven parts to the Magnificat, sung in the week before Christmas. These are often known as the Seven Os.

7 = number of virtues
Faith, hope, charity, fortitude, justice, prudence, temperance. James Bond has them in abundance.

7 = number of wonders of the world, hills of Rome and seas
Just to jog your memory, the Roman hills are: the Palatine, Capitoline, Quirinal, Caelian, Aventine, Esquiline, and Viminal. And there are seven seas if you split both the Atlantic and Pacific oceans into two parts, north and south.

7 = number of points you get for the letter D in Scrabble, in Finland
Not many people know that.

7 = the luckiest number
Since Pythagoras, in around 500BC.

CIA (Fleming was a confidant and ally of 'Wild' Bill Donovan, one of the leading lights in the CIA and its forerunner, the OSS).

Peace released Fleming from his duties but renewed the old dilemma, what was he to do? His personal life was almost as disordered as Bond's: his dalliance with **Lady Ann Rothermere**, the wife of media mogul **Lord Rothermere**, led to her pregnancy, divorce, and subsequent marriage to Ian. This dramatic chain of events led, in some degree, to the birth of James Bond. Fleming downplayed his writing (although he cared enough about his prose to ask **Raymond Chandler** and **Noel Coward** for their thoughts on his hero), yet Ian also admitted he was struggling to come to terms with the dramatic change to his lifestyle, telling friends that writing enabled him to take his mind off the frightening prospect of his nuptials. It wasn't just about his own escapism, or his need to occupy his time, with Ann so focused on her unborn child's health, she abstained from sex.

He was also writing for one of the oldest and most common reasons in the world: he needed the money. Perhaps most of all, Ian felt he needed to prove to Ann she had made the right decision in leaving Lord Rothermere, one which would be acceptable to her and the social circle she immersed herself in. 'His book was both a present to her, and his entrée, however modest, into her grown-up world of letters and ideas,' notes Fleming's best biographer Andrew Lycett.

And so, at the turn of 1952, Ian began writing **Casino Royale**, possibly finishing it in as little as four weeks (a rate of 2,000 words a day). The initial reception to his hero was muted, Julian Symons calling it 'staggeringly implausible and thoroughly exciting' – two slightly contradictory characteristics that Bond has been famous for ever since.

By 1957, when Fleming was writing his fifth 007 novel *From Russia With Love*, he was so fed up with his creation's failure to take the world by storm that he considered killing him off, creating a cliffhanger ending which gave him that option.

Various attempts to translate Bond into other media stalled or flopped. But help was at hand, a swinging new decade (the 1960s) and a swinging new President of the United States in Bond fan **John F Kennedy**. His efforts to interest Hollywood in his character also finally paid off, with **Cubby Broccoli** and **Harry Saltzman** buying up the film rights. The deal ensured Bond's viability, in literary and celluloid terms, even if Fleming never seemed that impressed by any of the Bond movies he saw before his untimely death – at the age of 56 – in 1964.

Bond's popularity is apparently easily explicable and yet very mysterious. His lifestyle, his success with the opposite sex, his never having to worry about the mortgage, all appeal to men who secretly dream that they might be 007, that one day **Carly Simon** will sing 'Nobody does it better' about them. Fleming certainly understood this, telling an interviewer: 'James Bond is the author's pillow fantasy. It's very much the Walter Mitty syndrome – the feverish dreams of the author of what he might have been – the bang, bang, kiss, kiss, that sort of stuff. What you would expect of an adolescent mind, which I happen to possess.' Bond is, in many respects, an updated St George, a lone hero righting the wrongs of the world.

Critic **Tony Garland** says Bond's appeal lay in his accessibility to the average person. He is, 'a character who represents a one-million-dollar-man, but in actuality is a man like any other'. An indestructible superhero without the need to change in telephone boxes and whose powers, impressive though they may be, aren't super. He is, one critic noted, roughly the kind of hero you would expect to get if you put an advertising agency executive and a Freudian psychoanalyst in a room and asked them to create a hero who would appeal to the unconscious male psyche.

The Communist bloc was predictably enough not impressed, **Pravda** complaining that in Bond 'the laws are written with a pistol barrel and rape'. Other spy authors have been almost as sniffy, although **Len Deighton** worked on a Bond script, **John Le**

Carré once described them as 'cultural pornography'.

Some of Bond's success as a literary figure, as with his exploits in the bedroom, was a matter of timing. In 1952 Britain was just recovering from World War II, post-war austerity and rationing. Glamour and heroism were in short supply. Fleming as **Christopher Hitchens** noted in his essay in a new Penguin edition of Bond, paid 'loving attention to what we term the designer aspect of culture: the brand name and product placement… a daring refreshment in the post-austerity 1950s'. There are times when Fleming seems more at ease describing his characters' lifestyles than the characters themselves.

In *From Russia With Love*, Fleming writes lovingly of Bond's favourite meal of the day, breakfast: 'It consisted of very strong coffee, from De Bry in New Oxford Street, brewed in an American Chenex, of which he drank

Why 007?

Why indeed. Why not just, 'Number 7', or even 'Number 6' as the writers chose for Patrick McGoohan in *The Prisoner*? One theory has it that 00 was the prefix given to many Whitehall documents that Fleming saw on a day-to-day basis whilst working for Naval Intelligence. But there may be another explanation. The Duke of Marlborough (John Churchill, ancestor of Winston, the famous friend of Valentine Fleming, Ian's dad) used the 00 code with spies working for him in the War of the Spanish Succession (1701-1714 for those who didn't record the dates in their long-term memory banks in all those school history lessons). There's also the example of Elizabethan 007 spy Dr John Dee (see p23). Ultimately, as with so many questions about Bond, it's a case of you pays your money and you takes your choice.

17

The Duke of Marlborough: The first M? ▶

two large cups, black and without sugar. The single egg, in the dark blue eggcup with a gold ring around the top, was boiled for three and a third minutes.' Fleming didn't invent product placement but he would, you suspect, be quietly satisfied that his character's films rake in up to $100m from corporate sponsors.

In the early 1950s, with the Cold War at its height, it was possible to believe the Russians capable of the perfidy exhibited by SMERSH and SPECTRE, needing a 'blunt instrument' like Bond to sort them out. The films, created in the thaw of the early 1960s when Stalin's misdeeds already seemed like ancient history to many, were less hardline than the novels (in **From Russia With Love**, Fleming suggests that the thaw, initiated by **Nikita Khruschev**, is just a trick by the Russians to confuse the West). The movies conspicuously avoided the main hotspots of the Cold War: 007 was never sent to Berlin or to Cuba or, for that matter, Vietnam. When Fleming was devising 007, Britain had not yet begun to question its superpower status. The idea that the world's greatest secret agent was a Brit did not seem as daft as it might have done a decade later, when Britain's lack of superpower credentials was obvious to everybody except the Colonel Bufton-Tuftons who wrote to the **Daily Telegraph** pining for the good old days when the map of the world was dominated by the pink hues which signified the British empire.

As James Chapman, author of *Licence To Thrill*, a cultural history of the Bond films, put it, 'Fleming's Bond was in some ways the last of the great British imperial heroes. By the time the films are being made, the British empire is being dismantled at a pretty rapid pace. And Bond becomes this anachronism, this imperial hero in a post-imperial age.' The movies (and **Sean Connery**) stripped 007 of his imperial pretensions, making him more accessible and marketable. But the credit for creating the Bond myth must go to Fleming. In the last half century, the only other novelist whose fantasies have exerted a similar grip on a global audience of billions is probably **JR Tolkien**.

The original 007s

Ian Fleming always maintained that he created Bond in the mould of, 'an interesting man to whom extraordinary things happen'. As Fleming had spied for British Intelligence, had friends and contacts throughout British and US intelligence (with at least one CIA director, Allen Dulles, being a Bond fan) he had a head start when it came to spycraft. But Fleming's network of contacts and wealth of experiences means that naming the real Bond is a bit like identifying who shot 007's most famous fan, John F Kennedy. There's plenty of evidence, much of it contradictory, with no conclusive proof. But let's examine the real life models for Bond, apart, of course, from the ornithologist.

001 Ian Fleming

Who? The man himself

Probability rating 🔫🔫🔫🔫🔫🔫🔫

Although Fleming was the first to admit he was not the real James Bond, he did say that 007 was his slightly fantastic self-projection. Despite his denial that the Bond novels were in any way autobiographical, the parallels in the details of character and the life of author and agent are unmistakable. Fleming's novels pictured Bond as the same height as himself, with the same hairstyle and eye colour. They had both suffered the loss of a parent as child, held the same rank – that of Commander in Naval Intelligence – possessed a certain sartorial eloquence, smoked the finest cigarettes from a gunmetal case, and loved cars (Fleming was also partial to the odd vodka martini). Where women were concerned, Fleming liked his a certain way: very little make-up, maybe a touch of lipstick, and short, well-manicured but bare nails. They were generally around for as long as they remained detached from him, cast aside when they became too involved. The Bond of the novels preferred the same, although he was a little less fussy in the films. Fleming also littered his books with characters from his own past. (to give just two examples: M, the only man who Bond appears to respect, seems certain to have been based on Admiral Godfrey, Fleming's boss in Naval Intelligence (although Ian also called his mother M) while Miss Moneypenny could be the fictional incarnation of Fleming's own secretary, Paddy Bennett, although she denies she was ever in love with Fleming as Moneypenny was with Bond). To list every similarity between agent and author would take a book. Fleming first suggested David Niven and Cary Grant as potential movie Bonds, both of them surely idealised, glamorised, versions of how Fleming saw himself after a few vodka martinis.

002 Valentine Fleming

Who? Ian Fleming's father

Probability rating **FFFFF**FF

Killed during World War I when Ian was almost nine years old, Valentine Fleming remained a commanding influence on his son throughout his life. Like Bond, Valentine was a man of combat, his services during World War I praised by Winston Churchill who wrote his obituary in *The Times*, highlighting his 'loveable and charming personality', two traits frequently used in relation to Ian's literary creation (and Ian). In the Fleming family, Valentine became a mythical figure, eulogised by his widow Evelyn. That Valentine was not quite the saint in life he became in death is suggested by his will, which would have financially penalise Evelyn if she married again. When Ian was writing *Casino Royale*, he was in the midst of what we might now call a mid-life crisis: depressed, perhaps even envying his father's heroic early death. And in 007 he created a character as brave and as charismatic as his father had always seemed to Ian as a child.

003 Dusko Popov

Who? A double agent

Probability rating: **FFFFF**FF

Ivan to the Germans, Tricycle to the British (the nickname allegedly referring to his favourite sexual practice), Yugoslavian-born secret agent Dusko Popov had the trust of both Hitler and Churchill during World War II. Although his loyalties were said to lie firmly with the British, (he even refused payment from MI5, saying he was pleased to be working for a country which he had 'whole-hearted admiration for'), he was still a double agent. Popov was considered to be Britain's most important agent during World War II, successfully communicating false information to the Germans time and time again, as well as bringing information to the FBI of Japanese plans to attack Pearl Harbour months before the event occurred. It wasn't just his secret operations that led critics to believe Popov is Bond. Infamous as the playboy of the secret service, Popov counted Hollywood starlet Simone Simon as one of his countless conquests. His love of women extended to a love for the finer things in life and Popov was once described as an, 'intelligent, cultured man [who] would feel at home in society circles in any European or American capital, being much the usual type of international playboy.' Unfortunately, his lavish lifestyle had a price: he reputedly managed to spend $80,000 ($1m in today's money) in just 14 months while on a counter-espionage operation in New York.

The early Bond spin-offs

Although Cubby Broccoli and Harry Saltzman would like audiences to believe they happened to get it right first time when 007 first uttered the words, 'The name's Bond... James Bond' in *Dr. No*, by 1962 there had already been a few unsuccessful attempts to bring Fleming's spy hero to life.

Climax!

In October 1954, James Bond made his debut on the *Chrysler Climax Mystery Theater* series. A live TV version of *Casino Royale* saw CBS making use of poetic licence, with Bond (Barry Nelson) as a fast-talking American secret agent, a far cry from the suave, cool British spy, aided by British agent Clarence Leiter (Michael Pate). Peter Lorre as villain Le Chiffre stole the show when he came back to life, getting up moments after being killed by Bond, in order to head back to the comfort of his dressing room.

James Bond, the cartoon strip

Although Fleming's fifth 007 novel, *From Russia With Love*, had the approval of President Kennedy, it was the support of Edward Pickering, managing editor of the *Daily Express*, which led to James Bond the cartoon strip. Fleming initially had misgivings, but eventually yielded to the inevitable. Written by Anthony Hearne and Henry Gammidge with illustrations by John McLusky, McLusky's James Bond was based on an amalga-mation of Hollywood actors such as Robert Taylor and Gary Cooper, a hard, very masculine hero and a million miles away from Fleming's own vision, deemed outdated by McLusky. The stories were close enough to the novels to maintain the original fan base whilst attracting new readers. An immediate success, the cartoons may have provided the visual groundwork for the films. Despite its success, the strip came to an abrupt end in the middle of *Thunderball*, when Fleming angered *Express* owner Lord Beaverbrook by signing another deal with the *Sunday Times* for the rights to *The Living Daylights*. The rift was eventually resolved in 1964, the *Express* starting up again with *On Her Majesty's Secret Service*, with a new-look hero who was the spitting image of Sean Connery.

James Gunn, the TV series

Although Fleming was on his fourth Bond novel by 1956, it didn't stop him penning a similar character for TV in an attempt to take 007 from page to screen. Producer Henry Morgenthau III commissioned Fleming to write a pilot, the author coming up with a 28-page script entitled *James Gunn: Secret Agent*, with Commander Bond pitted against super-villain Dr No. The pilot eventually ran aground, but Fleming went on to develop the script into his fully-fledged sixth novel, *Dr. No*.

004 Sir Fitzroy Maclean

Who? Diplomat, soldier, politician, writer, photographer and friend to Fleming
Probability rating: $\mathbf{F F F F F}$

Throughout his life, **Brigadier Sir Fitzroy Hew Maclean** of Dunconnel always refused to comment on the recurrent rumours that he was the 'real' James Bond, which in itself ranks him fairly highly in the list of probable candidates. Of all of Fleming's compatriots in British Intelligence, the link to Fitzroy may be the most convincing. A founding member of the SAS, his exploits included parachuting into Nazi-occupied Yugoslavia as Churchill's personal envoy, in order to aid **Josip Broz-Tito** against the Nazis. When he died in 1996, aged 85, obituaries singled out his bravery in fighting behind enemy lines in both North Africa and the Balkans as having inspired Fleming's spy books. Maclean's rip-roaring auto-biographical account of his exploits, **Eastern Approaches**, has all the sweep and the gusto of a Fleming Bond novel. He even consulted with Fleming over their relative deals as authors, Fleming complaining sniffily to his publisher Jonathan Cape that a 'younger author' (he meant Maclean) had got much better royalties than he had been offered for his first Bond book *Casino Royale*. Maclean's help in this matter didn't, however, affect Fleming's opin-ion of his friend's book. After being sent a copy of *Eastern Approaches*, Fleming refused to write the usual complimentary letter so useful for filling up space on book jackets. The tone was, he insisted, 'patronising' and the book was 'not in the tradition of such books by Englishmen'. He also felt that Maclean had claimed too much credit for his wartime exploits, a strange thing for Fleming to accuse someone of given some of the fancies woven around his own time in Naval Intelligence. Maclean remained a friend of Fleming's, learning early on that the author shared at least one trait with his creation. In the 1930s, he once walked into Fleming's hotel room in Moscow to invite him to dinner, only to catch him in flagrante delicto. With Bondian irony, Maclean informed his wife that Fleming was 'sorry he could not accept the invitation because he was very, very busy.'

005 Patrick Dalzel Job

Who? A member of Fleming's '30 Assault Unit' team in Naval Intelligence
Probability rating: $\mathbf{F F F F}$

Unlike Fleming, Patrick Dalzel Job experienced more than his fair share of action working for Naval Intelligence. Before joining Fleming's '30 Assault Unit' in 1944/45 where he directed a reconnaissance team working on operations ahead of Allied lines in France, Belgium and Germany, he performed his own Bond style one-man mission in Norway. In

1940, having already led a force of 10,000 soldiers of the Allied North West Expeditionary Force safely into Norway without a single loss of life, he then, against the orders of his superiors, used the same boats to take the women, children and elderly of the town of Narvik to safety, just before it was bombed by the Luftwaffe. Unlike Bond, Job was monogamous. In a previous mission he had taken a young Norwegian girl to safety, only to track her down and marry her six years later. Dalzel Job, in his book *From Arctic Snow To Dust Of Normandy*, describes combat in very Bondian terms: 'It may seem terrible and inhumane that anyone could have in any way enjoyed that half hour; yet it would be dishonest to deny that I did enjoy it and I was tactless enough to say so.'

006 Peter Fleming

Who? Ian's older brother

Probability rating: 🔫🔫🔫🔫🔫🔫🔫

Did Bond represent Peter Fleming, the brother Ian revered throughout his youth and tried desperately to live up to? If so, Ian was never likely to admit it. Peter entered military intelligence before Ian, was a noted journalist, and wrote a novel sending up the bureaucratization of the security services, The Sixth Column, before Ian began Casino Royale (although Peter did dedicate it to his younger brother). Peter was more genuinely at ease with women than his brother and led the daring life Ian longed for. While Ian lived the good life, Peter was travelling the world, writing books set in almost as many locations as his brother's spy novels (*Brazilian Adventure*, *News From Tartary* and *One's Company*) full of the kind of derring do which Ian never got around to derring doing, but which would symbolise his creation. Peter's prose style reads like something a more sophisticated Bond might have written. He even wrote a light novel, The Flying Visit, about the problems posed by Hitler's unexpected arrival in England, which seemed terribly prescient when just over a year later Hitler's deputy Rudolf Hess unexpectedly flew to England. He also acted as 'Dr Knittpik' picking up mistakes in Ian's novels that his editors and proofers missed.

007 Dr John Dee

Who? The first British secret agent

Probability rating: 🔫🔫🔫🔫🔫🔫🔫

As strange as it may sound, Dr John Dee may have been the first ever British spy, serving Queen Elizabeth I. Dee was a learned, well-travelled man, very much like Fleming's creation, and well-respected for his work in mathematics and philosophy, as well as for his talents as an alchemist and astrologer. It was as an astrologer that he first served the Queen, asked by her to determine the most favourable day for her coronation. Elizabeth took a liking to him, as many women did, (so Bondian) and used Dee to help defeat the Spanish, sending him on secret missions to unearth King Phillip II's plans. The first recorded British spy, Dee even used the 007 code on messages to the Queen, the double zero said to represent a pair of eyes (signifying to the Queen that the document was 'For Your Eyes Only'), and the seven being the luckiest number.

008 Michael Mason

Who? A member of the Special Branch of British Naval Intelligence
Probability rating: 🔫🔫🔫

Like Merlin Minshall and Job, Michael Mason was recruited by Fleming to carry out special operations during the war. Of the three, Mason's tough rugged character was somewhat closer to Bond's. Mason had previously been a boxer before working as a trapper in Canada and was one of the agents Fleming drew on for his portrayal of 007, although Bond always looked better in his winter gear than Mason did.

009 Merlin Minshall

Who? A member of the Special Branch of British Naval Intelligence
Probability rating: 🔫🔫

An unlikely candidate if only because Minshall was the first to suggest the link, although he would later answer questions about the rumour with 'I don't know. I didn't find Fleming a very likeable fellow.' A member of Naval Intelligence, he worked with Fleming on a mission in the Danube, Minshall working undercover to chart the river's waters. Unfortunately, Minshall's account of this and other wartime exploits were slightly exaggerated. Yet he was the kind of character to make an impression on people, with a love of danger and adventure exemplified by his desire to be the first Englishman to do whatever he set his mind to, even if it be crossing the Sahara desert on a motorcycle.

010 James Boone

Who? British diplomat
Probability rating: 🔫

Possibly the strangest candidate comes from Miles Copeland, the ex-CIA agent and former manager of the rock group, the Police. Copeland, in his 1974 book *Without Cloak Or*

British agent Michael Mason, looking almost as elegant on the slopes as 007 ▲

Dagger, says that James Boone, a diplomat with the foreign office, was the real James Bond. Despite his day job as an admin inspector where he spent each day monotonously examining the inventories of supplies at British missions, Boone told prospective female conquests a different story, insisting that his mundane duties were merely a cover for his real, ever-so-glamorous secret role in the foreign office. Boone became something of a hero in diplomatic circles after he killed a man (who later turned out to be a heroin smuggler) in a fight over a girl in Tehran. It's a cracking story, which Copeland credits to friends of Fleming's in British intelligence. But that's probably as far as it goes.

0011 Sir Peter Smithers

Who? Member of Naval Intelligence

Probability rating: 🔫🔫🔫

Like Mason and Wilfred Dunderdale, Sir Peter Smithers isn't viewed as the 'real' James Bond, but the exploits of Smithers and his fellow naval commandos were used by Fleming as inspiration for his novels. Originally a barrister with a First from Oxford in History, Smithers met Fleming when the latter began working as assistant to Admiral Godfrey in naval intelligence. Taken out of active service after getting measles, Smithers was keen to help the war effort and so began working for Fleming on operations in France and Mexico. He was a friend and confidant to Fleming – 007's inventor often wrote to Smithers detailing his recent exploits and thoughts.

0012 Wilfred Dunderdale

Who? Commander in Naval Intelligence

Probability rating: 🔫🔫🔫🔫

The fact that Dunderdale was better known to his friends as Biffy suggests he and Bond were significantly different in character, (Bond would never have allowed anyone to call him by anything other than Bond, James – if it was a girl – or 007). The Odessa-born Biffy, however, was certainly a character, never without a pair of Cartier cuff links and so eager to get into the war that he financed his own espionage operations. As SIS station chief in Paris, the dashing commander was infamous for his bullet-proof Rolls Royce, which he drove around the city in a strangely high-profile fashion, his credentials being about as secret as 007's in the books. He was also one of the key players in the cracking of the German Enigma code. Dashing, with a love of elegant (bullet-proofed) cars, the similarities to Bond are fairly obvious.

002
THE BOOKS
All the novels, from Ian Fleming
to Raymond Benson, and more

007

'He was good-looking in a dark, rather cruel way...'

Vivienne Michel, The Spy Who Loved Me

James Bond, according to his author, was a cardboard dummy and the books were piffle. Ian Fleming's contemporaries agreed with him, one editor noting: 'We stand firmly against the things represented by Mr Fleming. We find his writings disgusting drivel.' If you had asked any of Fleming's peers (even his friends like **Noel Coward**) which British novelist from the 1950s and 1960s would have had an international following half a century later, they would have nominated **Anthony Powell**, author of *A Dance To The Music Of Time*, or **Angus Wilson**, whose most famous work was *The Old Men At The Zoo*. Or perhaps **Graham Greene**; Fleming's spy fiction was regarded, as Greene used to describe some of his novels, as 'entertainments'.

The conventional explanation for the fact that these books have sold over 50 million copies is that Fleming's novels are well written. (The cynical – that we only read them because of the movies – just doesn't hold up any longer.) The novels are written energetically, confidently and are full of the kind of knowledge which feels as if it can only be gained by actual experience. Yet in many of his books, Fleming runs out of steam – but none of this

◀ Ian Fleming at Goldeneye, the only place he could ever write a Bond novel

matters because he has created a hero who intrigues us; more complex than the dummy Fleming (in moments of despair) described, and more real than the movie hero. In the books Bond hurts, is afraid ('his stomach crawled with the ants of fear'), has scruples (he doesn't like to see a man killed in cold blood) and his weakness for the ladies seems less like a hormonal exercise than the desperate need of a loner to take love where he can find it. Fleming, knowing a hero is judged by the quality of his opposition, created a fantastic cast of villains (perverted or blessed with some physical oddity but always talkative, often cheating at cards) for Bond to combat.

Italian critic and novelist **Umberto Eco** famously reduced the Bond novel to a series of nine moves. He lists these moves as:

A M moves and gives a task to Bond;

B Villain moves and appears to Bond (perhaps in vicarious form);

C Bond moves and gives first check to villain or villain gives first check to Bond;

D Woman moves and shows herself;

E Bond takes woman (possesses her or begins her seduction);

F Villain captures Bond (with or without woman, or at different moments);

G Villain tortures Bond (with or without woman);

H Bond beats villain (kills him or kills his representative or assists in their killing);

I Bond, convalescing, enjoys woman, whom he then loses. Eco notes that some moves may occur more than once and they may not always occur in the same order. He is right, of course: this sequence is at the heart of the best Bond novels. But, as he also notes, this pattern adds to the books' appeal.

All the Bond novels and short stories, as well as a selection of books about or connected to 007, are reviewed in this section. First there is an attempt to place Fleming in the context of **spy fiction**. The reviews of the Bond novels, written by Fleming and his appointed successors, start on p35.

A potted history of spy fiction

Spy novels are often seen as a product of the Cold War but the genre can be traced at least as far back as 1823 and the publication of The Spy, a historical romance by James Fenimore Cooper, the American novelist more famous as the author of the Last Of The Mohicans. The Spy, which focused on British spy Major Andre in the War of Independence, was not critically acclaimed but then, noted one of Cooper's friends, 'it has been found impracticable to raise the spy into a hero'.

Despite its title, the novel was something of a false start for spy fiction. Although spies were used as devices by Victorian novelists like Wilkie Collins, it wasn't until the very end of the 19th century that spies returned to the fore with British writer William Le Queux's The Great War In England in 1897. The first of a series of best-selling novels which focused on the threat of German spies to Old Blighty, it was publicised by the Daily Mail and did much to create the hysteria which led Parliament to agree to the creation, in 1909, of a secret service. Le Queux was outsold, globally, by E Phillips Oppenheim, whose best-known novels such as The Kingdom Of The Blind, dwelt on high society and seductresses in a way that appealed to North American readers.

Joseph Conrad's The Secret Agent (1907) was a completely different calibre of spy novel reeking, as it did, of a moral ambiguity which both Eric Ambler and John le Carré would later develop. Conrad's novel, like many of its successors, gave the reader the satisfying feeling that the fiction was studded with secret fact, the plot being loosely based on a spectacularly unsuccessful attempt by anarchists to bomb the Greenwich Observatory in 1894. Conrad's spies were anti-heroes, the polar opposites of Hannay, the hero of John Buchan's The Thirty Nine Steps, published in 1915 and probably the most enduring spy novel of World War I. Sapper and Bulldog Drummond have since fallen out of favour for their xenophobic and anti-Semitic tendencies.

The anti-hero dominated spy fiction for most of the next 30 years, with Somerset Maugham, himself a secret service agent, bringing spy fiction back to realism with his Ashenden stories. (His very unBondian credo: 'The work of an agent in the Intelligence Department is on the whole monotonous. A lot of it is uncommonly useless.') At best, the hero of Eric Ambler's spy novels was an innocent protagonist trapped in the Machiavellian machinations of others. Fleming even drops in a gag in one of his novels at Ambler's expense: in From Russia With Love, Bond falls asleep reading Ambler's A Coffin For Dimitris. Ambler's natural heir, in many ways, was Graham Greene. Greeneland, as it became known, was a weary duplicitous world where the

Reading a Bond novel always sent Graham Greene scurrying for the whisky. ▲

A potted history of spy fiction

hero never knew who to trust. In The Confidential Agent, the 'hero', D, shirks from a fight, has trembling hands (the consequence of too much time in prison) and doubts even the justice of the cause he is acting for, but feels that, having chosen his side, it would be churlish to change his mind. Subsequent Greene 'heroes' may not have been quite this miserable but if they were active (like Pyle in The Quiet American), they were horribly naïve, liable to end up causing the deaths of innocents. More usually, they were plagued by self-doubt or, as in Our Man In Havana, spinning a fantasy.

Fleming's Bond changed the gravitational force of spy fiction, offering the genre's most convincing hero since Buchan's Hannay and inspiring such diverse writers as Frederick Forsyth (who recently said he could never write a Bond novel) and Tom Clancy, whose Jack Ryan is an obvious American version of 007. Forsyth, especially, brought some of Fleming's meticulous observation to novels like The Day Of The Jackal.

Fleming's success prompted several CIA agents, notably Watergate conspirator Howard Hunt, to write their own spy novels. Greene, perhaps realising the way Fleming had reshaped the spy genre, was not a fan of Bond's, a sentiment he shared with John le Carré whose books are as full of ennui, betrayal and ambiguity as Conrad and Greene's. Le Carré, two decades after Fleming's death, said on a visit to the Soviet Union that the Fleming novels were 'cultural pornography' and complained about the 'Superman figure who is ennobled by some sort of misty, patriotic ideas and who can commit any crime and break any law in the name of his own society. He's a sort of licensed criminal who, in the name of false patriotism, approves of nasty crimes'. He has a point, though some maintain that le Carre's ambiguity and betrayal have become monotonous and that his novels are often much harder to read than Fleming's without offering many of the compensations of truly great literature.

Len Deighton created the second most popular spy of the 1960s, an agent unnamed in the novels but christened Harry Palmer for the movies, which were produced by Harry Saltzman, Cubby Broccoli's fellow producer on the first Bond movies. Deighton's hero lives in a small flat south of the Thames, wears horn-rimmed glasses and is not spectacularly attractive to the opposite sex. Yet he is not a complete anti-Bond; he has more self-belief to his role than, say, Leamas in le Carre's The Spy Who Came In From The Cold and he brings an 007-like efficiency to his tasks.

Fleming's legacy is most obvious in the mass market, with writers such as Clancy

A potted history of spy fiction

and Robert Ludlum. At the heavyweight end, writers such as Alan Furst, author of historical spy fiction, have built on the legacy of Greene and le Carré.

Charles McCarry, himself a former CIA agent, has become a cult author although sadly not enough of a cult to keep all his works in print. His novels, four of which focus on CIA agent and poet Paul Christopher, are probably the most literary novels published in the genre since Greene. Tears Of Autumn (1974) is often cited as his best, possibly because it offers a chilling explanation for the assassination of JFK. The troubling aspect of the novel is that, at times, it reads like a well-crafted, subtle, piece of CIA propaganda. Christopher's colleagues are the professionals, the politicians are the amateurs, blissfully unaware of the laws of cause and effect or wilfully blind to them. It's hard to believe that Christopher works for the same agency which tried to kill Castro and helped usher in the horror that was the Pinochet regime.

So, if 007 arouses your curiosity you could do worse than check out the following:

Heroes
Archangel Robert Harris (Arrow) A classic amateur spy thriller.
Greenmantle John Buchan (Oxford) The second Hannay novel may just be better than the more famous *The Thirty Nine Steps*.
The Miernik Dossier Charles McCarry (Arrow). His debut novel: surprisingly easy to read for a novel of documents. Out-of-print but available used.
Havana Bay Martin Cruz Smith (Pan) Starring *Gorky Park* hero Moscow policeman Renko, this time embroiled in some realpolitik in Castro's Cuba.
The Quiller Memorandum Adam Hall (Rosetta) The 1960s' most underrated spy novel.
Funeral In Berlin Len Deighton (Flamingo) Simply a pleasure to read.

Anti-heroes
Ashenden Somerset Maugham (Vintage) A quietly seductive set of short stories, derived from Maugham's own time in the British secret service.
Night Soldiers Alan Furst (Harper Collins) A Bulgarian agent tries to survive two wars: 1939-1945 and the Cold War.
Our Man In Havana Graham Greene (Vintage) The best spy comedy.
The Secret Agent Joseph Conrad (Penguin) The definitive spy novel of betrayal.
The Spy Who Came In From The Cold John le Carré (Hodder & Stoughton). His best, and most thrilling, a more satisfying read than the George Smiley novels.

The Bond fiction

All Bond novels and short stories are reviewed and rated except for novelisations of the movies. Completists will want to collect them all, some purists consider anything post-Fleming as irrelevant, an understandable reaction although that would exclude Kingsley Amis' *Colonel Sun*. If you wanted to start with a handful of Bond titles, we would recommend *Casino Royale, Live And Let Die, From Russia With Love, Goldfinger* and *Colonel Sun*. (The name of the publisher of each book has been left out due to the complex publishing history attached to Bond books.)

Casino Royale (1953) Ian Fleming

The plot Bond must neutralise a Russian agent known as 'Le Chiffre' by ruining him at the baccarat table, thus forcing his 'retirement'. But a beautiful female agent leads him to disaster – and a saviour...

The book *Casino Royale* marked Bond's debut. Fleming insisted it was written to take his mind off the horrific prospect of matrimony, yet it introduced enough of the Bond trademarks – the villain, the 'shaken not stirred' dry martinis, the enticing femme fatale Vesper Lynd – to suggest that although it was written in weeks, he had been piecing together the elements in his mind for some time. Bond's luck with girls already seems double-sided: they find him irresistible but they either betray him or are taken away from him. At the end of this adventure, Bond notes bitterly 'The bitch is dead now', the girl had got under his skin, and he vows to 'stop playing red Indians'.

There's an emotional depth and a political subtlety here which may surprise those who only know 007 from the films. Some critics, notably **Simon Raven** who wrote dialogue for the film *On Her Majesty's Secret Service*, baulked at the torture scene, but the **Times Literary Supplement** (in the author's favourite review) called the book 'exciting and extremely civilised'. His least favourite review was from brother-in-law Hugo Charteris who deemed it neurotic and disgusting. Families, eh?

Verdict 𝆑𝆑𝆑𝆑𝆑𝆑

Live And Let Die (1954) Ian Fleming

The plot Bond goes to Harlem – the kingdom of Mr Big, criminal mastermind, voodoo baron and head of the Soviet espionage operation in the Caribbean – and the treachery, terror and torture leads inexorably to an island in the sun owned by Mr Big and unlike any island Harry Belafonte ever sang about.

The book In later years Fleming would, defensively, dismiss his novels as mere entertainments but he started out with more serious intent. *Live And Let Die* was supposed to be a more serious novel than its predecessor (hence the original title **The Undertaker's Wind**) with Fleming meditating, through Mr Big, on the nature of evil. But his natural instinct for pace, local colour and events overwhelmed the book, the *Observer* reviewer noting, enthusiastically: 'Don't blame me if you get a stroke!' (*The Times*, less impressed, noted that the book lived on the 'edge of flippancy'. Tut tut.)

Fleming was proud of the way his black characters talked, but this part of the book hasn't aged well. Indeed, even for the first US edition, it was edited heavily. His wife Ann's friends, notably **Evelyn Waugh**, disapproved mildly but Fleming was delighted to hear from his idol Raymond Chandler that some of the American scenes were 'amazing for a foreigner to accomplish'. The Irish authorities weren't as impressed, banning it. This book is also notable for the moment where Bond tells Solitaire, 'We have all the time in the world.'

Verdict 𝄢𝄢𝄢𝄢𝄢

Moonraker (1955) Ian Fleming

The plot Hugo Drax plans to use a rocket, originally developed to give Britain 'an independent say in the world', to destroy London.

The book The best review is probably from Fleming's friend **Noel Coward** who noted: 'It is the best thing he has done yet, very exciting and as usual too far-fetched. His observation is extraordinary and his talent for description vivid.' Although in some ways the plot harked back to the V2 rockets of the 1940s, as so often with Fleming it's mildly ahead of its time – the Russians wouldn't send the Sputnik into space

until 1958. His villain must have got his first name from Fleming's brother-in-law Hugo, while Drax is derived from 'drache', the German word for dragon, and possibly from the marvellously named Admiral **Sir Reginald Plunkett-Ernie-Erle-Drax**, an old acquaintance. One of the original titles was *Mondays Are Hell*, an amusing sentiment for an author who rarely suffered the drudgery of a nine-to-five, Monday to Friday working week. The American title, **Too Hot To Handle**, made it sound like a Mickey Spillane novel. A radio adaptation was broadcast in south Africa (and later on the BBC) starring future TV quiz show host **Bob Holness**. The one-word title came to Fleming after much work (he discarded, among others, 'The Infernal Machine' and 'Wide Of The Mark', which would have been, well, wide of the mark for a Bond novel.) One of the book's charms is the sense you get of Bond's London life, but it isn't as suspenseful as its predecessors.
Verdict 🔫🔫🔫🔫🔫

Diamonds Are Forever (1956) Ian Fleming

The plot Bond is assigned to break a diamond smuggling operation and calls on the beautiful Tiffany Case to help him.

The book It's hard to think of this book without hearing Shirley Bassey singing the movie theme but, for once, Fleming's work isn't as convincing as the film derived from it. **Raymond Chandler** criticised it mildly in the *Sunday Times*, complaining Fleming was trying too hard to make Bond human, and said he preferred 007 when he was 'exposing himself to half a dozen thin-lipped killers and neatly dumping them into a heap of fractured bones'. Another of Fleming's heroes, **Somerset Maugham**, praised his ability to get 'the tension to the highest possible pitch'.

The problem with the novel is often said to be the frequent changes of locale but it also violates the author's golden rule about giving Bond a suitably impressive villain. Jack Spang is supposed to be the mastermind but appears too infrequently and we have to make do with his henchmen, well drawn thugs but thugs for all that. Their aim isn't to control or destroy the world but to get rich, a rather modest

ambition for Bond criminals. Tiffany Case, though, is a cut above the usual Bond girl, rebuking him for his cynicism about marriage: 'You can't be complete by yourself.'
Verdict 🔫🔫🔫

From Russia With Love (1957) Ian Fleming

The plot SMERSH, the Soviet organ responsible for vengeance and violence, decides to use an innocent girl and the bait of a cipher to lure and destroy Bond.

The book Is this the best Bond novel? It's probably a toss-up between this and *Goldfinger* – the argument can be pursued endlessly but without profit or clear conclusion. As he wrote this, fearing he was 'too old to cut the mustard', Fleming was reading a 10-year-old copy of *The Crack Up*, **Scott Fitzgerald**'s frank confessional of his own break-up, and some of that epigrammatic style permeates the book. It isn't just a matter of style though: the supporting cast is memorably drawn, from repulsive lesbian villainess Rosa Klebb to celibate psycho Red Grant and the innocent girl Tatiana Romanova plus our man in Istanbul, Darko Kerim. Fleming's well-honed observations are mingled with, as reviewer **Anthony Price** noted, the right flavour of 'sex, brutality and death'.

The beginning and the end of this novel are among the most memorable in Fleming's fiction, with the author giving himself the option of killing off his character. The finale also, unlike in the films, emphasises 007's human fallibility: he falls for a pretty obvious trap and is poisoned by Klebb. No wonder Fleming later felt that this was his best Bond novel to date. After being selected by **John F Kennedy** as one of his favourite reads, this was the first Bond novel to really make an impression in the US.
Verdict 🔫🔫🔫🔫🔫🔫🔫

Dr. No (1958) Ian Fleming

The plot Still recovering from the denouement of his last assignment, Bond is given a soft option by M: to investigate the disappearance of the head of our man in Jamaica. The obvious suspect is a local bird-dung merchant with his own island, Dr No.

The book Nitpickers might note that the plot is, in essence, a reprise of that in *Live And Let Die*: 007 investigates some malfeasance and finds the solution on an evil magnate's private island in the Caribbean. But that (and the general air of implausibility) are virtually the only flaws in Bond's sixth outing. Chandler returned to the fray, praising Fleming's unBritish (in Chandler's eyes) willingness to escape from conventional English, his sense of place and his 'acute sense of pace', concluding that it was 'masterful' and 'beautifully written'. Chandler's review set the general mood with **Cecil Day-Lewis** weighing in for the BBC; he called it 'wildly thrilling, packed with convincing technical detail'.

  Paul Johnson (then a critic on the left rather than the right) called it 'the nastiest book I have ever read' and added, with a snobbery the English excel at, it was 'the sadism of a schoolboy bully, the mechanical two-dimensional sex-longings of a frustrated adolescent and the crude, snob-cravings of a suburban adult'. You have to admire the way Johnson calls Fleming a snob but goes on to sneer at him as 'suburban' – only a critic with Johnson's self-belief could fail to see the contradiction. **Dr. No** was Fleming's attempt to emulate the Sax Rohmer villain **Fu Manchu**. The attempt may have been too obvious as one critic felt Dr No was 30 years out of date. But he did say suitably fiendish things like, 'You have both put me to a great deal of trouble. Now I intend to put you to a great deal of pain.'

Verdict 🔫🔫🔫🔫🔫🔫🔫

Goldfinger (1959) Ian Fleming

The plot Bond is called in to investigate cheating at cards but soon realises that the villain has bigger things on his mind: like stealing all the gold from Fort Knox and taking it to Russia.

The book British novelist **Anthony Burgess** (later called in to write a script for *The Spy Who Loved Me* which was subsequently rejected) ranked this as one of the 99 best novels since 1939. He put it in some pretty exalted company (with the likes of Norman Mailer, Saul Bellow and Ernest Hemingway). Yet this is not always a favourite with Bond fans who find it a little slow, querying the amount of space devoted to the game of golf (roughly 30 pages) and musing, for once, about the unlikely plot: would any villain really threaten to kill the inhabitants of Fort Knox with a deadly toxin and blow the fort open with a nuclear weapon? Yet for non-Bond fans, the fact that this isn't your average Bond novel is what makes it such a cracking read.

Without trying to sound as snobbish as Paul Johnson, *Goldfinger* actually feels and reads like a proper novel, albeit with some rather fantastical elements. Fleming devoted particular care to the villain: his first name 'auric' is derived from the Latin word for gold and his surname comes from architect **Erno Goldfinger**, a distant relative of Fleming's, famous for his brutal high-rise buildings and reputed to be as attached to concrete as the novel's villain was to gold. Erno later threatened to sue to stop publication but mercifully changed his mind, so that Fleming didn't resort to plan B which was to call his baddie, at **Cyril Connolly**'s suggestion, Goldprick. He also gave him a wondrously lethal henchman, hat-dispensing Oddjob. The reviews were indifferent but Burgess would later make amends, cheering 'a patriotic lecher with a tinge of Scottish Puritanism in him, a gourmand and amateur of vodka martinis, a smoker of strong tobacco who does not lose his wind... against... megalomaniacs'.

Verdict 🗡🗡🗡🗡🗡🗡🗡

For Your Eyes Only (1960) Ian Fleming

The plot There were five short stories in this collection: in **From A View To A Kill**, enemy agents are ambushing dispatch riders; in **For Your Eyes Only**, 007 volunteers to eliminate the villains who have slain M's friends; in **Risico**, 007 breaks up a dope-running scheme; in **The Hildebrand Rarity**, our hero joins an American couple for fishing and murder; while in **A Quantum Of Solace**, Bond has a distasteful mission stopping arms reaching Castro and takes a well-earned break with the Governor of Bermuda.

The book There is no real connection (other than the title) between the story and the movie *View To A Kill*, while the movie of *For Your Eyes Only* draws on both the story of that name and *Risico*. This collection was originally entitled 'The Rough With The Smooth'. For those addicted to the tension and the plots of the novel, the rough was *A Quantum Of Solace*, essentially Fleming's attempt to craft a story like his mentor **Somerset Maugham**. He doesn't quite match Maugham but the exercise works and the usual Fleming touches abound. In *The Hildebrand Rarity*, the beautiful wife whom 007 lusts after is beaten by her villainous husband Krest with a 3ft whip called 'the Corrector', a taste he probably shared with the story's author. Nobody is too surprised or peeved when Krest is found dead with a rare fish in his throat.

Verdict 🔫🔫🔫🔫

Thunderball (1962) Ian Fleming

The plot Bond is in disgrace and poor health and is sent off to a clinic to be restored to his former physical glory. His curiosity about a fellow patient's tattoo leads to a contretemps and 007 is forced to kill the chap, inadvertently interfering with the plans of SMERSH, a criminal organisation run by Emilio Largo which includes **Ernst Stavro Blofeld** among its gallery of rogues.

The book The genesis of this book is almost as tortuous as a Fleming plot. Suffice to say it can be traced back to a short story written by Ernest Cureo, a friend of Fleming's, which was rewritten by Fleming and earmarked for a film produced by **Kevin McClory**. This is, in some ways, the book of the film which McClory produced twice: once using the same name with Cubby Broccoli and Harry Saltzman. And once by himself, with **Sean Connery** in the lead, as **Never Say Never Again**.

The plot, about a terrorist group planning to hijack an atomic bomb, has become

The critics on Bond

Eric Ambler
The Bond books definitely deserve to be read as literature.

Raymond Chandler
Bond is what every man would like to be, and what every woman would like to have between her sheets.

Umberto Eco
The reader finds himself immersed in a game of which he knows the pieces and the rules – and, perhaps the outcome – and draws pleasure simply from following the minimal variations by which the victor [ie Bond] realises his objective

Christopher Hitchens
The staying power of the books is partly and paradoxically attributable to their departure from standard Cold War imagery. Bond confronts not just the unsleeping evil of Moscow-directed communism, but also a metastasised sub-species of monsters in human form who are, in some sense, in business on their own account.

Stuart Jeffries, The Guardian
Fleming writes breezily, but most of the pleasures of reading the Bond books have little to do with the quality of the writing, but with their unwitting silliness.

Philip Larkin
So far from being orgies of sex and sadism, the books are nostalgic excursions... England is always right, foreigners are always wrong... Girls are treated with kindness and consideration... Life's virtues are courage and loyalty, and its good things an aristocracy of powerful cars, vintage wines, exclusive clubs, the old Times, the old five-pound note, the old Player's packet.

William Rees Mogg
With Bond we are back in barbarism. If one met him, he would be a sinister bore. The Bond cult suggests our age may not be as modern as we like to think.

Will Self
I can think of few other fictional characters whose stock has fallen as low – in my estimation – as Bond's.

familiar as a tabloid scare story, repeated irregularly ever since the book's publication, and has provided the plot for many movies, including the George Clooney-Nicole Kidman yarn *The Peacemaker*. Perhaps because it was originally intended for the movies, the novel contains enough of the usual Bond ingredients to be satisfying, with Fleming piling on the violence (characters are eaten by barracudas, electrocuted, and tortured with an ice cube and a cigar). Good but not top-notch Bond.

Verdict ✱✱✱✱

The Spy Who Loved Me (1962) Ian Fleming

The plot A beautiful girl with a sensual past, Vivienne Michel, is confronted with two evil killers – there's only one man who can save her now, who can that be?

The book The most controversial Fleming novel, not least because the woman who narrates the book suggests, 'All women love semi-rape'. This is Fleming's desperate attempt to break out of the trap he senses is about to spring. Unlike its predecessors, this novel is narrated, in the first person, by the girl and Bond doesn't appear until relatively late in the novel. At times it sounds like Fleming is trying to ape Mickey Spillane ('Nothing makes one grateful for life except the black wings of danger') or his idol, Raymond Chandler.

As **Anthony Burgess** noted, the novel was 'a failed experiment in shoving Bond to the margin of the narrative and making the protagonist an English girl looking after an American motel'. Fleming later admitted his failure, allowing only the title to be used for the movies and restricting its reprints of the book. One critic called it 'one of the worst, most badly constructed novels we have read'. The point was underlined when the story was published in **Stag** magazine, under the title *Motel Nymph,* though the alleged pornography, which got it banned in several countries, may seem mild to anyone who's read a **Jackie Collins** novel. The novel is probably not as bad as critics would suggest – like most of Fleming's stuff it is plenty readable – but it deviated too sharply from Eco's formula for comfort for no

43

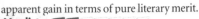

apparent gain in terms of pure literary merit.
Verdict 🕵️🕵️

On Her Majesty's Service (1963)
Ian Fleming

The plot Bond is growing as dissatisfied with his usual *modus operandi* as Fleming but regains his old verve when he realises that Ernst Stavro Blofeld, the villain he's been tracking, is planning to commence biological warfare against England.

The book This novel wouldn't, you suspect, have been anywhere near as successful if it had been called, as Fleming mooted once, 'The belles from hell'. (The villains in this book were not of the St Trinian variety.) Critics were, on the whole, relieved that Fleming had given up the idea of experimenting with his hero or trying to be the next Mickey Spillane, although he again suggests women like to be raped.

The Bond family motto, it is revealed, is 'The world is not enough', a motto which might be said to fit, more accurately, Blofeld's nefarious ambitions. By this time Fleming was not in brilliant health, and there are a number of unusual factual errors (a half bottle of **Pol Roger** champagne appears – even though that brand was never sold in half bottles) and you sense a certain ennui. Once again he builds to a tragic climax, with Bond marrying Contessa Teresa di Vicenzo (you can see why he prefers to call her Tracy) only for his bride to be killed as they start off for their honeymoon. Less radical a departure than *The Spy Who Loved Me*, this still presents a different Bond as if Fleming is trying to save his hero from the rather one-dimensional image created by the hype surrounding his creation.
Verdict 🕵️🕵️🕵️🕵️🕵️

44 You Only Live Twice (1964) Ian Fleming
The plot After Blofeld brutally murders James Bond's bride, 007 loses the plot and almost becomes a security risk. M gives him a last chance

to redeem himself, sending him to Japan to retrieve a secret ciphering method. This apparently simple job becomes complicated when he notices a doctor who persuades people to commit suicide.

The book It's probably worth recapping a bit here: Bond started *Thunderball* in disgrace because of his dodgy health; he didn't start *The Spy Who Loved Me* at all, appearing later in this untypical 007 novel; in *On Her Majesty's Secret Service* he is growing tired of the game; and in *You Only Live Twice* he is understandably gutted by the murder of his new bride. You don't have to be a conspiracy theorist to spot the coincidence here: it's as if Bond is afflicted by the same kind of melancholy which was plaguing his creator. (Fleming's wife Ann would later recall him often asking her: 'How can I make you happy when I am so miserable myself?')

It's as if since *From Russia With Love*, Fleming has been trying to plot an escape route for himself and his hero. Yet always he is pulled back, perhaps (as his wife noted) by the need to provide some yellow silk for the drawing room walls.

The agony continues for Bond here as, by the end of the novel, he is presumed dead but found on a remote Japanese island suffering from amnesia. Death, perhaps unsurprisingly as this is Fleming's last completed novel, is an obsession throughout the book; shortly after publication he told a friend he could smell 'the undertaker's wind'.

The American novelist **EL Doctorow**, then an editor at New American Library which was publishing Fleming's novels, felt that Bond's sadness was affecting Fleming's writing although it might have been more accurate to say that Fleming's sadness was affecting his character.

Fleming's friend **Cyril Connolly** was quite severe when he reviewed it, suggesting that Bond's antics had become just too ludicrous, and calling for 007 to return to the 'exact science' that was espionage. The real problem, as Doctorow noted, is that the scene-setting first half, fascinating as it is for those who want to learn about Japan, is too slow for a novel of tension and thrills.

45

Verdict 🔫🔫🔫🔫🔫

007 in New York (1964) Ian Fleming

The plot 007 travels to the Big Apple to warn a former MI6 employee that her lover is a KGB agent.

The book Only available in the US edition of Fleming's collection of travel writings, **Thrilling Cities** (although republished in the *Sunday Times* in 1999), this is the shortest Bond story, of interest mainly as a curio and possibly because 007's good buddy Felix Leiter has been telling him about sado-masochistic bars. Bond is laid low not by some arch fiend but by a lunch of smoked salmon and scrambled eggs.

Verdict 𝓕𝓕𝓕𝓕

The Man With The Golden Gun (1965) Ian Fleming

The plot The man with the golden gun, Scaramanga, needs to be dealt with on account of him being an agent of Fidel Castro, who has plans to wreck the world's sugar cane industry and a habit of killing innocent birds.

The book The basic problem with this book is obvious from the synopsis. If a villain like Scaramanga really wanted to take over the world, surely there are more obvious commodities to target: gold, oil, even water. It's hard to imagine a criminal mastermind working for Castro, after considering all the options for evildoing very carefully, and announcing: 'Yes, that's it, we're going to hit 'em where it hurts, we'll deprive the free world of sugar.' Granted, Scaramanga is an unusual bloke, what with his third nipple and the fact that his disposable income is large enough for him to be able to use silver-jacketed gold-core bullets as a hitman. Surely these can't be tax deductible? That said, you have to give Fleming credit for an arresting opening with a brainwashed Bond being sent to London in a KGB plot to kill M. In most secret services, this would be enough for the agent concerned to be terminated with extreme prejudice, but kindly old M tries to improve Bond's mental health by giving him the chance to redeem himself and assassinate Scaramanga.

Fleming hadn't finished the book when he **died in August 1964**

Literary ancestors

The character of James Bond is a blend of many literary figures, the oldest being Saint George, dragon conqueror and patron saint of England, Georgia, Aragon and Moscow. The cult of George goes back to the 4th century which makes 007 seem a neophyte in the icon business. More recent precursors of Bond include Rudolf Rassendyll, the chivalrous hero of Anthony Hope's twice-filmed adventure yarn The Prisoner Of Zenda, who revelled in daring exploits in a similar vein to 007. Bond also owes a debt to John Buchan's Hannay and Bulldog Drummond, the cheerfully ugly hero who escaped death and matrimony in a series of 1930s adventures.

Captain WE Johns' Biggles was as popular in his day as Bond. In 98 adventures, Biggles globetrotted like 007 and his recruitment to a special elite unit in the later novels seems very Bondian. And Johns says of his hero in Biggles Flies North: 'He could not settle down to a humdrum occupation, the only relief he could find to relieve nerves strung to a high pitch was to go on living dangerously.'

'I have been trying to make a picture of a man. Fantastic, improbable-perhaps. Quite worthless, quite irritating, if you feel that way. Or a slightly cockeyed ideal, if you feel differently. It doesn't matter so long as you feel that you would recognise him if you met him tomorrow.'

CLASSIC THRILLERS

ANTHONY HOPE

THE PRISONER OF ZENDA

Was Bond a return to Zenda? ▲

This was how Leslie Charteris, creator of The Saint, described his hero in 1939 and Simon Templar would have been one of the most obvious models for Bond even if Roger Moore had never played both heroes. The motto on the back cover of the second Templar novel, confusingly entitled Enter The Saint, was 'On the side of the law yet outside the law' which almost sums up 007's modus operandi. Templar was, of course, nominally a thief but how many real villains could wear a halo? Besides, like Bond, he spent much of his time rescuing damsels in distress. Like Fleming, Charteris also wanted Cary Grant to play his hero on screen.

47

and **Kingsley Amis**, a decent novelist and a Bond fan, was called in to fix the manuscript. He suggested that Scaramanga was a rather thin character and found it even more ludicrous than was the norm for him to hire a man, Bond, who he didn't know, to help him with his security. Amis' suggestion, that Scaramanga was sexually attracted to Bond (is that what the third nipple meant?), was repudiated by Fleming's editor **William Plomer**. The book was published to respectful (if not warm) reviews with the **Scotsman** saying it was 'as fast moving as ever'. Many of the flaws in the book would become apparent when it was turned into a film.

Verdict   🔫🔫🔫

Octopussy (1966) Ian Fleming

The plot This collection consists of three short stories: **Octopussy** in which 007 tracks down a major who has been living off stolen Nazi gold in Jamaica; **The Property Of A Lady** in which he is sent to spy on the KGB's London chief who may be bidding for a Fabergé egg at Sothebys and **The Living Daylights** in which Bond is assigned to kill a KGB executioner called Trigger (who himself has been sent to Berlin to kill a double agent), a nickname which presumably has nothing to do with Roy Rogers' horse,

The book Fleming has become one of the world's richest dead fiction writers, thanks to the continuation of his literary legacy through **John Gardner** and **Raymond Benson**, the posthumous publication of books like this and the continuing interest in his work provoked by the movie franchise

The collection of these three stories seemed like a logical way to keep the bandwagon rolling and the Fleming and Bond names in the public eye. At this point, of course, no-one knew quite how durable the Bond franchise was to prove on celluloid and on paper. In **The Living Daylights**, 007 shockingly considers visiting a brothel, a rather desperate step for the man every woman would want between the sheets. Trigger turns out to be a lovely cellist whom 007, in reckless disregard for his duties, has fallen in love with and cannot bring himself to kill. It's as well, at this point, to consider what kind of photos Bond must have on M, given the fact that he's tried to kill him, disobeyed orders, become a virtual security risk etc etc.

The Property Of A Lady was written for inclusion in *The Ivory Hammer*, the yearbook for Sotheby's auction house – hence the scenes at an auction – and Fleming wouldn't take a fee for it because he wasn't really happy with it. The Fabergé egg motif would later appear, in transmogrified form, in the film **Octopussy**.

Octopussy itself is a taut story which draws on Fleming's love for the Austrian Alps (where he escaped as a young man after quitting Sandhurst, partly because of a genetic inability to take orders and partly out of his embarrassment at contracting gonorrhea), the exotic fish to be found in the Caribbean and the mysterious activities of commandos at the end of the war. The story is so entitled because Major Smythe has a pet octopus. Communicating with his pet is the retired officer's chief pleasure in life – so presumably death at the hands of a poisonous fish must have come as something of a relief.

For many fans of Bond the literary hero, the real story ends with this collection. There are two very short excerpts of unfinished Fleming stories, the first of which is obviously about Bond, which were published for the first time in **John Pearson**'s biography. After that, our secret agent becomes subject to the whims of Messrs Amis, Gardner and Benson.

Fleming has become something of a stick to beat his successors over the head with, not always fairly. Obviously he created Bond so he deserves the lion's share of the credit. And all his Bond novels have that distinctive voice, so that even when they're being infuriating, ludicrous or terribly irrelevant, they are almost always entertaining. Yet sometimes the slavish attention paid to the essential luxuries of life can be a bit excessive. True, Bond did announce, 'I take a ridiculous pleasure in what I eat and drink' but sometimes Fleming's enthusiasm

49

007 great openers

Ian Fleming, like James Bond, certainly knew how to make an entrance, as these opening lines prove.

001 The Spy Who Loved Me
I was running away.

002 A Quantum Of Solace
James Bond said: 'I've always thought that if I ever married I would marry an air hostess'.

003 From Russia With Love
The naked man who lay splayed out on his face beside the swimming pool might have been dead.

004 Thunderball
It was one of those days when it seemed to James Bond that all life, as someone put it, was nothing but a heap of six to four against.

005 Live And Let Die
There are moments of great luxury in the life of a secret agent.

006 Moonraker
The two 38s roared simultaneously.

007 Goldfinger
James Bond, with two double bourbons inside him, sat in the final departure lounge of Miami Airport and thought about life and death.

seems to run away with him and the novels, at their worst, lack the tension which is implied in the very name of the genre, 'thriller'. All of Fleming's successors also had to struggle with the fact that they weren't inventing 007 but overhauling him for a very different age and competing with (rather than defining) the agent in the movies. The novels that follow are not without their rewards, but at their worst they lack that very distinctiveness which Fleming brought to his hero and his fiction.

Verdict 𝄢𝄢𝄢𝄢

The Adventures Of James Bond Junior 003½ (1967)
R D Mascott

The plot Famous Five-style antics during the school holidays with James Bond Junior as he investigates a sinister-looking chap who bought junior's old house.

The book Glidrose can't be accused of not trying everything to perpetuate the Bond literary brand. This book, which later inspired an awful cartoon strip, asks us to accept that Bond has an offspring – some leap in itself.

That shock apart, it's sub-Enid Blyton all the way. There are two mysteries attached to this manuscript: why Glidrose passed it for publication in the first place. And which author is hiding behind the pseudonym R D Mascott.

Various potential authors have been suggested, including Kingsley Amis and Roald Dahl. We'll leave the list of candidates there as, frankly, if we pointed the finger at any living writers, they'd probably sue us for libel. Two websites have identified the author as **Arthur Calder Marshall**, a British novelist, scriptwriter and writer who is best remembered for his novels *The Fair To Middling* and *The Scarlet Boy*. In other words, he's not that well remembered at all, but the latter, a variant on **Henry James**' ghost story *The Turn Of The Screw*, did win praise from Fleming's old mucker **Cyril Connolly**. If you're interested in the reasoning behind the identification, log on to www.007forever.com/literary_intrigues_007/investigative_reports/ the_search_for_rd_mascott_james_bond_junior_003.htm where you will find a mere 6000 words on this subject. We recommend that you read them, but we also recommend that you take a stimulant after the first 2000. If only the book was as intriguing as the search for the identity of the author.

Verdict

Colonel Sun (1968) Kingsley Amis

The plot M is kidnapped, at the behest of Chinese agent Colonel Sun Liang-tan, in the hope that 007 will feel obliged to try to rescue him and walk into a trap.

The book 007's peripatetic post-Fleming existence starts here with this book by Amis, a respected British novelist (best known, at this point in his career, for his debut novel **Lucky Jim**) and a fan of Fleming's who had been brought in to fix **The Man With The Golden Gun** – and then cheekily reviewed the fruits of his labours in the *New Statesman*. The relatively poor standing of this Bond novel can be judged from the fact that, unlike almost every other 007 novel (and, for that matter, almost every other Amis novel), it is at this moment out of print in the UK. The reviews were mixed and sales disappointing, both good reasons (it seemed to Glidrose) why Amis should not be invited back. In retrospect, this seems like one of those critical turning points in Bond's literary career.

The critics had already begun to take potshots at the very idea of Bond even while Fleming was still alive and writing. His death, after the usual period of critical mourning, freed some like **Malcolm Muggeridge** to weigh in with their bitter criticism of the Bond canon. Muggeridge, whose mild-mannered appearances on TV were obviously deceptive, described Bond as an Etonian **Mickey Spillane**, calling him 'utterly despicable; obsequious to his superiors, pretentious in his tastes, callous and brutal in his ways, with strong undertones of sadism, and an unspeakable cad in his relations with women, toward whom sexual appetite represents the only approach'. In short, our Malcolm wasn't a fan of our hero. It was quite an attack for someone whom, Ian Fleming's brother Peter noted, admitted he had only read one Bond novel. But that set the tone for the intellectual revisionism which put Bond beyond the literary pale (even as the movies were plundering the box office). Amis was a victim of similar thinking so his first Bond novel was bound to draw critical fire.

The novel (not that it mattered in the critical climate surrounding its launch) was good, better than any subsequent Bond novel and better than some of Fleming's weaker efforts. Amis' prose was more disciplined than that in Fleming's later novels, and the plot was less elaborate, making this a more genuine page turner than any Bond novel since **From Russia With Love**.

Quite simply Amis brought Bond back to earth. There was less fussing about having the right brand of salmon and less focus on the marvels of gadgetry. But he kept some Fleming traditions. M was kidnapped and hidden in an island off the coast of Greece and the locale was described with care and

007 camp, mocked and X-rated

Bond Strikes Camp

Cyril Connolly's spoof of his friend's hero was certainly different. In this story, first published in *London* magazine, M orders 007 into drag and tricks him into bed. As for the gadgets, suffice to say they include a child's water pistol with a small screw-top ink-bottle full of some transparent liquid, a jockstrap and foam rubber falsies with electronic self-erecting nipples. Fleming bought the manuscript for £100, not finding it as funny when Connolly read it out to him as he later claimed to. It's not a very finely observed parody and the humour is as crude as any of the 1970s Bond films ('That's my comma', 'I'm afraid I make more use of the colon') but it has curiosity value, and suggests that under Bond's machismo there was indeed something horribly camp about 007 – certainly in *From Russia With Love*, there is a rather camp account of Bond's typical breakfast.

Alligator

From the people who brought us Sesame Street, Michael Frith and Christopher Cerf, came this National Lampoon, er, lampoon of 007. With more accuracy than Connolly, the authors created a purple-faced, steel-toothed villain (Lacertus Alligator) some 15 years before Jaws appeared in the film *The Spy Who Loved Me*. This was published by Vanitas in the US but only twice, possibly because at times the book crosses the line between affectionate parody and slavish imitation of the original.

For Your Sighs Only, Nautipussy

Writer William Knowles so liked Bond that he wrote sexy/soft porn novels about the antics of 008, Trevor Anderson. They sold well in paperback but are now very rare. Knowles is rumoured to have committed suicide in 1972.

in detail. He presented Bond with a love interest: the beautiful Ariadne, who can't reconcile her belief in Communism (the Russian variety) with her love for 007. There's also a chilling torture scene in which Colonel Sun, in accordance with the rules of **Talking Killer Syndrome**, describes the pains he has in store for our hero. (Amis got the ideas for the torture from his physician, returning the favour by naming a doctor in the novel after him.) Heck, Amis even drops in a few Fleming-style swipes at foreigners (in this instance, the Albanians). Still, in the end Amis took £10,000 and went back to writing his own novels. Shame.

Verdict

Kingsley Amis

As the author of just one James Bond novel (under the pseudonym, Robert Markham), Kingsley Amis is often dismissed as the George Lazenby of Bond fiction. The comparison does Bond, Amis and his 007 novel, *Colonel Sun*, a disservice. Amis was a genuine Bond fan who said of his own 007 novel: 'The Bond of the books was always a guns and fists man...and although he was mostly a fantasy hero... he never lost elements of realism... My Bond tips the scales towards the latter figure. I am tired of gloss and gadgetry.' But Fleming's widow Ann snobbishly wrote, in a review the *Sunday Telegraph* never published for fear of being sued for libel, that Amis would create a 'petit bourgeois red brick Bond'.

Licence Renewed (1981)
John Gardner

The plot Anton Murik tries to blackmail the major powers by threatening to cause meltdown in nuclear plants around the world.

The book Before Gardner assumed the Bond mantle, Glidrose had accepted the right of thriller writer **Geoffrey Jenkins** to write a Bond novel based on diamond smuggling in South Africa, (which Jenkins had discussed with Fleming) but vetoed the project after seeing the manuscript. Gardner's first Bond novel loses points for having a heroine called Lavender Peacock (at least Fleming's daft names for his female characters were funny) and another for christening Major Boothroyd's assistant Q'ute which, whatever else it is, isn't cute. But Gardner does bring Bond's employers into the real security world. Overall, this is a decent thriller, lacking Fleming's spark as a writer but more credible than some of his fanciful plots.

Verdict 🔫🔫🔫🔫🔫🔫🔫

For Special Services (1982) John Gardner

The plot Bond meets and falls for Felix Leiter's daughter as they investigate the possibility that SPECTRE has reformed.

The novel Probably Gardner's finest Bond thriller, though marred – like many of his Bond novels – by indifferent writing. The other objection: even Bond might not be enough of a cad to fall for his old friend Felix's daughter. But the plot, in which SPECTRE tries to take control of America's military satellite network, is credible, suspenseful and anticipates Ronald Reagan's Star Wars defence plan (see page 244). Pity 007 is driving a Saab. Nena, Blofeld's illegitimate daughter (bit of a turn up – he was reputed to be uninterested in sex) has only one breast, homage presumably to Scaramanga's third nipple.

Verdict 🔫🔫🔫🔫🔫

Icebreaker (1983) John Gardner

The plot A new National Socialist army poses such a threat the Russians, Americans and British unite to investigate.

The book The idea of reborn Nazis is an old standby of desperate thriller writers. The double crosses, with the CIA and the KGB both pursuing their own agenda, are more intriguing and the attempt on Bond's life with a snow plough shows some Flemingesque ingenuity. The novel rattles along, even if 007 is peripheral at times. And there's a final twist on a twist. You just wish Gardner had a better grasp of the English language. 'The warnings were cauterised in the conflagration as their lips touched' being a case in point.

Verdict 🔫🔫🔫

Role Of Honour (1984) John Gardner

The plot SPECTRE want to disarm America's nuclear capability.

The book Skip over the fact that one character laughs 'like an angry cobra' and the fact that Gardner seems almost as obsessed by 007's dead bride Tracy as 007, and this is a good Bond novel. Gardner's third foray makes up for an occasional lack of thrills with its feel for Bond's character (even if it does give him an uncle whose existence had previously been unsuspected). The plot is reasonably simple and convincing(ish) until the moment **SPECTRE**'s evil genius Tamil Kahani can't find a pilot for the airship which is central to his plot. Gardner even throws in a literary allusion – the training camp to which Bond is taken is called 'Erewhon', clearly the chaps at SPECTRE are big fans of **Samuel Butler**, author of the satire of the same name.

Verdict 🔫🔫🔫🔫

55

Nobody Lives Forever (1986) John Gardner
The plot SPECTRE, understandably, want to kill 007.
The book There's a certain formulaic quality to the title and to
Bond's character in this book. *Nobody Lives Forever* (it was originally
called *Nobody Lives For Ever*) sounds like a spin-off **Diamonds Are
Forever** and **Nobody Does It Better**. (The same disease would
later infect the films with *Tomorrow Never Dies* and *Die Another Day*.
You can almost mix them up without noticing: *Tomorrow Is Not
Enough, The World Never Dies, Die Another Day Tomorrow*). We don't
learn that much about Bond (although Gardner harps on about Tracy

Guess who's coming to dinner

If you were lucky enough to have Bond around for dinner, you'll know he's arrived when he turns up in a Bentley. Forget the Aston Martins in the movies; for Fleming his vehicle of choice is a 4.5 litre Bentley. If you've got an American car, hide it, the only American car 007 likes is a Studebaker. If you've got an Italian sports car, leave it outside and he'll purr over it as he strolls past.

Don't serve him smoked salmon from anywhere but Scotland. If Scottish salmon was hard to find you could distract him with some pink champagne, eggs benedict or tender stone crabs, with lightly buttered toast and pink champagne. Or beluga caviar (only $49 an ounce). Or cold roast beef with potato salad.

Apart from pink champagne, Bond is not averse to brandy and ginger ales, dry martini, vodka martini, 10-year-old calvados, gin (English preferably,

definitely not American, served with tonic and lime, not lemon), most champagne and whisky. But don't offer him Pernod. Offer him any kind of cigarette. As he's enjoyed Macedonian cigarettes in his time whatever you offer him will be luxurious by comparison.

If 007 stayed until 0700 hours, serve him two cups of black coffee, an egg boiled for three and a third minutes, strawberry jam, marmalade and honey, preferably from Fortnum & Mason followed by three scrambled eggs and bacon. Best to have a pint of orange juice on hand too and some Pinaud shampoo ($8.99) in case he needs a shower.

Some final advice: never use the word 'actually' especially if you pronounce it 'ectually'. For more info on Bond track down Kingsley Amis' fine *The Book Of Bond*, out of print but still available in some good used bookshops.

again). The simplicity of the plot works although various elements echo earlier Bond novels: M was kidnapped to lure Bond in *Colonel Sun* – this time Moneypenny is taken hostage. And instead of Mr Big's island (or Dr No's island) we have Shark Island, which is SPECTRE's HQ. Efficient but not memorable.

Verdict 🔫🔫🔫🔫

No Deals Mr Bond (1987) John Gardner

The plot Two members of a spy team Bond helped rescue from East Germany are murdered; M asks him to find the three surviving agents from the same mission.

The books After reviving SPECTRE, Gardner now brings back SMERSH in this complex (as is often with Gardner, there is one double cross too many), intriguing novel which ends in a surprising, and slightly clichéd, gladiatorial contest between KGB general Konstantin Chernov and 007. It's hard to know if the inclusion of a Russian character called Semen is a joke or an oversight.

Verdict 🔫🔫🔫

Scorpius (1988) John Gardner

The plot Father Valentine, alias Vladimir Scorpius, thinks that if his cult manages to assassinate all the Western leaders, the stock markets will crash.

The book In this book Gardner reveals that **Sean Connery** is one of Bond's favourite actors. He also shows the secret agent's more sadistic side as he orders Scorpius into a swamp of poisonous snakes. He investigates Scorpius with Harriet Horner who (like M, Moneypenny *et al*) is captured and then, as in **Colonel Sun**, Bond is deliberately captured so that he can rescue her – although why some fans wonder why he bothered. This is a Bond without an Aston Martin or expensive cigarettes but with nylon socks. Some, including this reviewer, regard this as an act of literary vandalism.

Verdict 🔫🔫🔫

John Gardner

'Thank you, but no thank you,' was John Gardner's initial reaction to the suggestion by Bond's literary protectors, Glidrose, that he continue Fleming's legacy. He changed his mind although he admits, 'I didn't even like Bond that much, I thought he was po-faced.' But he brought an air of reality to 007: 'I made sure I handled and tested the gee-whiz technology 007 used in the books and tried to make sure I visited everywhere he sent him'.

Gardner tests gizmos for Bond ▲

Gardner announced at the age of eight that he wanted to be a writer, (dad handed him a notebook and pencil). Twenty five years later, in 1959, his debut novel Spin The Bottle based on his experience of alcohol addiction, appeared.

Gardner, like Fleming, brought a wealth of experience to Bond. He was in the Home Guard at 14, entertained the war wounded as a magician, joined the Royal Marines, and briefly followed his father into the clergy. He wrote his second book, The Liquidator, in 1965, the first of a series featuring Boysie Oakes, a cowardly hitman, fearful of aircrafts who contracts out his killings. This Bond send-up made the leap to film with the release in 1965 of The Liquidator, starring Rod Taylor and British comedy writer Eric Sykes as a villain.

Die-hard fans and critics attacked him but Gardner ignored them. But then he has come back from cancer, the loss of a wife, bankruptcy and the complaint by two fans that he wasn't dashing enough to write about 007. He wrote 14 Bond novels between 1981 and 1996, before handing Bond over to Raymond Benson.

Win Lose Or Die (1989) John Gardner

The plot BAST (Brotherhood of Anarchy and Secret Terror) plan to kidnap world leaders and hold the world to ransom.

The books Gardner may never have seen the movie spin-off of the 1960s TV series **Batman** but in an episode the caped crusader and boy wonder foil a plot by Penguin, Catwoman, and the Riddler to dehydrate the members of the equivalent of the UN security council and hold the world to ransom. Twenty three years later BAST plot to kidnap Gorby, Thatcher and Bush Senior and the organisation's four

leaders are known as the Man, the Cat, the Viper and the Snake. This is one of those Gardner novels which reads more like a screenplay.
Verdict 🔫🔫🔫

Brokenclaw (1990) John Gardner
The plot The eponymous Chinese-native American villain offers two plots for the price of one: he wants to give the Chinese access to the West's nuclear submarines and wreak havoc on Wall Street.

The book The thumb on **Brokenclaw**'s left hand is on the wrong side of his palm, symbolic of something or other. Bond is assisted by the beauteous Sue Chi-Ho, known as Chi-Chi, presumably (the story's Chinese roots are showing) in honour of a panda. But she is then kidnapped (like M, Moneypenny and Harriet Horner) and Bond has to go to Brokenclaw's reservation to win her back in combat. Gardner's minor baddies have names like Bone Bender Ding and Gory Fox. There's a strange passage where 007 worries about the number of alcohol-related deaths: in character for Gardner, as a man who overcame his addiction to booze, but not, surely, for an agent so fond of vodka martinis. For all that, many fans find this a gripping book, some even suggesting it's the best Bond novel not yet made into a movie.
Verdict 🔫🔫🔫

The Man From Barbarossa (1991) John Gardner
The plot General Yevgeny Yuskovich wants to reinstate Communism in Russia, help Iraq, and destroy America with a nuclear strike.

The book Yuskovich is the Russian general from hell, the kind of figure conjured up by paranoid tabloid writers with space to fill and readers to terrify. Gardner uses him here to change tack, playing up political intrigue, in an attempt, presumably, to answer those critics who insisted that his Bond novels were becoming ever more irrelevant. The book seems a retread of Gardner's *Icebreaker*, only this

time the villain who unites the intelligence agencies against him is not a Nazi nostalgia freak but a Communist nostalgia freak. Bond's love interest, Nina, turns out to be a double agent, like **Vesper Lynd** in *Casino Royale* and, like Fleming's double dealer, pays with her life. Nina has a nice line in oral sex, apparently, although Gardner coyly describes this as 'things at which many wives would draw the line'. Full marks for trying to break the mould, shame it doesn't work.
Verdict 🔫🔫🔫

Death Is Forever (1992) John Gardner

The plot A network of British agents in East Germany vanished two years ago, and are now turning up dead. Bond is sent to Germany and soon realises that there is a plot to blow up the Eurotunnel at the very moment a train with world leaders on board will speed through.

The book The dead agents with a link to East Germany sounds uncannily like the plot for **No Deals Mr Bond**, the threat to world leaders sounds like **Win, Lose Or Die**. The title is the third time the word 'forever' has been used in a Bond novel (and the second time Gardner has used it.) **Sean Connery** gets another namecheck. There's also a baddie nicknamed The Poisoned Dwarf. Gardner sharing Fleming's suspicions about short people. Yet after the relative failure of the previous novel, Gardner piles on the action and the violence. Apart from CIA agent (and love interest) Elizabeth Zara 'Easy' St John, none of the characters have conspicuously daft names. A better read than any of his Bond novels since **Role Of Honour**
Verdict 🔫🔫🔫🔫

Never Send Flowers (1993) John Gardner

The plot Bond investigates the death of an MI5 agent to see if it is connected to four mysterious assassinations around the world.

The book Don't be put off by the title, with its presumably unconscious echoes of the Neil Diamond-Barbra Streisand hit and the **Doris Day** sex comedy *Send Me No Flowers*. Don't be put off either by the fact that Bond admits to liking Disney theme parks or

that the villain is called David Dragonpol, and Bond's love interest (who starts off as a lust interest) is called Fredericka von Grusse. Bond chasing a serial killer is, at least, novel. As serial killer novels go, this doesn't quite match the tension of **Patricia Cornwell** but it never loses momentum. That said, the killer's list of targets is puzzling: **Kiri Te Kanawa**? Still, at least this time Bond's girl lives, under Gardner their survival rate has been lower than that of Henry VIII's wives.
Verdict 🔫🔫🔫🔫

Seafire (1994) John Gardner
The plot Mysterious tycoon Sir Max Tarn tries to bring back the Third Reich and create a massive oil slick
The book There are those who felt that Gardner's penultimate Bond novel went downhill after the title. Certainly, it's a case of *déjà vu* all over again. The Fourth Reich plot is straight out of Gardner's own *Icebreaker*: the villainous Tarn fakes his own death (as Bond's love interest Beatrice Maria da Ricci did in **Win, Lose Or Die**, as did Dr Jay Autem Holy and General Zwingli in **Role Of Honour**) and Bond's girl is captured (like Chi Chi, Harriet Horner, Moneypenny and M), although he rescues her and proposes to her, prompting (for Gardner) inevitable memories of Tracy. This novel is not without its adherents but not many. Why is Tarn deluded enough to think a massive oil slick will help him take over the world?
Verdict 🔫🔫

Cold/Coldfall (1996) John Gardner
The plot Retired American general Brutus Clay is plotting to take over America in a Fascist coup.
The book This is a chin-up, stomach-in, pull-yourself-together performance by Gardner, as he bids farewell to Bond. There's another cult (as in **Scorpius**), the Children Of The Lost Days being manipulated by Clay in Operation Blizzard. Mercifully the chilly villain is iced, but not before M has been kidnapped again (thank you **Colonel Sun**) and 007's old friend Principessa Sukie Tempesta turns

61

out, like four characters in previous Gardner novels, not to be dead after all although she is murdered after warning Bond about COLD. Fredericka von Grusse is dying, like every potential 007 bride. The novel ends with M retired and the reader wondering why 007 is investigating a plane crash. But Gardner does keep up the tension.
Verdict 🔫🔫🔫🔫🔫🔫🔫

Blast From The Past (1997) Raymond Benson
The plot Irma Bunt (remember her?) wants revenge on 007 for the things he did to her and Blofeld.
The book This short story, published in *Playboy*, is essentially a sequel to *You Only Live Twice* and received a rapturous welcome from Bond fans tired of Gardner's sometimes lame attempts to update 007. The only real problem is that it's a short story and the issues raised here (Bond's relationship with an illegitimate son) and some of the scenes (Bunt torturing 007 with a poisoned razor) are worthy of a longer read. Good to see Major Boothroyd and the Walther PPK back.
Verdict 🔫🔫🔫🔫🔫🔫🔫

Zero Minus Ten (1997) Raymond Benson
The plot Guy Thackeray is so upset by the handover of Hong Kong (and its effect on his family business) he wants to nuke it.
The book Benson's first Bond novel features a female M, a demotion for 007 (to captain, no reason given) and a villain who fakes his own death. The villain isn't in the book very much and the girl, Sunni Pei (you have to say it carefully), is as peripheral or as pointless. But the plot has plenty of twists and Benson's enjoyment comes through.
Verdict 🔫🔫🔫🔫🔫🔫🔫

The Facts Of Death (1998) Raymond Benson
The plot A sinister group, who are behind mysterious deaths caused by an unknown plague, try to start war between Greece and Turkey.
The book A cracking title, a cracking, complex plot and an almost obsessive need to emphasise continuity characterise Benson's second

Boris, Avaokoum, Israel & James

The name's Stolitsky, Boris Stolitsky
He's the hero of three novels by Finnish writer (and translator of Ian Fleming's novels) Arto Tuovinen in the 1960s. A Soviet spy, Stolitsky likes vodka (without martini), doesn't believe in Leninism, is deemed a misfit by his superiors and spends the first two books investigating a Nazi organisation run by Hitler's old mate, Martin Bormann. The third novel, set in the arms trade, wasn't such a success. Tuovinen died when he was just 35 in 1968, only two years after his first Stolitsky novel was published.

The name's Zakhov, Avakoum Zakov
Bulgarian writer Andrei Gulyashki took such great offence at the Bond novels' portrayal of the Bulgars as thugs for hire that he wrote a novel in which his hero, Bulgarian secret service officer Avakoum Zakhov, takes on a 'decadent but handsome agent of a corrupt Western power' called 07. Originally, Gulyashki called his hero James Bond before Glidrose, as the literary protectors of Bond, stepped in. For all of Gulyashki's bravado, Zakhov fails to kill agent 07, making his hero Zakhov just as ineffectual as the Bulgarian hitmen in From Russia With Love.

The name's Bond, Israel Bond
Sol Weinstein gave the world probably the most unusual Bond spoof. Step aside Austin Powers, Oy Oy Seven is in town. Agent Israel Bond starred in four literary adventures (from 1965 to 1968). Loxfinger (which like some Bond novels was published in Playboy), Matzohball, On The Secret Service Of His Majesty and the amusingly entitled You Only Live Until You Die.

The name's Bond, James Bond
Jim Hatfield's The Killing Zone doesn't appear in many lists of Bond novels even though its hero is called James Bond. The reason: it was not approved by Glidrose and is, if not illegal, certainly a bootleg Bond. That caveat aside, this US writer's novel is better than some of the later official Bond novels with a genuinely shocking ending.

Bond novel which is also notable for the amount of Anglo-Saxon used by the characters. Nothing against the odd swear word but somehow it doesn't quite sit with Bond.
Verdict 𝄢𝄢𝄢𝄢𝄢

Midsummer Nights Doom (1999) Raymond Benson
The plot Vital secrets are being sold to the Russian mafia at parties held by *Playboy* magnate **Hugh Hefner**.
The book This short story is vanity publishing for Hefner, and reads

at times like a Bond spoof. Thoroughly silly.

Verdict 🔫

High Time To Kill (1999) Raymond Benson

The plot Mercenaries try to sell a top-secret formula, which would enable aircraft to travel at five times the speed of sound, to sell to the Chinese government.

The book There are some obvious homages to Fleming, especially to **A Quantum Of Solace**. But the writing sometimes recalls Gardner's worst: 'She was studying him, attempting to figure him out with a spontaneous first impression'. There are a few other errors in this 300-page novel which make you feel Benson is being just too darned prolific. A pity because the plot is suitably sinuous (he has created a new SPECTRE, Union) and the global sweep is reminiscent of Fleming. Oh and Bond's girl gets it – again. You'd think he'd have trouble getting dates by now.

Verdict 🔫🔫🔫

Live At Five (1999) Raymond Benson

The plot On his way to a date with an American TV commentator, 007 remembers helping a Russian ice skater defect.

The book This very short story in *TV Guide* is too short to breathe. Still, an intriguing idea.

Verdict 🔫🔫🔫

Doubleshot (2000) Raymond Benson

The plot Enraged villain le Gerant wants to frame 007 for various murders, kill him and start war between the UK and Spain.

The book The last bit of the plot already echoes one of Benson's earlier novels but give him full marks for using a 007 double in what, it turns out, is the second in what is known as the Union

trilogy. This Bond weighs in at some 275 pages and Benson makes use of the extra space to get into 007's character. *Kirkus Reviews* concluded that 'despite some nifty bullfighting scenes, this is for diehard fans only', which is probably a bit harsh although Bond seems strangely witless for much of the book.
Verdict ₣₣₣

Never Dream Of Dying (2001) Raymond Benson
The plot Terrorists plan to attack the Cannes film festival.
The book Benson's final instalment of his Union trilogy is better than the in-a-nutshell plot might suggest. His writing is no worse than, say, Tom Clancy's, his plots are complex and ingenious (he pulls off a nice twist at the end here) and in the Union (run by a Japanese villain Yoshida), he has fulfilled Fleming's rule about giving 007 worthy adversaries. His nods to Fleming don't feel as mechanical as some of Gardner's did.
Verdict ₣₣₣₣

The Man With The Red Tattoo (2002) Raymond Benson
The plot Yoshida plots mass assassination at a G7 summit with a 'biological' weapon.
The book Benson's arrival as the new Bond author was greeted with some apprehension by Bond fans who learned that he'd never written a novel before (although he had written a bedside companion to Bond) and was a computer games geek. And some of that nerdiness comes across here when he devotes too much space to, for example, the life cycle of genetically engineered mosquitoes. But the same thoroughness makes his villains credible, the demise of the girls genuinely upsetting and his Bond human. **Robert McCrum**, reviewing this book in the *Observer*, probably summed it up best when he said: 'What's missing is Fleming's inimitable voice, that languid, Fleet Street drawl as smoky and cynical as the morning-after atmosphere of a Mayfair nightclub'.
Verdict ₣₣₣₣

Other Bond related books

Biographies

With a distinct lack of interest in writing about Bonds two (Lazenby) and four (Dalton), these are the best biographies written about the people that played and made Bond or played alongside him.

Ian Fleming Andrew Lycett (Phoenix)

Definitely the most recent and arguably the best biography of the man who invented Bond. Lycett had access to Fleming's family and friends and produced an affectionate, readable, yet realistic account of the man's life. It's much easier, after reading this, to see how and why Fleming created Bond. Lycett also makes judicious use of the amusing and enlightening testimonies of friends and peers like Noel Coward and John Betjeman. The earlier biography by John Pearson, published in 1966 by Jonathan Cape, is not without merit – Pearson then went on to write a biography of James Bond (published in 1973 by Sidgwick & Jackson and later in paperback by Pan), an accumulation of the biographical data littered through Fleming's novels.

Sean Connery Michael Feeney Callan (Virgin)

Read about Connery as a milkman, bodybuilder and superstar. Most of Connery's biographies are short on revelations, yet Callan mercifully avoids portraying the world's sexiest pensioner as purer than the driven snow. After all, you don't go from 13-year-old school dropout to Hollywood superstar without upsetting someone. Not the most up-to-date book on the market but more honest than most although it doesn't quite explain why a man who wears a 'Scotland forever' tattoo, and campaigns for the Scottish National Party, visits his homeland even less frequently than the other great expat patriot Scot, Rod Stewart. The biography has just been reissued by Virgin.

Roger Moore His Films & Career Gareth Owen & Oliver Bayan (Robert Hale)

The only Moore biography is recommended by Richard Kiel, aka Jaws from the Bond series – and who are we to disagree with him? Casual enthusiasts probably won't find it that entertaining, but a good buy for fans of the raised eyebrow. You might, though, find out more about Moore by reading his own account of the filming of Live And Let Die.

Pierce Brosnan Peter Carrick (Robert Hale)

Lacking both an imaginative title and any real new information about the current Bond. But Carrick gets our vote because he concentrates on different aspects to other Brosnan biographies, mainly focusing on his struggle for professional recognition. Others might prefer the York Membery biog (Virgin).

Q – the Authorised Biography of Desmond Llewelyn **Sandy Hernu & Pierce Brosnan (SB Publications)**
When Llewelyn was cast as Q in *From Russia With Love*, neither he nor the producers
expected the character to become such a feature of the films. However, as Hernu and
Brosnan point out, there was more to Llewelyn than Q.

When The Show Melts: An Autobiography **Cubby Broccoli & Donald Zec**
As the producer and controller of the Bond franchise, Cubby Broccoli holds a unique
place in cinematic history. You have to wait until midway through to get to the Bond bits
but his tales of Hollywood in the 1940s and 1950s, and his friendships with luminaries
such as Cary Grant (best man at Broccoli's wedding) and Howard Hughes make for

Playboy and Bond

1953 saw the birth of two literary phenomena (and we use the word 'literary' in the
loosest way for the latter), the Bond books and *Playboy* magazine, both products which
would hit the target Ian Fleming aimed his books at – 'somewhere between the solar
plexus and the upper thigh'. Both offered a vision of a hedonistic, luxurious, heterosexual existence which tapped into many men's fantasies.

The magazine's founder **Hugh Hefner** soon lived a Bondian lifestyle (without the need to
sort out some megolamaniacal monster). Bunny girls offered similar ideals of feminine
perfection as did the Bond girls in the films, just more ludicrous. Even Fleming didn't
make his female characters wear rabbit's tails, and the idea was too risible even for
the Roger Moore movies of the 1970s – in which Bond did indeed get to roger more.

Hefner was quick to see the advantage of pairing his mag with 007 and Fleming's
books were serialised in *Playboy*, beginning with the short story the Hildebrand Rarity,
printed in 1960. Each subsequent book received the *Playboy* treatment, serialised and
illustrated in the magazine. When the film franchise took off, *Playboy* extended the
association, running pictorials of films, such as 'Oriental Eyefull', to promote For Your Eyes
Only, accompanied by naked centrefolds of Bond girls, and pictures of **Lois Maxwell** (Miss
Moneypenny), who didn't appear naked but did expose more flesh than usual. Even
press-shy Connery was interviewed by *Playboy*; as was Fleming, in 1963.

Since the 1960s *Playboy* has maintained its ties with 007. In 1987, his 25th anniversary was marked by a special edition featuring every Bond girl since the films began.
The magazine even featured its own parodies, accompanied by surreal
artwork – such as Toadstool, the hero surrounded by psychedelic rabbits. For more on
the Playboy link, try www.artofjamesbond.com/playboy.htm.

good reading. And when it gets to Bond, there's an amusing refrain where, with each new actor cast in it, Broccoli muses about how he made them what they are today, that success has gone to their head, and that don't they realise how lucky they are. Like Broccoli himself, the book is larger than life and never dull.

For Our Eyes Only John Glen (BT Batsford)

The director of five Bond films (who was also involved in the making of three others) tells, if not all, enough to justify the cover price. There's an amusing foreword by Moore who insists that Glen would make a movie of all of the actor's worst takes, 'for their eyes only', at the end of every film. Glen also includes some decent rarely seen books.

Golden Girl Shirley Eaton (BT Batsford)

Mickey Spillane, creator of Mike Hammer, a crime-fighting hero whose penchant for violence was exceeded only by Bond villains, has written the foreword to this memoir by the actress chiefly famous for being dipped in gold paint. Pity the designer chose a gold border for the cover – it clashes horribly with Eaton's gold portrait. In the book, our Shirl insists: 'The reason why people are huge stars is nothing to do with acting. It's the magic. Charisma is a word that's used too often, it's something special and it's what makes stars. It's luck and basically it's genes.' So now we know.

John Barry The Sound Of The Sixties Eddi Fiegel (Constable)

Preferable to *John Barry His Life And Music*, mainly because it gives you a much better flavour of what Barry is like to work with. The behind-the-scenes feel gives this book something extra and if you're intrigued by Barry, this is for you. The book is also available in paperback from Boxtree.

Making It Big in the Movies Richard Kiel (Reynolds & Hearn)

Inspirational autobiography of the man with the metal teeth, say some. Just a cut above a schoolboy's 'What I did on my summer vacation' essay, say others. Probably more interesting to those who share his religious views than to those who want inside info on the making of Bond movies. We say this, fully aware of the danger that a 7ft man with metal teeth may turn up on our doorstep one day and ask us to explain ourselves.

General

The Bond Files Andy Lane and Paul Simpson (Virgin)

One of the co-authors is the namesake of this guide's text editor, but that coincidence aside, this is a thorough run through of books, films, comic strips and role-playing games. The authors quote Oscar Wilde ('It is a very sad thing that nowadays there is so little useless information') and this book is full of it. The only caveat is that the authors

Roger protects Jane on the *Live And Let Die* set ▲

don't always seem to like Bond that much. Still worth the price of entry.

Dressed to Kill: James Bond – the Suited Hero (Flammarion)
Novelist Jay McInerney, author of *Bright Lights, Big City* and *Brightness Falls*, is among the heavyweight contributors to this gorgeous coffee table book, which looks at the influence Bond and his imitators have had on popular culture and fashion. Complete with a rundown on the sartorial eloquence, or otherwise, of all five actors to play 007.

Il Caso Bond (aka The Bond Affair) Del Buono and Umberto Eco (Macdonald)
Sadly out of print, this wonderful book by the man who would, in the 1980s, have a worldwide best-seller with The Name Of The Rose (in the film of which a certain Mr Connery would play the monastic crime-solving hero) analyses Bond to within an inch of his life. A good provoking read. This essay was reprinted in Popular Culture: Past and Present published by Croon Helm.

The James Bond Bedside Companion Raymond Benson (Publishing Online)
The book that earned Benson his shot at writing 007 novels. You can see why. It's chock-full of delights for a true Bond fan. Published in 1988, and not yet updated, – Mr Benson having other books to finish – this is still essential reading.

James Bond: The Secret World of 007 Alastair Dougall Dorling Kindersley
It's big, it's lavish, it's loads of fun for kids from nine to 49. Among other things, this runs through every mission Bond

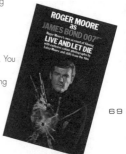

has ever undertaken in enough detail to be informative but not so much that it's tedious. Buy it for a younger sibling or just own up and buy it for yourself.

The Little Book of Bond (Boxtree)

Small, perfectly formed and strangely addictive little tome – almost the literary equivalent of a snack. This selection of Bond's finest lines has been a steady seller and it's the perfect beginning to a Bond collection or an inexpensive but nifty present for a friend. A sample of the wisdom on offer: 'Most girls just paddle around. You swim like a man'.

The Politics of James Bond Jeremy Black (Praeger)

As the title suggests, this is not the book to peruse if you're after on-set scandal or two-bit trivia about your favourite Bond films and stars. Black, a professor of history, writes in an academic style which doesn't quite conceal the fact that he hasn't really made any startling connections between Bond as a literary hero and movie star and politics – ideological or even sexual. Ironically, the book is almost more effective running through the movies and the casting than it is when drawing parallels between fact and fiction.

Kiss Kiss Bang! Bang! Alan Barnes, Marcus Hearn (BT Batsford)

In-depth analysis of each of the Bond films (up to The World Is Not Enough) charting their transition from page to screen, with refreshing accounts of casting calls, location shoots and those theme songs. For 'unofficial', read, more interesting than most, with details on Connery's refusal to play ball with the press, and Moore's dissatisfaction with the lack of acting the role took. A must for Bond fans.

The books

The Devil with James Bond Ann S Boyd Greenwood Press

007 as St George – the parallel between the two is probably the highlight of this book, originally published in 1967 when it seemed obligatory for a publisher to have a title which had an intellectual angle on Bond.

My Name's Bond, James Bond: editor: Simon Winder (Penguin)

A lovely, slender volume of prose culled from Fleming's Bond novels under various themes, which doesn't gloss over the book's idiosyncrasies (the chapter sub-titled 'this country of furtive stunted little men' being a magnificent round up of the books' prejudices against johnny foreigner) yet contrives to make the books and the world of Fleming/Bond seem hugely entertaining.

The 007 Dossier: Your Assignment Into the Literary World of James Bond B.S. McReynolds (BS Books)

A quick flick through Bond books, with handy sections such as, Bond Girls, Chick

Charts, Bonded Habits and 007 Gourmet to dip in and out of. Not for anyone looking for a deep and meaningful examination of 007 – and don't hold the fact that they can't spell 'service' on the back cover against them.

The movies

The Complete James Bond Movie Encyclopedia Stephen Jay Rubin (Contemporary Books)
If you only buy one book about Bond's movie career, this is the one. Simple as that.

The Essential Bond: An Official Guide to the World of 007 Lee Pfeiffer and Dave Worrall
Buy it for the photos, many of which haven't been seen elsewhere, this having EON's blessing. The text is okay – about up to the standard of John Gardner's *The Man From Barbarossa*, with disappointingly little inside info.

Goldfinger The Ultimate Film Guide Adrian Dunbar
As *Goldfinger* was the film which perfected the Bond celluloid formula, as well as being the movie in which the former coffin polisher Sean Connery made the Bond role conclusively his own, it probably makes sense to have a guide to this Bond movie more than any other. It is better value than its size (78 pages) might suggest.

James Bond Movie Posters – the Official Collection Tony Nourmand (Boxtree)
Bond has been responsible for some of the finest movie posters of the last 40 years, at their best, typifying the flair and confidence which has made the movies such a success. The inclusion of oddities such as the Italian poster for *The World Is Not Enough* adds to the value, as does the decision to include the posters for the unofficial movies, *Casino Royale* and *Never Say Never Again*.

Live And Let Die Roger Moore
Roger Moore's debut as Bond in *Live And Let Die* is documented by the man himself, with a certain degree of no-holds-barred frankness (obviously he couldn't be too frank or he might not have been recalled for the next film). Simply brimming with on-set gossip of fights, arguments, the card games and the artistic wranglings. Bond girl Gloria Hendry, says Moore, needed to relate all her dialogue to her own experiences, this trait unfortunately meaning that it took her 12 takes to say 'useless'. A fabulous insight into the films, entertaining for both avid fans and casual observers.

Licence to Thrill James Chapman Columbia University Press
An intriguing examination of Bond's cultural impact and his development through the last four decades. Particularly interesting is the analysis of other film movements upon Bond, for example the influence of the 'blaxploitation' movement on *Live And Let Die* in 1972.

The author clearly knows his stuff and so will you by the end. Sometimes slips into such nonsense as 'While the narrative ideologies of *GoldenEye* and *Tomorrow Never Dies* have much in common through their reassertion of the patriotic code of the Bond series, the films are quite different in style' – but it still deserves a place on your bookshelf.

The rest of Fleming

Chitty Chitty Bang Bang Ian Fleming (Puffin)

You've seen a horse fly but have you ever seen a car fly? This charming children's book, turned into a memorable film with Dick van Dyke and Julie Andrews substitute Sally Ann Howe, was originally a bedtime story for Fleming's son Caspar. It is beguiling proof of Fleming's love for his son, cars and technology. He even managed to have the head of the Potts family tell his kids: 'Never say "no" to adventures. Always say "yes". Otherwise you'll lead a very dull life.' The car is a composite of two cars, one of which Fleming had owned and, in a never-say-no to adventures kind of way, driven into a train.

The Diamond Smugglers Ian Fleming (Amereon)

Fleming's real account of skulduggery in the international diamond trade is not without interest but given that it was based on research conducted almost half a century ago, may only be worth buying for completists.

Thrilling Cities Ian Fleming (Amereon)

Ian Fleming's travelogue with a difference. For a start, few travel writers spend as much time focusing on dung beetles in Naples as Fleming does here. And he's thrilled by prostitution, stripteases and the crimes passionels in cities like Geneva. But he brings the same experienced, observant eye to these cities as he does to the locales in his Bond novels, which makes this well worth a read.

Miscellaneous

Birds Of The West Indies James Bond (Petersen)

The book that gave Ian Fleming the name for his blunt instrument of a hero. Wonderfully sub-titled, *An Account With Full Descriptions Of All The Birds Known To Occur Or To Have Occurred On The West Indian Islands,* and first published in 1936, it has been rarely out of print since – possibly because of the 007 connection. Now available, mainly in the US, as a Petersen Field Guide although, as the ornithologist has been dead since 1989, you wonder how much he's had to do with the 1999 edition. At least one ornithologist is not placated by the link to 007, complaining on Amazon.com, 'The plates are sporadically placed throughout the book, and some species of birds are not illustrated. For example, what does a greater antillean grackle look like?'

Brazilian Adventure Peter Fleming Northwestern University Press
It would be remiss not to include at least one book by Ian's brother Peter. The Flemings' inability to write a dull line was obviously genetic, with Peter's travel books being some of the most entertaining ever written. This book almost has a Bondian plot: Fleming goes off on an expedition to solve the mystery of the missing Colonel Fawcett, who had gone into the Amazonian jungle in search of a lost city. This is probably, just, Peter's best travel book although News From Tartary and One's Company are both worth buying.

Eastern Approaches Fitzroy Maclean (Penguin)
There are three cracking adventure books in one here, the added bonus being that written by Fitzroy Maclean, friend of Fleming and possible model for 007, it's all true. His understated style brings his experiences (being in Moscow for the show trials of the 1930s and working with Tito in Yugoslavia) wonderfully to life.

From Arctic Snow To Dust Of Normandy Patrick Dalzel-Job (Nead-an-Eoin)
Tersely written, stirring account of the author's wartime adventures, including his work for a naval commander called Ian Fleming. Full of understated Bondian derring do.

From Stockport with Love Dave Bowker Sceptre
An odd book this: dad John Bryce goes to see GoldenEye on the eve of his son's birth, musing on the discrepancies between his life and Bond's. The next day his son is born with a serious heart defect. This sounds like the recipe for a perfectly awful tear-jerker but Bowker manages to avoid the schlock and produces a novel that is at times both humorous and heart-breaking that works even for those readers, like this reviewer, who have an in-built suspicion of father-and-son bonding scenarios in fiction.

James Bond's London Gary Giblin (Daleon)
If you want to retrace the steps of Commander Bond, as he appears in the Fleming novels, through the city affectionately known to locals as 'The smoke', this is the book for you. Lovingly prepared, lavishly detailed – almost to the point that you begin to wonder about the depth of the author's obsession – this is a fine work.

Your Deal Mr Bond Phillip and Robert King (Batsford)
A collection of bridge fiction which is named after Bond because it includes a story in which Bond impersonates bridge expert Zia Mahmood. As the book comes with a foreword by Mahmood, he obviously approves of the impersonation. Curiouser and curiouser.

The next Bond novelist?

It's not our place to tell Glidrose, the guardians of the Bond literary heritage, what to do. Nor do we have any special wish to stop the estimable Raymond Benson continuing his profitable work. But the literary side of 007's existence is in dire need of either some serious spin-doctoring or a high-profile author to weigh in on our hero's behalf. The obvious solution, from a legal and literary standpoint, would be to bring in Martin Amis as he is a) legally entitled to write one thanks to his dad and b) himself in need of some subject matter since the failure of his novel, The Information, to justify the huge advance which lured him to switch publishers.

Martin is, like Fleming, constitutionally incapable of writing a dull sentence and his imagination is almost as grotesque as Fleming's. Amis' early novel Dead Babies is full of creatures so macabre Fleming could have incorporated them into his fiction (once he'd added in a few bits about how they wanted to take over the world). And he's written about sex almost as frequently as Fleming has, albeit with more emphasis on the role played by bodily fluids than you find in any of Fleming's Bond novels. The only serious difficulty, apart from the fact that Amis Junior would have to shelve his pretensions to literary greatness for a while, might be that for all his prowess, he struggles to create male characters the reader can actually warm to. His Bond might turn out to be a sad, slightly nerdy, loner who only has any success with women in his dreams.

If Martin's not interested, there's always his ex-mate Julian Barnes, who could knock out A History Of James Bond In 7 1/2 Chapters. It's a pity Elmore Leonard wasn't born British, as he has the vocabulary and the worldliness which were such essential parts of Bond's charm. Nearer to home, both in genre and geography, Glidrose could do worse than ask Ian Rankin, who has already proved he knows the patch with his pseudonymous Jack Harvey novels.

Martin Amis, aged 007 years ▲

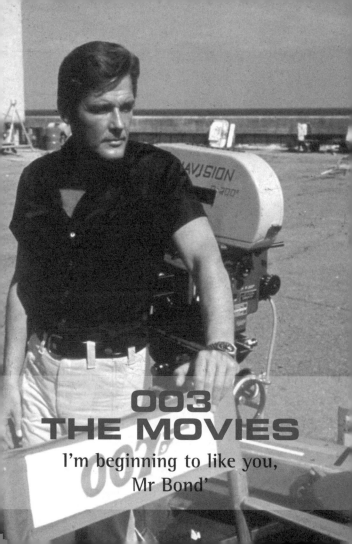

003
THE MOVIES
'I'm beginning to like you,
Mr Bond'

007

'World domination... The same old dream'

Dr. No

The James Bond film phenomenon is the longest, most successful and highest grossing movie series in the history of cinema. From 1962 to 1999 it had grossed over $3 billion for its makers and distributors, and the cash cow looks set to continue with *Die Another Day*. It is now 40 years since Sean Connery walked onto the big screen as 007, and even though at times it has looked like Bond might be about to retire from film life, it's never long before he's resurrected and more successful than ever.

There has been extraordinary continuity in the series in terms of the people responsible for bringing each story to the screen, and the main thread of this is the producer, **Albert Romolo Broccoli**, known as Cubby after a childhood friend named him after a popular cartoon character, Abie Kabibble. A win at the races allowed the young Broccoli to move from Queens in New York to Los Angeles where he soon made his way in the movie business, eventually teaming up with director **Irving Allen** to make films under the very favourable terms set by the British government in the 1950s. Although none of the films he made were particularly successful (check out *The Gamma People* starring **Leslie Phillips** if you're wondering why), Cubby had a knack for knowing what audiences wanted. When he became interested in **Ian Fleming**'s novels, he found out that most of the film rights were owned by Canadian producer **Harry Saltzman**, an option that had cost the producer $1,000. Saltzman and Broccoli teamed up to form EON Productions and persuaded United Artists to put up the $1m it cost to make *Dr. No*. Dana Broccoli, Cubby's wife, spotted **Sean Connery** (after hubby was turned down by **Cary Grant**) and the casting ensured the film was to be a success. Just how much of a success, nobody – perhaps not even Cubby – could have predicted.

The early Bond movies blasted through the box office all over the world (13 of them topped the British box office for their year of release), and even those that had a mixed critical response still made a healthy profit. EON seemed unstoppable, and even the flurry of legal deals that surrounded the making of *Thunderball*, with Broccoli and Saltzman eventually sharing credits with Kevin McClory who owned the rights to Fleming's story, hardly dented its momentum.

Lazenby was best known as a model in a chocolate advert

When Connery quit after *You Only Live Twice* (he believed the spy craze was on the wane), the search for a new Bond unearthed both **Timothy Dalton** and **Roger Moore**. Dalton was actually offered the part but turned it down feeling that, at 25, he was too young. As it transpired, both lost out – to a dapper Australian playboy who raced cars and wore a dinner jacket with terrific style. When it turned out that George Lazenby was not really a playboy, but a model best known for a chocolate commercial, it was too late. Riding high on 007's aura, Lazenby decided he might become too famous as Bond and quit the series after only one film, *On Her Majesty's Secret Service*. This was possibly the worst decision he (or any other actor) ever made – his subsequent career 'highlights' have been 1977's **Kentucky Fried Movie** and several *Emmanuelle* films.

The producers

Cubby Broccoli didn't just produce Bond movies. Before 007 his most enduring contribution to the movies was probably his role in producing The Trials Of Oscar Wilde starring Peter Finch as the Irish poet and playwright and Lionel Jeffries as his persecutor, the Marquis of Queensberry. Jeffries later played inventor Caractacus Potts' dad in Chitty Chitty Bang Bang – which Broccoli also produced (and also sprang from the fertile brain of Ian Fleming) – singing the song 'Posh posh travelling life' to great effect while suspended in a phonebox from an airship. Jeffries also starred in Call Me Bwana, the 1963 Anita Ekberg-Bob Hope comedy which was the only other film (apart from Chitty) that Broccoli produced to completion after the Bond series kicked off. A 1970 film of Nijinsky, the ballet dancer not the horse, starring Rudolf Nureyev and written by Edward 'Who's Afraid Of Virginia Woolf?' Albee, was not finished. Broccoli's long-time partner as Bond producer, Harry Saltzman, did make a film based on the dancer's life story, starring George De la Pena in the title role, though, given the mixed reviews and poor box office, probably wished he hadn't bothered. Saltzman's non-007 career is more interesting than Broccoli's: he was responsible for such 1950s classics as Look Back In Anger, as well as The Ipcress File (and its sequels in the Len Deighton spy series) and Yugoslav director Emir Kusturica's masterpiece, Time Of the Gypsies.

Connery initially refused all efforts to get him back, to the point where EON had already hired American actor **John Gavin** (who later played Cary Grant in a TV movie of Sophia Loren's life) as Bond. Gavin was dumped when Connery was lured by the promise of a huge fee, which he donated to a Scottish charity. After *Diamonds Are Forever* another round of Bond casting began (despite an offer of £5m to Connery). This time Moore got the role, starting his 12-year run with *Live And Let Die*.

Broccoli and Saltzman co-produced the Bond films until *The Man With The Golden Gun* (despite having to alternate duties as hands-on producers for the last few films due to what are known in Hollywood as 'creative differences'), after which Saltzman, under financial pressure in his other businesses, sold his stake in the Bond franchise to United Artists. Initially the split was good news for EON. For *The Spy Who Loved Me* a vast film stage was built at Pinewood Studios (it was rebuilt after a fire, but the Albert R Broccoli 007 Stage is still the largest purpose-built film stage in the world), and the film raked in more than double the box office of *The Man With The Golden Gun*. Its successors, *Moonraker* and *For Your Eyes Only* (the first Bond film to have no credit for Ian Fleming), did equally well.

After that, however, times got tough for Bond. *Octopussy* and *A View To A Kill* suffered from budget cutbacks by MGM/UA, as well as a Bond overload: **Kevin McClory**, prevented from producing anything based on his *Thunderball* material for 10 years, had finally realised his dream of getting Connery to play the role once again, in *Never Say Never Again*, but as one of three Bond films released in just over two years, it proved to be a less than spectacular success.

The Albert R Broccoli sound stage in all its pomp and glory ▲

Broccoli continued producing the Bond films alone until *The Living Daylights* when he teamed up with **Michael G Wilson**, his stepson, who, after a career in law, had gone to work as Cubby's assistant and been groomed to take over. They took Bond in a new direction, with the casting of **Timothy Dalton** – who brought the franchise a darker, more Fleming-like edge – and some spectacular action. Sadly, audiences liked their Bond a little on the lighter side, and Dalton's two films were not great successes.

The six-year gap between *Licence To Kill* and *GoldenEye* was partly due to the former's poor box office, and partly because EON was locked in a lawsuit with MGM/UA and Pathé over television licensing for the earlier Bond films. By the time the writs had stopped flying, and it was clear Dalton was not going to make another Bond movie, the search was on again. Happily, despite rumours that **Sean Bean** was being considered, there was a clear choice in **Pierce Brosnan**, who had been offered the role after Moore but was unable to get out of his TV contract for *Remington Steele*.

> There were rumours Sean Bean was considered for 007

With **Barbara Broccoli** now co-producing with half-brother Michael G Wilson (ill health forced Cubby to step down in the early 1990s), 007 has been truly revived, with lots of new faces on screen, fresher scripts, bigger action and better stunts than ever. It remains very much a family affair, though, with at least a dozen crew members for the later Bonds sons and daughters of crew members from the earlier films. Cubby Broccoli died in 1996 (*Tomorrow Never Dies* is dedicated to his memory) but he was able to glimpse the new Bond family in *GoldenEye*. *Die Another Day*, with Oscar-winner **Halle Berry** as the new Bond woman (in one scene her outfit is a definite homage to Ursula Andress in *Dr. No*), looks set to be another blockbuster. We're sure Cubby would approve.

Casting

Much of the ongoing success of James Bond is due to his on-screen partners. The calibre of the girls, the villains and the recurrent characters has added to the sense that a Bond movie is unlike any other, an exclusive club where you can spend some time just by buying a cinema ticket.

The three main recurring characters, the stalwarts of MI6, are **M**, **Miss Moneypenny** and **Q**. M was played perfectly by Bernard Lee up until his death in 1981, with *Moonraker* his last Bond outing. He was a prolific actor, featuring in more than 100 films, including British classics like *Whistle Down The Wind* and *The Blue Lamp*. After Lee died, M was given leave during *For Your Eyes Only*. For *Octopussy* Robert Brown, who had previously played Admiral Hargreaves, was promoted to the leather chair and remained there until **Judi Dench** broke through the glass ceiling and nabbed the role on behalf of all the feminists Bond had annoyed over the years. The casting of Dench as a female M gave the series scope for personal development of the character, as well as for some stunning put-downs of Bond's occasional macho posturing. Let's face it, if Judi Dench told you to do something, you'd do it, wouldn't you?

Sadly, David Bowie refused to play Max Zorin

Lois Maxwell famously played Miss Moneypenny, M's capable and flirtatious secretary, in the first 14 Bond movies. In the early Bonds she even wore her own clothes as the character seemed to suit her so well. When Maxwell retired in 1989, a new Moneypenny was found for Dalton but **Caroline Bliss** was not an inspiring choice. The idea of Moneypenny listening to Barry Manilow is a bit too sad even for such a confirmed spinster, so it came as a relief when the role passed to the sparkier **Samantha Bond** in the Brosnan era. And while the new incarnation is fluent in double entendres Lois

Maxwell never dared utter, Miss Moneypenny seems in safe hands.

Most beloved and longest-serving of the cast regulars is Desmond Llewelyn. He first appeared in *From Russia With Love* as Major Boothroyd, the armourer, but from then on was known only as Q. His fondness for Bond was only outweighed by his love for his work, and it's testament to his acting that he established a believable rapport with all five of the Bonds. Nobody could deliver all those lines on the theme of 'Try not to break it, 007', with such hope mixed with resignation. Sadly, he was killed in a car accident in 1999 at the age of 85, but not before introducing his assistant, R (**John Cleese**), who has been promoted to replace Q in *Die Another Day*. At least Llewelyn kept his promise to continue in the role 'as long as the producers want me and the Almighty doesn't'.

All the other characters – the girls, the villains and the strange henchmen – have also been cast with care, although sometimes it's more interesting to look at who didn't play the part than who did.

Raquel Welch was cast as Domino in *Thunderball* but was released from her contract as a favour to the makers of *Fantastic Voyage*. **Brigitte Bardot** and **Catherine Deneuve** were asked to play Bond's ill-fated wife Tracy, and Tom Mankiewicz wrote the part of Solitaire in *Live And Let Die* for **Diana Ross**.

> Blofeld was to have either a limp, hump or a facial scar

Similar changes of mind affected the villains. The best refusal was probably **Noel Coward**'s. Offered the part of Dr No, Fleming's chum sent a telegram saying 'Dr No? No! No! No!' **Gert Fröbe** was at one point set to return as Goldfinger's vengeful twin brother, but the script never got written. When **Donald Pleasance** took the part of Blofeld, he dithered about whether to have a hump or a limp before settling on the facial scar – the right choice, we think. Several actors were considered for the Jaws role, including **Dave Prowse**, the Green Cross Code man who also occupied Darth Vader's robes, before the producers hired seven-foot two-inch giant Richard Kiel. Sadly, **David Bowie** turned down the chance to play Max Zorin, which would have given an interesting twist to the background story that he had been the result of Nazi genetic experimentation ('Dammit, ve got ze eyes wrong again!'). New Zealand rugby star **Jonah Lomu** was offered the role of Bullion in *Tomorrow Never Dies*, but declined.

Dr. No
1962

Cast	Sean Connery, Joseph Wiseman, Jack Lord, Ursula Andress
Director	Terence Young
Screenplay	Richard Maibaum, Johanna Harwood, Berkely Mather
Rating	♟♟♟♟♟♟♟

Bond is sent to Jamaica to investigate a colleague's disappearance. He tracks the killer to remote Crab Key where he finds **Honey Ryder** (Andress) rising from the waves in her white bikini (the point at which, for many, Bond reached a cinematic peak never to be scaled again). They are both captured by Dr No, a reclusive, brilliant scientist belonging to SPECTRE (Special Executive for Counter-intelligence, Terrorism, Revenge and Extortion), who is sabotaging the US space programme. After a miraculous and daring escape, Bond triumphs.

Even the most hopeful producer could never have dreamed *Dr. No* would be the first of a movie franchise still going strong 40 years later. In-jokes, like the Goya painting of the Duke of Wellington (which had recently been stolen in real life) hanging on Dr No's wall, became a staple of the series, and the early appearance of CIA agent Felix Leiter (played by **Jack Lord**, who never repeated the role because he demanded equal billing with Connery) set him up as an intermittent character for stories to come. Good reviews, word of mouth and a special communiqué from the Vatican condemning the film's lack of morality, ensured the first Bond wouldn't be the last.

Title sequence An early attempt at cinematic psychedelia with strips of celluloid and flickering lights, complete with silhouette of a dancing woman. Nice touch with the assassins walking from the titles straight into the film.

Best lines Miss Moneypenny 'Flattery will get you nowhere, but don't stop trying.'

Honey 'Are you looking for shells too?'

Bond 'No, I'm just looking.'

Famous last words Dr No 'You are just a stupid policeman whose luck has run out.'

Notable stunts Nothing truly spectacular, but Bond's escape (surviving electrocution, burning and near drowning) is vintage.

Goofs/in-jokes Besides Felix's chameleon suit, which changes colour between our first and second glimpse and the next shot,

The name's Carmichael, Hoagy...

In the search for the perfect celluloid 007, Cubby Broccoli never really considered the man whom Ian Fleming had first seen as his inspiration for the character: Hoagy Carmichael. Just as well really, as by the time Dr. No was filmed, Carmichael was 62. Best known as a singer/songwriter (and creator of such classics as Stardust and Georgia On My Mind), Carmichael did a modest career as a movie actor, often playing a musician (he was Cricket, the piano player, in the Bogart and Bacall classic To Have And Have Not) and occasionally himself (as he did in the late 1940s William Bendix crime drama Johnny Holiday). When Fleming gave the go-ahead for a Bond comic strip, he sent an illustration of his ideal hero to the Daily Express describing him as a dashing, good-looking, 'sort of Hoagy Carmichael type'. Born in Bloomington, Indiana, Carmichael was a good friend of jazz great Bix Beiderbecke (starring in a movie of his late friend's life), had parallel careers as actor, singer and radio star for a time in the 1950s and died, after a heart attack, in 1981. He had something of a Bondian physique in his prime, combining elegance and a certain masculinity. For more on Hoagy, try www.dlib.indiana.edu/collections/hoagy/index.html.

and Bond's disappearing tie in the scene with Professor Dent (perhaps it was an early Q prototype), *Dr. No* has some fine plot holes. How can Dr No have detected Honey's sail boat on his radar when radar cannot pick up either wood or canvas? And why doesn't the decontamination lab flood when water is pouring down the ventilation shafts?

From Russia With Love

1963

Cast	Sean Connery, Robert Shaw, Lotte Lenya, Daniela Bianchi
Director	Terence Young
Screenplay	Richard Maibaum, 'adapted by Johanna Harwood'
Rating	𝄢𝄢𝄢𝄢𝄢𝄢

A SPECTRE plot to avenge Dr No's death lures Bond to Istanbul with the promise of a Soviet encryption device. Unwitting double agent **Tatiana Romanova** helps Bond steal the Lektor, but then he is plunged into a nightmare as he tries to get the machine back to England. A miraculous and daring escape from a low-flying helicopter, a speedboat chase, and a villainous lesbian, ensures Bond is free to pursue SPECTRE another day.

Despite its complex plot, this is one of the best Bond movies – a real thriller where Bond is a spy first and stylish superhero second. The script serves up some wonderful English snobbery (SPECTRE agent Donald 'Red' Grant is condemned for drinking red wine with fish rather than for being a psychopath) and the doubled budget is put to good use with more gizmos. The villains are top notch too, with exemplary paranoid psychosis provided by Grant and Rosa Klebb. Watch out for the gypsy dance sequence which turns into a Cold War gun battle – a scene sometimes cut from TV versions. First appearances are made by

Connery and Daniela Bianchi get some technical advice from director Terence Young ▶

Blofeld, complete with white Persian cat, and Q (Desmond Llewelyn), brandishing the obligatory booby-trapped attaché case. *From Russia With Love* justifiably topped the UK box office in 1963 and established the release of a Bond movie as an event.

Title sequence No sign of the real Sean yet, just a macho mish-mash projected onto the stomach of a belly dancer.

Best lines Bond 'Your mouth is the right size… for me that is.'

Famous last words Blofeld 'Let his death be a particularly unpleasant and humiliating one.'

Notable stunts Bond being chased by the tiny, low-flying SPECTRE helicopter (a sequence that nearly killed Connery), followed by his flawless shooting of the oil barrels that explode and destroy his pursuers on their boats.

Goofs/in-jokes Bond never turns off the shower he is about to take when Tatiana arrives. For all we know, it's still running. Plus, if you look very carefully in the gypsy sequence, you can see Kerim applying his own fake blood.

Goldfinger
1964

Cast	Sean Connery, Gert Fröbe, Honor Blackman
Director	Guy Hamilton
Screening	Richard Maibaum, Paul Dehn
Rating	🎬🎬🎬🎬🎬🎬🎬

Bond is sent to check out toad-like **Auric Goldfinger** (Fröbe) who is no longer satisfied with his impressive gold smuggling operation and is planning to irradiate the US gold supply at Fort Knox, causing global economic meltdown. Despite being captured fairly early, Bond uses his considerable talents to persuade Pussy Galore (Blackman), Goldfinger's secret weapon, to agree a counter-plot, overseen by Felix Leiter and the US Army. After his miraculous and daring escape from being

Over-dressed Fleming meets Connery on set ▲

chained to a nuclear warhead, followed by some quality time with Oddjob, the lethal, bowler-hatted henchman, Bond decides not to save the world himself but let the bomb disposal guy do it for him. Goldfinger tries a last hijack but he has lost his Midas touch and gets sucked out of Bond's private plane.

This established the recognisable template for all subsequent Bond movies with its opening action sequence (Bond's destruction of a heroin plant), a sacrificial lamb (**Shirley Eaton**) to establish the ruthlessness of the villain and a touch of humanity for Bond, its jokes and puns, and its increasing number of explosions and deaths. Plus, of course, it had the first appearance of Bond's fully-loaded Aston Martin. The film also, as critic **Roger Ebert** notes, contains arguably the finest example of a Hollywood cliché known as Talking Killer Syndrome.

Title sequence Now what is the perfect follow up to the near-naked woman in the previous titles? Lots of near-naked women, this time, wait for it, painted gold. Scenes from the film (some missing from the final cut) are projected as they writhe around, presumably under the impression that Bond will be joining them very soon. He doesn't.

Best lines Bond 'Ejector seat, you must be joking!'

Q 'I never joke about my work, 007.'

Bond 'My dear girl, there are some things that just aren't done, such as drinking Dom Perignon '53 above the temperature of 38 degrees Fahrenheit.'

Famous last words

Bond 'You expect me to talk?'

Goldfinger 'No, Mr Bond, I expect you to die.'

Notable stunts Not really a stunt but an image: Jill Masterson's gold birthday suit is an iconic movie moment to rival the best. Oddjob's slicing of the statue with his hat isn't bad either.

Goofs/in-jokes We particularly like the fact that the in-car scanner helping Bond track Goldfinger after their Miami golf match is showing a map of Southend, but the film's classic goof involves the elastic nuclear countdown, with time ticking by in an infinite loop. The bomb timer originally stopped at 003, but was later changed to 007, making a nonsense of Bond's line 'just three more clicks'. And those who have way too much time on their hands might be interested to note that the car Oddjob has crushed, swaps from a 1964 Lincoln Continental to an engineless 1963 model halfway through.

Thunderball
1965

Cast	Sean Connery, Adolpho Celi, Claudine Auger, Luciana Paluzzi
Director	Terence Young
Screening	Richard Maibaum, John Hopkins, (story by Kevin McClory, Jack Whittingham)
Rating	🎞🎞🎞🎞🎞

SPECTRE is back with a clutch of new recruits from the school for disgruntled egomaniacs, this time managing to steal a couple of warheads the British happened to leave lying around. Bond tracks the weapons to the Bahamas (no one ever tries to

007 best (or worst) taglines

1 'Far up, far out, far more'. With taglines like this, George Lazenby never had a chance as 007 in *On Her Majesty's Secret Service*.

2 'Meet James Bond, secret agent 007. His new incredible women... His new incredible enemies... His new incredible adventures...' The tagline for *From Russia With Love* didn't leave much to the imagination. The shorter alternative was 'James Bond is back!'

3 'Yesterday is a memory, today is history, tomorrow is in the hands of one man: Bond...You know the rest!' The tagline that feels as if it's almost as long as the script. Luckily *Tomorrow Never Dies* was better than the slogan.

4 'Where all other Bonds end, this one begins.' A high falutin' way of saying that *Moonraker* is set in space.

5 'It's the biggest. It's the best. It's Bond. And B-E-Y-O-N-D!' We prefer the Carly Simon derived alternative for *The Spy Who Loved Me*,: 'Nobody does it better.'

6 'James Bond's all time high'. The *Octopussy* slogan, about as inspired as the film.

7 'Everything he touches turns to excitement.' *Goldfinger* was a class product: the song, the baddie, the scary bowler hats, even the tagline, all had that certain something other 007 odysseys would only aspire to.

take over the world from Scunthorpe) where he meets Domino, whose lover, Emilio Largo, is the key. After a daring underwater battle, Bond recovers the nukes and saves the world.

The laid-back mood of the Bahamas permeates the whole of *Thunderball*, drawing unfavourable comparisons with the drive and excitement of *Goldfinger*, particularly since Connery seems to be sleepwalking through his lines. However as villainesses go, Volpe (Luciana Paluzzi) is one of the best, hot-blooded and ruthless, next to whom Domino (Claudine Auger) seems a bit of a cold fish (understandable considering how much time she spends underwater). The seabed fight sequences go on too long, but a villain with an eyepatch is always good, and Q's pineapple print shirt is a reason to rewind in itself. On the whole, a well-deserved winner of Best Visual Effects Oscar.

Title sequence In case we're in any doubt about the place of women in Bond's world, here is the obligatory near-naked woman getting a harpoon fired between her legs while out swimming. Oh, and it is finally Sean himself doing the gun-barrel pose at the beginning.

Best lines Bond 'Most girls just paddle around. You swim like a man.'

Famous last words Volpe 'James Bond, who only has to make love to a woman and she starts to hear heavenly choirs singing: she repents and then immediately returns to the side of right and virtue – but not this one.'

Notable stunts The RAF Vulcan bomber landing on the seabed, complete with underwater runway, and the yacht that converts to a nippy hydrofoil are real Bond moments, while the rocket-pack escape hints at ludicrous plot devices to come.

Goofs/in-jokes An opening conversation identifies SPECTRE as having consulted on the Great Train Robbery, which took place a couple of years earlier. Also, Felix Leiter's still having trouble keeping his clothes in order as he swaps between shorts and trousers during the helicopter search. Similar problems afflict Bond's flippers in his first scene with Domino, and the licence plates of his and Count Lippe's cars.

Casino Royale
1967

Cast	David Niven, Peter Sellers, Ursula Andress, Orson Welles and pretty much anyone else you can think of
Director	Val Guest, Kenneth Hughes, John Huston, Joseph McGrath, Robert Parrish
Screenplay	Wolf Mankowitz, John Law, Michael Sayers
Rating	𝅘𝅥𝅮𝅘𝅥𝅮𝅘𝅥𝅮𝅘𝅥𝅮𝅘𝅥𝅮𝅘𝅥𝅮

Sir James Bond, a reformed character, comes out of retirement to avenge the murder of M, and finds that life as a spy has moved on since he was granted his licence to kill.

Despite the Bond franchise being a rich vein from which to

mine a good spoof, this is a poor mish-mash of a few entertaining ideas overrun with bad acting and a tortuous and embarrassing plot. Considering the talent pooled on and off screen, with input from **Woody Allen**, **William Holden**, **Jacqueline Bisset**, **Orson Welles**, **Peter Sellers** and, er, **Ronnie Corbett**, plus uncredited input from **Billy Wilder**, it should have been a triumph. Instead it's a double oh dear.

You Only Live Twice
1967

Cast   Sean Connery, Donald Pleasance, Akiko Wakabayashi, Mie Hama
Director   Lewis Gilbert
Screenplay Roald Dahl, Harold Jack Bloom (additional story material)
Rating

SPECTRE has given up stealing nukes in favour of getting East and West to blow each other up by sabotaging both their space programmes. Investigating the Japanese island that seems to be the source of the problem, Bond sleeps with several geisha girls, passes Ninja 1.0 with flying colours and reveals a handy First from Cambridge in Oriental Languages. After a miraculous and daring infiltration of SPECTRE's secret volcano, Bond averts World War III but loses Blofeld. Again. Damn.

The first Bond film to bear little resemblance to the novel on which it is based, *You Only Love Twice* is often slated for being campy and over the top. All we can say is, have these critics seen *Octopussy*? Yes, the script slips into terrible racial and gender stereotypes – more likely a reflection of **Roald Dahl**'s own preoccupations than anything else – and no attempt is made to keep the story within the bounds of believability. But hey, a guy gets eaten alive by a pool of piranhas, Bond gets a body wax and we get to see Blofeld for the first time – and he turns out to be **Donald Pleasance**. Great stuff!

The OTT action in *You Only Live Twice* devoured a then-astronomic $9.5m budget ▲

Title sequence Nubile Japanese women and exploding volcanoes oozing lava. Yeah, we get it.

Best lines Moneypenny 'Bond, the password chosen for this mission is: "I love you." Say it back to me so I can be sure you've got it.'

Famous last words Blofeld 'Give him his cigarettes. It won't be the nicotine that kills you, Mr Bond.'

Notable stunts The SPECTRE spaceship swallowing the US and USSR rockets whole, plus the car chase that culminates in the Japanese Secret Service dumping Bond's pursuers in the sea using a huge electromagnet mounted on a helicopter.

94

Goofs/in-jokes It's amazing how much like Surrey the Japanese countryside looks in the scene with Helga Brandt and the stricken airplane. Similarly, would the Japanese police really use British-made tape recorders? Also, it's ever so lucky that the lethal gas that overcomes Bond and Kissy when they swim into the volcano caves has completely dissipated by the time they swim out again.

On Her Majesty's Secret Service
1969

Cast	George Lazenby, Telly Savalas, Diana Rigg
Director	Peter Hunt
Screenplay	Richard Maibaum, Simon Raven (additional dialogue)
Rating	🎬🎬🎬

Still on Blofeld's trail, Bond gets involved with a criminal overlord, Marc-Ange Draco, when he saves his daughter, Tracy, from a suicide attempt. In return for Bond marrying Tracy to protect her, Draco will lead the spy to Blofeld, now esconced in the Alps and developing lethal viruses with which to hold the world to ransom. After a miraculous and daring escape from Blofeld's remote control avalanche Bond and Tracy marry, although it's not long before life proves that, sadly, Bond is simply not the marrying kind.

It's hard to know what to say about this one. Most of its problems lie in the fact that Lazenby cannot help but be compared to Connery and lose. Yet **Diana Rigg** and **Telly Savalas** are both excellent, classy and believable. If it were a stand-alone film it would probably be seen as a serious, entertaining spy movie, as there is far less cartoon action than in previous or subsequent Bonds and a much more psychological plot. Unfortunately that's not what most people are after from James Bond (Timothy Dalton suffered a similar reaction 20 years later).

If you can forget Connery, you'll enjoy it. If not, a bit of judicious fast-forwarding (especially through the long, long exposition at the beginning) may help. But don't forget to look out for a young **Joanna Lumley** at Blofeld's clinic.

Title sequence In an attempt to convince the audience that this is still the Bond they know and love, images from the previous films are inserted willy-nilly. Desperate or what?

Best lines Slim pickings, but we do like Bond's line, 'He had a lot of guts' about the assassin churned up by the snow blower.

Famous last words Bond (to Tracy) 'We have all the time in the world.'

Notable stunts The ski chase sequence is good, but it was later eclipsed by various snow-bound Roger Moore sequences.

Goofs/in-jokes The kilt has got to be a joke. And why doesn't Blofeld recognise Bond after meeting him in the previous film?

Not so friendly off-screen: Rigg reportedly ate garlic before love scenes with George ▲

Diamonds Are Forever
1971

Cast	Sean Connery, Charles Gray, Jill St John
Director	Guy Hamilton
Screenplay	Richard Maibaum, Tom Mankiewicz
Rating	🎬🎬🎬🎬

What appears to be a simple diamond smuggling operation gets a lot more complicated when Bond finds out that the inevitable Blofeld has taken over with the intention of launching a powerful laser into space and training it on whoever has the most money. Once again the Americans launch a gung-ho attack on Blofeld's oil-rig base, during which Bond effects a miraculous and daring destruction of the whole thing. And Blofeld. Maybe.

Bond is back on song here, with Connery taking his final official crack at the role for a $1.25m fee, donated to a Scottish charity for deprived children. **Guy Hamilton** fails to recapture his own Midas touch and we're left with a cartoonish caper, a few flashes of style and terrible puns with outfits to match (white suit and pink tie? Please, Sean, no). Thankfully the minor bad guys are exceptional, especially the double acts, Bambi and Thumper (psychotic babes), and Mr Wint and Mr Kidd (twisted, gay and as politically incorrect as they come). Sadly, Felix Leiter (Norman Burton) makes spying about as thrilling as accountancy and Charles Gray, with two very tough acts to follow, is a weak, dull Blofeld, who isn't even bald.

Title sequence A lot of sparklers. No one could ever accuse the Bond producers of ignoring the obvious.

Best lines Bond (on being disturbed while making love to Tiffany) 'Gentlemen, I'm afraid you've caught me with more than my hands up.'

Famous last words Blofeld 'Surely you haven't come to negotiate, Mr Bond?'

The beginning of the end for 007?

You could argue that Cubby Broccoli and Harry Saltzman did something Ernst Stavro Blofeld failed to do: killed off Ian Fleming's James Bond. And the horrible irony was that Fleming had spent the best part of a decade chasing TV or movie deals before Saltzman and Broccoli stepped in. The première of the first Bond movie should have felt like the crowning glory of Fleming's career, yet at a private screening in Soho and at the glitzy official première, he seemed at best ambivalent about the film.

His reaction may partly be explained by his health. He had suffered a massive heart attack in 1961, when he was just 53, and he never quite recovered his old bonhomie (although, ironically, his sister-in-law, Celia Fleming, thought he was much nicer after this reminder of his own mortality). The première of *Dr. No*, a year later, may just have seemed like a triumph come too late. It may also have been overshadowed by the legal dispute with Kevin McClory over the film rights to *Thunderball*.

It is reasonably well known that Fleming didn't, initially, warm to Sean Connery as 007. He seemed to change his mind yet still never really expressed massive enthusiasm for the movies. He stepped aside from the filming, which suited Broccoli who told director Guy Hamilton that he was going to fix *Dr. No* for the movie because the book was 'full of nonsense'. At the première of *From Russia With Love*, Fleming made a Bondian gesture, hiring the front row of the dress circle at the London cinema for his friends. He then turned up in a lounge suit, while his male friends arrived in the expected tuxedos and retired 'beaten to the ground' at 1am.

While the films boosted sales of the novels, they took the character away from Fleming. Novelist EL Doctorow, author of *Ragtime*, was a reader at Fleming's US publisher and noted of *You Only Live Twice*, published after the first two Bond films: 'It is as if Bond's sadness and apathy had affected Fleming.' While writing *The Man With The Golden Gun*, he confided, 'This is alas the last Bond because I have run out of both puff and zest.' It was indeed his last Bond: he died in 1964. His complaints that his books were 'piffle' and that 007 was a 'cardboard dummy' seemed to grow more frequent in his last years. To be fair, he had been plagued by doubt before, notably when writing *From Russia With Love*, his fifth novel, where he left himself the option of killing 007 with a cliffhanger ending; *The Spy Who Loved Me*, written from the point of view of the Bond girl before *Dr. No* was filmed, was another obvious bid to tweak the formula. Maybe seeing Connery on the screen simply convinced him that the movies would make it harder than ever for him to break out of the formula.

Notable stunts Nothing amazing, but the car chase through Las Vegas is fun and inventive. The final showdown is poor, compared to the others in the series.

Goofs/in-jokes The moon buggy chase and the moonscape film set are a nod to the popular conspiracy theory that the Apollo moon landings were faked by NASA. *Diamonds Are Forever* is littered with continuity problems, but the biggest mistake must be the fact that Blofeld's diamond-encrusted satellite would never work as a laser. If Bond had simply pointed this out, we would have been spared a lot of angst.

Live And Let Die
1973

Cast	Roger Moore, Yaphet Kotto, Jane Seymour
Director	Guy Hamilton
Screening	Tom Mankiewicz
Rating	𝅘𝅥𝅘𝅥𝅘𝅥𝅘𝅥𝅘𝅥𝅘𝅥

After three Secret Service agents are assassinated, Bond is sent to investigate. He uncovers a plot to flood the USA with heroin, hatched by a voodoo-practising gangster who also happens to be prime minister Kananga of St Monique. Aided by the gangster's virginal (although not for long) tarot reader Solitaire, Bond manages several miraculous and daring escapes from life-threatening situations, until he faces Kananga and kills him while his colleagues destroy the heroin supplies.

A new Bond and a new era. While the villains are solidly earthbound, smuggling drugs rather than taking over the world, Bond himself is now firmly ensconced in the fantastic, a superhero for the Seventies with casual sex and a dodgy wardrobe as his secret weapons. Despite all this, and despite the fact that Bond doesn't drink a martini or have a chat with Q, *Live And Let Die* is a terrific movie, with great villains and

99

a speedy pace. Yes, the blaxploitation elements look a bit suspect these days, and yes, stereotypes abound (Sheriff J W Pepper, please stand up), but the Bond franchise has taken on its own momentum and nothing, not even the women's movement, Fleming die-hards, or even SPECTRE, is going to stop it.

Title sequence No Bond, just a collage of clichéd tokens from a holiday resort voodoo theme night.

Best lines Bond (about a voodoo amulet) 'It's just a hat darling, belonging to a small man of limited means who lost a fight with a chicken.'

Famous last words Kananga 'On Solitaire's first wrong answer, you will sever the little finger of Mr Bond's left hand. On the next wrong answer, you will move on to more… vital parts of his anatomy.'

Notable stunts Bond using the crocodiles as stepping stones is one of the most memorable Bond moments ever, but the airboat chase through the bayou is a corker too.

Goofs/in-jokes It's a good thing that Solitaire's tarot cards have a 007 motif on the back, in case she forgot who she was dealing with. And when Baron Samedi attacks Bond with a machete, Bond could just shoot him instead of picking up another machete. Or is he leaving that joke for Indiana Jones?

The Man With The Golden Gun
1974

Cast	Roger Moore, Christopher Lee, Britt Ekland, Hervé Villechaize
Director	Guy Hamilton
Screening	Richard Maibaum, Tom Mankiewicz
Rating	🔫🔫🔫🔫🔫🔫🔫

Scaramanga (Lee, in a part originally turned down by **Jack Palance**) is the world's greatest assassin and the only man he fears is 007. Bond is led to believe that he is on the assassin's hit

Roger Moore brings his own brand of laconic charm to the 007 set and 007 seat ▲

Bond movies in a nutshell or two

Dr. No
The one with Ursula Andress and her bikini.

From Russia With Love
The one with the yellow helicopter and the lesbian in poisonous shoes.

Goldfinger
The one with the girl in a golden birthday suit and the weirdo with the killer bowler hat.

Thunderball
The one with the shark-infested pool and the rocket backpack.

Casino Royale
The crap one.

You Only Live Twice
The one with the Ninjas, the volcano, and the death by poisonous string.

On Her Majesty's Secret Service
The one without Sean Connery.

Diamonds Are Forever
The one with the gay assassins and the coffins.

Live And Let Die
The one with the crocodiles, the air-boat, and the guy with the metal hand.

The Man With The Golden Gun
The one with the house of mirrors and the psychotic French dwarf.

The Spy Who Loved Me
The one with the Union Jack parachute and the amphibious Lotus Esprit.

Moonraker
The one where Jaws gets a girlfriend.

For Your Eyes Only
The one with Sheena Easton and the bullet-ridden 2CV.

Octopussy
The one with the knife fight on the plane wing and the deadly yo-yos.

Never Say Never Again
The one we could probably have done without.

A View To A Kill
The one with the mink-lined submarine and the chase up the Eiffel Tower.

The Living Daylights
The one with sex on the Ferris wheel and the stun gas keyring.

Licence To Kill
The one with the Hasselblad-cum-gun gun and the exploding toothpaste.

GoldenEye
The one with the tank chase and the renegade 00 agent.

Tomorrow Never Dies
The one with the henchman who's into torture and the lighter that's really a grenade.

The World Is Not Enough
The one with the X-ray glasses and the Millennium Dome.

list after a gold bullet engraved with 007 arrives in London. While tracking, Bond discovers a link to his previous incomplete case concerning a top secret solar-engineering project. After various traps and counter traps, involving a Hong Kong businessman, a vital gadget called a solex and Sheriff Pepper (**Clifton James**) who, luckily considering his audience popularity, is on holiday in Bangkok, Bond makes a miraculous and daring raid on Scaramanga's Island, fights a duel, retrieves the missing solex and runs off with Britt Ekland. It's a tough job but somebody had to do it.

Moore really gets into his stride with this one, countering his naturally light touch with a bit of un-PC machismo, particularly in the early fight scenes.

The plot is a little tortuous and following all the links between assassins and secret agents can make your head hurt, but it's slick throughout and **Christopher Lee** is perfect as Scaramanga, with the evil Nick Nack (**Hervé Villechaize**) doing the dirty work before heading off to *Fantasy Island*. They get away with most of the humour (although the return of Sheriff Pepper is shameless), we just think it's a shame they cut Hai Fat's sidekick Lo Fat out of the final draft.

Probably a bit underrated, its treatment of women hasn't dated brilliantly and there is a streak of cruelty which some find hard to accept, but this is one of the better Moore Bond movies, despite its disappointing box office. Still, in at least one market, this flick broke new ground for Bond: it was the first in the series to be screened in the Kremlin.

Title sequence Dancing girls, fireworks and firearms. Scaramanga's fun house made celluloid.

Best lines Bond 'Who would pay $1m to have me killed?'

M 'Jealous husbands, outraged chefs, humiliated tailors… The list is endless.'

Bond 'There's a useful four-letter word, and you're full of it.'

Famous last words Scaramanga 'A duel between titans.

My golden gun against your Walther PPK.'
Bond 'One bullet against my six?'
Scaramanga 'I only need one, Mr Bond.'
Notable stunts It's got to be the car taking a mid-air 360 degree spin across a broken bridge.
Goofs/in-jokes Bond's status as a secret agent seems pointless here as everyone knows who he is, especially Scaramanga. Hai Fat has a home in Bangkok, but it turns out to be on a hill, quite a feat as hills are about as rare in that part of Thailand as mountains are in Florida. There are a lot of minor errors (eg silenced weapons sounding unsilenced) but nothing too irritating.

The Spy Who Loved Me
1977

Cast	Roger Moore, Curt Jurgens, Barbara Bach, Richard Kiel
Director	Lewis Gilbert
Screening	Christopher Wood, Richard Maibaum
Rating	𝆕𝆕𝆕𝆕𝆕

US and Russian subs are going missing, and a submarine detector is on the black market. Joining forces with Soviet agent Major Anya Amasova (Bach), Bond finds that shipping magnate Karl Stromberg (Jurgens) has converted a tanker into a sub-swallowing device, hoping to provoke a World War III scenario where the surface of the earth is nuked, returning life to the seas. After a miraculous rescue of the captured Amasova from the undersea base, Bond shoots Stromberg and escapes. But he doesn't do such a good job on Stromberg's seven-foot henchman, Jaws.

Now where have we seen this plot before? Oh yes, it's **You Only Live Twice** underwater. Still, it's a good plot and sustains a revisit. Thankfully, Bond's slide into terminal misogyny is halted here by a stronger, brighter Bond girl than we've seen in a long time, but the certifiable Stromberg, a lunatic even by Bond villain standards, is somewhat overshadowed by his excellent metal-toothed sidekick (Kiel). The gadgets are back in top form though, and the movie passes an enjoyable, if not particularly memorable, couple of hours.

Title sequence Oh my God, a bouncing Bond. Bring back the near-naked women.

Best lines Bond 'When one is in Egypt, one should delve deeply into its treasures.'

Bond 'Well, you did save my life. Thank you.'

Amasova 'We all make mistakes, Mr Bond.'

Famous last words Stromberg 'Farewell, Mr Bond. That word has, I must admit, a welcome ring of permanence about it.'

Notable stunts The parachute ski jump, of course, but the submersible Lotus Esprit is another favourite.

Goofs/in-jokes Another sound joke: When Bond and Amasova are in the desert, the theme from *Lawrence Of Arabia* is played. Watch out for the scene where Bond is going to follow Fekkesh – several people change position in the frame between cuts.

Moonraker
1979

Cast	Roger Moore, Michael Lonsdale, Lois Chiles, Richard Kiel
Director	Lewis Gilbert
Screening	Christopher Wood
Rating	🎞🎞🎞🎞🎞

A space shuttle is hijacked in mysterious circumstances, leading Bond to its manufacturer, Hugo Drax, an eccentric (is there any other kind?) billionaire. One of Drax's scientists, Dr Holly Goodhead (Chiles), turns out to be working for the CIA and she and Bond reluctantly team up, getting caught, escaping, and getting caught again an improbable number of times. Along the way they discover Drax is planning to annihilate the world's

Moore the merrier: Fleming's first choice for Bond makes up for lost time ▲

population using globes of poison launched from space, and that he has been making his own rockets to carry out his plan. After a miraculous and daring (not to mention timely) escape from the blast chamber of Moonraker 5, Bond and Goodhead stow away on Moonraker 6 and are brought to Drax's space station where they foil all his plans and pal up with Jaws and his new girlfriend (proof that there's someone for everyone).

Even by Bond standards this plot is a mess, and silly with it. Locations flash by – London, California, Venice, Rio, the Amazon and space – all very impressive but hard to follow. It's a pity, as there's a lot of creativity in the gadgets, the stunts and the one-liners (Drax has the best), but suffice to say that Bond should forget cashing in on the *Star Wars* craze and keep his fantasies strictly earthbound. It's probably a few minutes too long, too.

Title sequence A positively Zen opening with Moore parachuting away from the stricken jet in the opening sequence, followed by shots of the earth from space. Oh, and some naked girls. Obviously.

Best lines Drax 'James Bond, you appear with the tedious inevitability of an unloved season.'

Holly 'You know him?'

Bond 'Not socially. His name's Jaws. He kills people.'

Famous last words Drax 'At least I shall have the pleasure of putting you out of my misery.'

Notable stunts The fight with Jaws on the cable car is a plus (despite the crappy blue screen effects), but a big minus is Drax having his illiterate female assistant torn apart by dogs, one of the most unnecessarily offensive scenes in the entire Bond series.

Goofs/in-jokes The keypad that unlocks the space lab and plays the theme from *Close Encounters Of The Third Kind* is a nice touch, but on the whole the science-fiction element is poor. It is only 1979 after all, and there are space marines who can get into orbit in a matter of minutes? Plus the zero-gravity effects are clearly just actors walking very, very slowly.

For Your Eyes Only
1981

Cast	Roger Moore, Julian Glover, Carole Bouquet
Director	John Glen
Screening	Richard Maibaum and Michael G Wilson
Rating	𝔉𝔉𝔉𝔉𝔉

Bond is sent to recover an encryption device, the ATAC, from a British warship that has sunk near the shore of a Warsaw Pact country. The Russians are also after it. Bond tries to track down their agent and meets Melina Havelock, a dab hand with a

Shaken, not stirred

James Bond, as we know, is a man who knows his mind, a trait particularly evident in his choice of alcohol. As the years have passed, Bond's tastes have changed a little (it would be churlish of us to suggest that this has anything to do with the growth of product placement in movies – a man is entitled to try something new, now and then), but on the whole his choice is always precise and impeccable. As long as he never ends up swigging a Bacardi Breezer, we don't mind.

The party starts in *Dr. No* when Bond threatens the villain with a champagne bottle. Dr No remarks, 'It's a Dom Perignon '55. It would be a pity to break it', to which Bond replies: 'I prefer the '53 myself.' He remains loyal to the '53 in *Goldfinger*, but by *Thunderball*, Bond orders the scorned '55 at the casino, and the '57 makes an appearance in *On Her Majesty's Secret Service*. By the time he reached *You Only Live Twice* Dom Perignon '59 was a tempting offer, but sadly Bond had to forgo a taste as he'd hidden a body in the drinks cabinet. Work getting in the way of a chap's simple pleasures again.

In later years Bond found it impossible to choose between Dom Perignon and Bollinger (poor fellow). In *Live And Let Die* Bollinger was on the table, but in *The Man With The Golden Gun* Bond is back with Dom Perignon, preferably the '62. In *The Spy Who Loved Me* a bottle of Dom Perignon '52 in Stromberg's escape sub puts the villain up in Bond's estimation ('A man who drinks Dom Perignon '52 can't be all bad'), but by *Moonraker* Bollinger is back on top with a '69 vintage, followed by a '75 in *A View To A Kill*. Timothy Dalton knocked back a bit of Bolly in *The Living Daylights*, even including a bottle in his shopping list for the defecting Russian, Koskov. *GoldenEye* sees Bond stowing a bottle of Bollinger '88 in his Aston Martin, and he is almost unable to continue with his mission after being offered the clearly sub-standard 'Mr Carver's champagne' in *Tomorrow Never Dies*.

Bond also changes allegiance over the years to various brands of vodka. Starting the trend in *Never Say Never Again*, Sean Connery displays a partiality to Absolut, although thankfully not any of the amusing flavoured ones. *A View To A Kill* sees Stolichnaya as top choice, followed later by a flirtation with Smirnoff in *Tomorrow Never Dies* (presumably because the champagne was so poor).

In between his high class tipples, Bond has always known the benefit of blending in and has drunk a fair selection of local brews including sake (at the correct temperature, of course) in Japan, Phu Yuck in Hong Kong, ouzo in Greece, a mint julep in Kentucky and even, distressingly, a beer in the Florida Keys. Of course Bond's favourite drink, the one everyone knows him for, is a medium dry **vodka martini**, shaken not stirred. To recreate the true Bond experience, just follow this recipe:

Take one cocktail shaker A proper silver one, please, this is not a recipe for novelty bar items.

Add 4 measures vodka A tablespoon measure will fill a single martini glass nicely.

Add 1 measure dry Vermouth Noilly Prat is a good one.

Shake with ice Do not stir. Shaking makes the liquid misty and much colder, as Bond prefers.

Put one green olive in the bottom of a martini glass and pour the cocktail over

Garnish with a thin slice of lemon peel

Serve on a silver salver And enjoy while wearing black tie.

crossbow and the vengeful daughter of parents murdered by the Russian contact. Aris Kristatos, initially introduced as a useful contact and supporter of winter sports, turns out to be the Russians' man and double-crosses Bond after he rescues the ATAC. After a miraculous and daring ascent of an unclimbable mountain, Bond thwarts the handing over of the ATAC to the Russians and saves the British fleet.

Moore only agreed to be in this one at the last minute and throughout it seems he's not quite sure he made the right decision. That's a shame, as **John Glen** takes Bond away from the absurdities of *Moonraker* and back to being a spy rather than a cartoon character (although he does use a parrot as a plot device). The lack of world-dominating billionaires is a plus too. Carole Bouquet does an excellent job as Melina, and without scars, gold bars or fluffy white cats to hide behind, Julian Glover is a deft and menacing villain – apart from his odd interest in ice skating. Robin Cousins has a lot to answer for.

Title sequence This time it's Sheena Easton singing her little heart out. Naked. Only kidding.

Best lines Bond (on turning down a willing girl for the first time) 'Now put your clothes back on and I'll buy you an ice cream.'
Bond (in a confessional) 'Forgive me Father, for I have sinned.'
Q 'That's putting it mildly, 007.'
Famous last words Kristatos 'You have shot your last bolt, Miss Havelock.'
Notable stunts Not so much a stunt as a two-fingered gesture to **Kevin McClory** with the opening sequence apparently killing off Blofeld (McClory owned the rights to him) once and for all. Also, note to the producers: Underwater fight scenes = dull. The action is saved by the outstanding ski chase.
Goofs/in-jokes The amazed extra from the beach in *The Spy Who Loved Me* and St Mark's Square in *Moonraker*, gets another eyeful when Bond skies through his dinner.

Octopussy
1983

Cast	Roger Moore, Louis Jourdan, Maud Adams, Steven Berkoff
Director	John Glen
Screening	George MacDonald Fraser, Richard Maibaum, Michael G Wilson
Rating	𝔽𝔽𝔽𝔽𝔽

With the USSR in disarray, renegade General Orlov is forging Fabergé eggs to finance his plan to frame the US for a nuclear attack on Europe and make way for a Russian conquest. When his latest forgery is intercepted by 009, Kamal Khan, Orlov's fixer, buys back the real egg. Bond follows Khan to India where he meets Khan's partner, Octopussy, who is surprisingly pleased to see him, and suggests a professional as well as personal liaison. Khan stops this, but only after Octopussy has tried to protect Bond. After a miraculous and daring escape from a crocodile-infested lake, Bond returns

Look who isn't talking

Bond movies have always been famed for their exotic female stars and their evil international villains. Unfortunately the producers' diligence in scouring the globe for just the right actress or actor to do justice to a role has often resulted in casting someone whose English leaves pretty much everything to be desired. Over the years the number of people in Bond movies whose voices have been dubbed is quite staggering. Here's a brief list:

Dutch actress Monica Van Der Zyl dubbed not only **Ursula Andress**, but all the other female voices in *Dr. No* (except Miss Moneypenny and a Chinese girl) for which she received the generous sum of £150 and a small part as a receptionist. She also went on to provide voices for **Shirley Eaton**, **Eunice Grayson** and **Claudine Auger**.

In *From Russia With Love*, **Daniela Bianchi** was dubbed by Barbara Jefford.

In *Goldfinger*, **Gert Fröbe** was dubbed by Michael Collins.

Even **George Lazenby** couldn't escape the vocal mania and was dubbed by George Baker for the scenes where he is pretending to be Bray (and you thought he was just a terrific mimic).

In *Diamonds Are Forever*, **Lana Wood's** California drawl was deemed inappropriate for Plenty O'Toole. Perhaps if she'd had the accent her real name, Svetlana Nikolaevna Zakharenko, suggested, she might have been considered exotic enough to speak for herself.

In *You Only Live Twice*, **Mie Hama** was originally cast as Aki, a role with more lines. When it turned out that she was struggling with her English, she swapped places with **Akiko Wakabashi** and took the almost silent role of Kissy. Robert Rietty, who also provided the voice of **Emilio Largo** in *Thunderball*, dubbed 'Tiger' Tanaka.

to Europe, finds and defuses Orlov's nuke, before returning with Octopussy to deal with Khan.

Octopussy is the film that gets slated by Bond reviewers, though we think that's a bit unfair. Granted, Moore is getting a bit long in the tooth to play the dashing hero, and the schizophrenic plot, with its European Cold War spy drama somewhat at odds with the Bollywood fantasies of the Indian storyline, is disconcerting at times. However, there are some terrific stunts and set pieces (the human tiger hunt is a good touch), plus a lot of classy casting, with everyone's favourite nutter, **Steven Berkoff**, doing a great job as Orlov. Plus we get lots more interaction between Bond and Q, which gives the film its best lighter moments. Look out for tennis player **Vijay Amritraj** as Bond's Indian contact.

Title sequence Quite cool really, with an octopus providing some respite from wall-to-wall naked women.

Best lines Vijay 'Is he still there?'

Q 'You must be joking! 007 on an island populated exclusively by women? We won't see him till dawn.'

Famous last words Khan 'Mr Bond is indeed a very rare breed – soon to be made extinct.'

Notable stunts The opening miniature jet chase through the hanger, with it then pulling up at a gas station. It could only happen to Bond. On the whole the chases are good but the fights are poor.

Goofs/in-jokes Vijay giving Gobinda's thugs a good whacking with a tennis racket (arf, arf). More importantly, no matter how fragile their government was, wouldn't the Russians have noticed that Sothebys was suddenly doing a roaring trade in state-owned Fabergé?

Never Say Never Again
1983

Cast	Sean Connery, Max Von Sydow, Klaus Maria Brandauer, Kim Basinger
Director	Irvin Kershner
Screening	Lorenzo Semple Jr, (story by Kevin McClory, Jack Whittingham)
Rating	𝔽𝔽𝔽𝔽𝔽𝔽𝔽

Sean needs a bigger rod than that if he's fishing for compliments about his gown ▶

The plot is basically the same as *Thunderball*, with Bond coming out of semi-retirement to take on SPECTRE again, plus a few variations in methods of assassination. And instead of Emilio Largo we have Maximillian Largo (personal assets $2.49 billion, including his yacht Disco Volante).

After his collaboration with Broccoli and Saltzman on *Thunderball*, **Kevin McClory** was under contract not to produce anything based on his own James Bond material for ten years. He started developing this project (originally entitled the yawn-worthy *James Bond Of The Secret Service*, and then the not much better *Warhead*) in 1976 but after much legal wrangling, during which Connery walked away from the project, it finally made it to the screen in 1983. And was it worth the wait? Well, sort of. The cast is magnificent, the direction excellent, locations glorious, and the action and quips as good as any previous Bond. It's pretty enjoyable, but you can't help feeling it's just a very expensive 'up yours!' to McClory's old partners.

Title sequence It doesn't have a gun barrel, so it doesn't count.

Best lines Fatima 'Oh, how reckless of me. I made you all wet.'

Bond 'Yes, but my martini is still dry.'

Famous last words Blofeld 'We have accomplished two of the functions that the name SPECTRE embodies: terror and extortion. If our demands are not met within seven days, we shall ruthlessly apply the third: revenge!'

Notable stunts The motorbike chase is good, and the horseback stuff impressive, but otherwise, like Domino's leg warmers, it's all a bit dated. A young Steven Seagal, in his second venture as a movie martial arts instructor, was responsible for the fight sequences.

Goofs/in-jokes Mostly just continuity stuff, with Fatima's waterskis going from one to two in a magic instant, while Felix Leiter, still dogged by sartorial trauma, keeps losing and gaining various items of scuba gear. Oh, and Q is hard up for the cash to develop his gizmos – a nice send-up of the official Bond movies.

A View To A Kill

1985

Cast	Roger Moore, Christopher Walken, Tanya Roberts, Grace Jones
Director	John Glen
Screening	Richard Maibaum, Michael G Wilson
Rating	

003 is killed retrieving an exclusive computer chip from a Siberian research station, and Bond tracks it to Max Zorin, billionaire industrialist. Zorin is also the biggest psycho Bond has encountered to date, and intends to aggravate the San Andreas fault and plunge Silicon Valley into the Pacific, thus ensuring his company monopolises the booming computer market. Aided by Stacey Sutton, a seismologist, Bond foils Zorin's plans, but not before Zorin has kidnapped Stacey. After a miraculous and daring confrontation with Zorin on the Golden Gate Bridge, Bond gets the girl and Zorin gets a watery death.

Those people with a low embarrassment threshold should watch this through their fingers. It lumbers along like a patronising dinosaur from a less-enlightened era, painfully revealing the age of the star (58) and the writer (76). Broccoli also complained that the film suffered from budget cuts, and it shows. You can't even find it entertaining as a camp classic, as the sight of Roger Moore on a snowboard is

Pussy Galore

Publicist Tom Carlile managed to persuade the American censors that the name Pussy Galore was acceptable for the great American viewing public. They had wanted to change the name to Kitty, but after Carlile arranged for Honor Blackman to be photographed with Prince Philip at the film's London première, and got the picture in all the papers captioned 'Pussy and the Prince', the US censors were satisfied that if it was good enough for royalty, it was good enough for them.

115

simply too shameful to enjoy. It's a waste of Christopher Walken, the only actor not sleepwalking throughout. It was responsible for introducing Dolph Lundgren to the big screen, and Tanya Roberts got the job from her role in *The Beastmaster* – two facts that speak volumes.

Title sequence Electronics are in, so the near-naked women shoot plastic laser guns at each other and glow in the dark. Imagine a Ready Brek commercial produced by the Playboy Channel, and you've just about got it.

Best lines Zorin gets some, otherwise little would sound out of place in a *Carry On* film.

Famous last words Zorin 'If you're the best they have, they'll more likely try and cover up your embarrassing incompetence.'

Notable stunts Hardly any, thanks to budget cuts, although the confrontation in San Francisco has a bit of the old Bond about it.

Goofs/in-jokes Bits of equipment and crew appear throughout: a taxi window reflects a mike; May Day pushes the Rolls into the lake… helped by a metal cable; two cameramen crouch on the back of the fire engine, and so on.

The Living Daylights
1987

Cast	Timothy Dalton, Jeroen Krabbé, Maryam d'Abo, Joe Don Baker
Director	John Glen
Screening	Richard Maibaum
Rating	🍸🍸🍸🍸🍸🍸🍸

A defecting Russian, General Koskov, tells of a Soviet plan to eliminate its enemies' spies, but is recaptured by the KGB soon afterwards. Bond gradually discovers, with the reluctant help of a young cellist called Kara, that Koskov set the whole defection up and is really working with lunatic arms dealer Brad Whitaker to escalate tension between East and West and so cash in on the increased arms spending. After a miraculous and daring raid on Russian forces in Afghanistan involving drugs, diamonds and the mujahedin, Bond kills Whitaker and returns Koskov to Moscow to face Soviet justice.

Another new Bond and another new tack. *The Living Daylights* sees James stripped of his superhero status – he even succumbs to a sleeping drug at one point – and back in the land of the Cold (only it's now just mildly chilly) War spy. Fans of the sun-soaked Bond surrounded by a bevy of beauties sipping colourful drinks with umbrellas in them, might feel cheated, but this brooding, maverick Bond is more like the original novels' character than many people realise, plus the plot is tight and rockets along. Thankfully the gadgets and stunts are still from fairyland, although a scene where Bond appears to ride a magic carpet – a rug held up by telegraph wires – over the rooftops of Tangiers sadly didn't make the final cut. Virginia Hey (Rubavitch) also becomes the first Bond girl to go (briefly) topless.

Title sequence Nothing out of the ordinary, but at least they spent some money. Dalton does a lovely gun-barrel swoop, too.

Best lines Check out Dalton's opening dialogue with the woman bemoaning the lack of real men in her life just before Bond parachutes onto her boat.

Famous last words Whitaker 'That's too bad, Bond. You could've been a live rich man, instead of a poor dead one.'

Notable stunts The escape through snowy Czech forests on Kara's cello case is great fun, plus the horseback Afghan fighters are a spectacular change from the usual transport methods.

Goofs/in-jokes No in-jokes (remember, this is serious Bond), and goofs are minor (although it does appear that Bond's car knocks down a hapless extra when parking in Tangiers). Also, in the days long before global terrorism, we guess the production crew thought that they could get away with the sign saying '325km to Islamabad' and '200km to Karachi' when the two cities are over 1,000km apart.

Ancestors and imitators

One of the earliest spy movies with a format we have come to recognise was *O.S.S.*, made in 1946 with a screenplay by none other than Richard Maibaum, clearly honing his creativity for subterfuge to come. Alan Ladd plays John Martin, an American spy sabotaging railways in wartime France with a few gadgets up his sleeve (like a pipe that becomes a gun), as well as a beautiful woman to rescue.

The closest we ever get to 'Bond: The Musical' is the Matt Helm series of movies, starting with *The Silencers*, made from 1966 to 1969. Dean Martin plays the laid-back playboy spy, saving the world from nuclear threat while cavorting with scantily clad women. And singing. When the original Donald Hamilton novels were adapted for television in the mid-1970s, they went back to their detective story roots with Anthony Franciosa in the lead role – more authentic, certainly, but a lot less fun.

The best spoof is probably the 1965 James Coburn flick, *Our Man Flint*, and its 1967 sequel, *In Like Flint*, in which US super spy, Derek(!) Flint, battles evil with his extraordinary abilities in everything, including talking to dolphins and teaching ballet. More recently, Mike Myers has mined the Bond seam for his trio of spy spoofs, *Austin Powers: International Man of Mystery*, *The Spy Who Shagged Me* and *Goldmember*.

The most jaw-dropping rip-off of Bond has to be *Operation Kid Brother* (1967) starring, you've guessed it, Sean Connery's real-life brother Neil Connery (and you thought the Baldwins were competitive). With its plot to eradicate the crime syndicate Thanatos, plus the astounding presence of Bernard Lee, Lois Maxwell and Adolpho Celi (scoring a perfect 10 on the what-were-they-thinking-ometer), this is a film that die-hard Bond fans must see. The terrible martial arts sequences, and the lounge music score by Ennio Morricone, can only add to its appeal.

The Bond bandwagon, however, is not confined to English-speakers, as 007 tributes have appeared in different languages all over the world. One of the most popular Greek comedians of all time, Thanassis Vengos, made two Bond spoofs in the late 1960s. The first, *Voitheia!.. O Vengos Faneros Praktor 000*, has Vengos making a farcical attempt to graduate from a Bond-style spy school, and the second, *Thou-Vou Falakros Praktor, Epixeirisis Gis Madiam*, sees the newly graduated Vengos duped into a trio of fake missions by a director wanting to film the botched and hilarious results. Reality TV meets the spy game with a surreal result. In Japan, they had Kokusai Himitsu Keisatsu, aka The International Secret Police in a trio of films

(*Interpol Code 8*, *Key Of Keys*, and *Driven To The Wall*). The 'Bond' character, Jiro Kitami, was played by Tatsuya Mihashi who later turned up as Phil Moscowitz, an agent tracking down a secret recipe for egg salad in Woody Allen's *What's Up, Tigerlily?* Sweden too, has got in on the act with its classy Carl Hamilton series featuring women, gadgets and nuclear weapons. The 1998 instalment, 'Hamilton', has Mark 'Feel The Force' Hammill as the bad guy and Lena Olin as the impressive love interest.

It's not only the character of Bond that offers a chance for filmmakers to have some fun – the villains also offer a rich vein of quirks and evil impulses which spoofers find hard to resist. The funniest of these is a Vincent Price movie made in 1965 called *Dr Goldfoot And The Bikini Machines* (far superior to the sequel, *Dr Goldfoot And The Girl Bombs*), where spying gets the beach blanket treatment and an army of gorgeous bikini-clad robots is out to take over the world. The poster tagline is possibly one of the best ever – 'Meet the girls with the thermo-nuclear navels'. Even Pussy Galore can't quite compete with that.

Licence To Kill
1989

Cast	Timothy Dalton, Robert Davi, Carey Lowell, Talisa Soto
Director	John Glen
Screening	Richard Maibaum, Michael G Wilson
Rating	**FFF**

Felix Leiter, now working for the DEA, is beaten and his wife killed, days after their wedding. Barred from pursuing the killer officially, Bond goes AWOL, coming up against Central American drug baron, Franz Sanchez. When a miraculous and daring attempt on Sanchez's life goes horribly wrong, Bond finds himself having to defend his actions to his bosses. Before long he is so embroiled in crossing and double-crossing that it takes all his powers to break free, destroy Sanchez's drug operation and hunt him down.

This is a very different Bond movie and, had it succeeded at the box office, things could have continued in this new direction. Rather than a lot of entertaining fluff until one big showdown when it all falls apart for the bad guy, here you have Bond picking apart the structure of Sanchez's empire bit by bit until it's just him and the drug lord face to face. It also gives Bond a much more personal motive, that of revenge. It's a good solid action flick, with some terrific performances, but perhaps it's not really a Bond movie. Maybe Dalton got a bit too serious, or maybe his slight vulnerability turned off devoted Bond fans, but whatever happened here, it won't happen again.

Title sequence More of the same really.

Best lines Bond 'Pam, this is Q, my "uncle". Q, this is "Miss Kennedy", my "cousin."'

The man with a golden pen

Richard Maibaum has a screenwriting credit on nearly all the Connery/Lazenby/Moore/Dalton Bond movies. The pipe-smoking writer began his prolific career as a stage actor and playwright in the 1930s, and then started writing screenplays for Hollywood. During World War II he served as director of the US Army Combat Film Division, and returned to Hollywood as a producer and screenwriter for Paramount (for whom he wrote O.S.S, see p118). In 1950, a tax loophole brought him to a working partnership with Irving Allen and Albert R Broccoli to make films in London. He liked the move, and continued to work with British film and television producers for the rest of his life. A couple of his more interesting credits include the storyline for Mel Gibson's 1996 film Ransom (actually released five years after Maibaum's death), and additional dialogue for Chitty Chitty Bang Bang (1968).

Over the years he teamed up with a number of excellent writers, like Johanna Harwood, Berkely Mather, Paul Dehn, Tom Mankiewicz and Christopher Wood, so we will never know exactly who wrote Bond's finest and most memorable lines, but Maibaum is certainly responsible for some top cinematic moments and iconic images.

In 1991, not long after the release of his 13th credited Bond film, Maibaum died back home in California.

Q 'Ah! We must be related.'

Perez (After Krest has spilt his innards all over a load of cash) 'What about the money, padrone?'

Sanchez 'Launder it.'

Famous last words Sanchez 'Señor Bond, you got big cojones. You come here, to my place, without references, carrying a piece, throwing around a lot of money… but you should know something: nobody saw you come in, so nobody has to see you go out.'

Notable stunts The final chase with the oil tankers, especially the wheelie in the big rig. Superb.

Goofs/in-jokes Apart from the stone fish statue that winks at the camera just before the end, it's all a bit po-faced.

GoldenEye
1995

Cast	Pierce Brosnan, Sean Bean, Izabella Scorupco, Famke Janssen
Director	Martin Campbell
Screening	Jeffrey Caine, Bruce Feirstein (story by Michael France)
Rating	𝕱𝕱𝕱𝕱𝕱𝕱𝕱

Bond tracks the theft of two highly secret GoldenEye nuclear satellites, capable of disabling all electronic equipment within their target area, to a Russian crime syndicate, Janus. He is astounded to find that Alec Trevelyan (Bean), a former 006 pre-sumed killed in action, is the head of Janus and intends to use GoldenEye to steal billions from the stockmarket as recompense for Britain's past wrongdoings. After a daring raid on Janus' Cuban control centre, Bond jams the satellite transmission and kills Trevelyan in a fight.

After a six-year hiatus, during which it seemed Bond had gone for good, Brosnan finally took up the role he had been offered years before. The change in studio, team, cast and star all seemed to work some kind of magic, and the release of a Bond film became an event again. Fair enough too, as Brosnan seems to be the wholly acceptable love child of Moore and Dalton, with just a touch of Connery about his delivery. Most importantly, he makes it possible to believe in this Bond – both the humour and the action suit him. The supporting cast is positively stellar with **Judi Dench** and **Sean Bean** both excellent, while minor baddie Zukovsky (**Robbie Coltrane**) is a great addition to the story. The plot is confusing in places, and perhaps a little time could have been shaved off some of the longer chase sequences, but for a bunch of first-timers, it's impressive stuff.

Title sequence It may be a new title designer, but it's the same old guns and girls.

Best lines M 'If I want sarcasm, I'll speak to my children.'

Trevelyan 'I might as well ask if all those vodka martinis silence

The penalties for not having a ticket on Trevelyan's train were rather severe ▲

the screams of all the men you've killed… Or if you've found forgiveness in the arms of all those women, for the ones you failed to protect?'

Famous last words Trevelyan 'Oh, please, James, put it away. It's insulting to think I haven't anticipated your every move.'

Notable stunts The chase in St Petersburg, where Bond hijacks a tank, and the bungee jump off the edge of an enormous dam.

Goofs/in-jokes Bond leans against a stone wall in the weapons factory and it buckles, plus he gets the fastest hair restyle ever, just by walking through the cabin door on the boat. Also, when the Tiger helicopter is being unveiled, the same boat passes by twice in the background.

Tomorrow Never Dies
1997

Cast	Pierce Brosnan, Jonathan Pryce, Teri Hatcher, Michelle Yeoh
Director	Roger Spottiswoode
Screening	Bruce Feirstein
Rating	𝄞𝄞𝄞𝄞𝄞𝄞

To complete his domination of the world's media, Elliot Carver needs to persuade China that he should be allowed to operate there. To accomplish this, he orchestrates the sinking of a British warship in Chinese waters, hoping to distract the Chinese with thoughts of war, while also buying himself a few juicy headlines. Bond is sent to investigate at the same time as the Chinese are sending their top agent, Wai Lin, to do the same, and their paths can't help but cross. After a tense finale on board Carver's stealth boat, Bond effects a particularly miraculous and daring rescue of Wai Lin (who has been dropped into the ocean in chains), kills Carver and manages to avert war.

One of the best plots in the whole Bond series, and one that lets Brosnan and **Jonathan Pryce** do their best work (it's about time Bond was up against an insane megalomaniac again). The pace is excellent, gadgets work beautifully, the script is stuffed with brilliant lines, and **Teri Hatcher** dies with terrific style – what more could we want? Well, it's a shame that Moneypenny seems to have turned into a one-woman double-entendre show, there's too much kung fu, and some of the fights come across as gratuitous and sadistic. But apart from that, it's a cracker.

Title sequence Not really sure about the woman made of computer circuitry who becomes flesh when viewed through a TV screen. Look out folks, we think the Bond movie may be in danger of trying to make a serious point.

Best lines Carver 'The distance between insanity and genius is measured only by success.'

Roebuck 'With all due respect M, sometimes I don't think you've got the balls for this job.'

Q: 'Your new BMW. Will you need collision cover?' 007: 'Yes' Q: 'Property destruction?'

M 'Perhaps, but the advantage is I don't have to think with them all the time.'

Famous last words Carver 'In a matter of minutes my plan will succeed and thanks largely to your efforts, the British Navy will destroy the evidence. And I'll be out of here in a Carver news helicopter, covering the event! It's going to be a fantastic show…'

Notable stunts The motorcycle and helicopter chase in Saigon, sorry, Ho Chi Minh City.

Goofs/in-jokes If you remember Robert Maxwell, the report on Carver's death that M instructs to be released will sound spookily familiar. However, the best goof seems to be the film's title – apparently it was supposed to be *Tomorrow Never Lies* (which would have been a lot better), but a typographical error switched it and they kept it that way.

007: 'Definitely' Q: 'Personal injury?' 007: 'I hope not, but accidents do happen'

The World Is Not Enough
1999

Cast	Pierce Brosnan, Robert Carlyle, Sophie Marceau, Denise Richards
Director	Michael Apted
Screening	Neal Purvis, Robert Wade, Bruce Feirstein
Rating	ргггг

After a botched mission, causing the death of his friend Robert King, Bond is assigned to protect King's daughter, Elektra, from Renard, a psychopath who has kidnapped her in the past. At first it seems that Elektra's attempts to complete her father's work, a vital strategic oil pipeline, are being targeted by terrorists. But after a miraculous and daring escape from a nuclear silo accompanied by Dr Christmas Jones, it becomes clear that Renard and Elektra are working together to sabotage her competitors. Bond manages to rescue M, who has been kidnapped, kill Elektra, avert Renard's plan to cause a meltdown in a nuclear submarine's reactor, and still escape with his loafers intact.

It's always good when a love interest turns out to be a vengeful psychotic (well, in movies) and this Bond film has some good twists and turns. Excellent performances from **Robert Carlyle** and **Robbie Coltrane** (returning as Zukovsky), and a cameo from **John Cleese** as Q's new assistant, cannot disguise a host of plot holes. Like, would M really fly to see Elektra? She's head of MI6, for God's sake. Also, **Denise Richards**, although initially passable in an I-can't-believe-she-could–be-a-doctor-but-she's-good-to-look-at sort of way, descends into petulant cheerleader mode when she has to share the screen with **Sophie Marceau**. Entertaining, but not one of the greats.

Title sequence Is it us, or does the oil-and-water look remind
you of the intermission screen at your local fleapit cinema?

Best lines Bond 'I've always wanted to have Christmas in Turkey.'

Renard 'Welcome to my nuclear family.'

Bond doesn't rule the world. Yet

Cubby Broccoli once boasted that half the world had seen a Bond movie. Yet when you pore over the box office takings of 007 it's rapidly apparent that, like Auric Goldfinger, he hasn't yet dominated the world. And that bit about Bond being the most successful movie series needs a tweak too: it is the most successful series starring a single character but Star Wars (five movies so far released and a cumulative box office take of $3.4bn compared to $3.3bn for Bond's 19 official movies) is the most successful series – though while the Bond franchise, with Brosnan, is gathering momentum, George Lucas's sci-fi extravaganza is gently declining at the box office.

All five Star Wars films are among the top 20 box-office performers of all-time. The best 007 can manage is number 67 on the same list with Pierce Brosnan's The World Is Not Enough, which raked in some $352m, almost exactly the same as his first outing GoldenEye. Bond's 'failure' is comparative: there have been 19 official Bond movies in 40 years and none have lost money, with four raking in more than $200m.

The Bond movies were the first event movies. The elements (hit theme tune, miraculous and daring rescues, barmy loquacious villains, dazzling girls, a steady supply of quips) were part of a ritual. We all knew exactly what to expect when we bought a ticket to watch a Bond film and what we expected, usually, was the same recipe served up with such craft and guile that it felt different. We wanted the formula, but we didn't want to feel we were watching something formulaic.

Most of the films have met these demands and yet, in the last 25 years, as Hollywood turned to the event movie to bring some predictability to a fiendishly unpredictable business, 007 has been left behind somewhat. Brosnan's stewardship has, at least, raised the possibility that an 007 movie might break the $500m barrier. Hollywood's rule of thumb is that a sequel should generate at least two-thirds of its predecessor's box office. So that gives Die Another Day a $230m 'start' at the box office. The problem for MGM and the producers is that Brosnan may only brandish a Walther PPK in one more film. And the riskiest moment in Bond's movie career is the handover of the tux to the next actor. It didn't work with George Lazenby (his film took in 27 per cent less than Connery's You Only Live Twice) or Timothy Dalton (whose films failed to match the performance of Roger Moore's The Spy Who Loved Me). But Moore and Brosnan both took the movies to new commercial heights. So if MGM and Barbara Broccoli get it right, the next 007 may be the actor who leads 007 to Indiana Jones-style world domination.

Famous last words Elektra 'You can't kill me, you would miss me too much.'

Notable stunts The ski chase over the peak, with snowmobiles pursuing and explosions raging behind, is stunning, as is the boat chase along the Thames. The helicopter chainsaw destroying Zukovsky's caviar factory is ludicrous OTT Bond, but great fun.

Goofs/in-jokes Is it really a good idea for Bond to carry his ID card in his shoe while working undercover? Look out for the portrait of Bernard Lee (the original M) on the wall of the Scottish MI6 headquarters. Similarly, the girlie pictures on the walls of Zukovsky's warehouse are all of former Bond girls.

007 at the box office

Film	Budget (in millions, US$)	Worldwide Box Office Gross (in millions, US$)
Dr. No	$1	$60
From Russia With Love	$2.5	$79
Goldfinger	$3.5	$125
Thunderball	$5.6	$141
Casino Royale	$10	$25
You Only Live Twice	$9.5	$112
On Her Majesty's Secret Service	$4.8	$82
Diamonds Are Forever	$8.0	$116
Live And Let Die	$9.0	$161
The Man With The Golden Gun	$10	$98
The Spy Who Loved Me	$13.5	$185
Moonraker	$30	$203
For Your Eyes Only	$20	$195
Octopussy	$20	$184
Never Say Never Again	$34	$160
A View To A Kill	$20	$152
The Living Daylights	$25	$191
Licence To Kill	$27	$156
GoldenEye	$50	$351
Tomorrow Never Dies	$75	$334
The World Is Not Enough	$100	$352

They could have been 007

The role of Bond is a lucrative one in acting circles. Brosnan has confirmed he'll return for another outing, yet speculation mounts as to who will be Bond number six. As natural as original star Connery seemed in the role, when casting *Dr. No* in 1962 Fleming failed to warm to the burly Scot. 'Not exactly what I envisioned,' was his initial opinion of Connery's portrayal of his hero. Connery remained philosophical about his big break, 'I got it because they could afford me. Ian Fleming wanted Cary Grant or Trevor Howard, but they couldn't afford either of them.'

Since Connery, countless names have been touted as potential Bonds, but here is a rundown of serious contenders for Bond over 40 years. Actors who claimed they were in the running merely to increase their profile are excluded.

Lucan would not audition for 007 ▲

David Niven Fleming's first choice, Niven encapsulated everything the author thought his hero should be: a stylish, educated English gent. But EON Productions wanted a Bond with a 'mid-Atlantic' image as Broccoli put it, to appeal to an American audience.

Cary Grant Broccoli's first choice, even if he was 57 when *Dr. No* was being filmed (the same age as Roger Moore when he made *A View To A Kill*). Grant turned down the role because of his age, his growing disinterest in movies and the fact that *Dr. No's* budget for the whole film ($1m) was about the same as his fee.

Trevor Howard Riding high from his Oscar nomination for *Sons And Lovers* in 1960, Trevor Howard was a star in the mould of Niven, and thus not what Broccoli wanted.

Rex Harrison In 1962 Harrison seemed like a natural choice. A well-spoken Englishman, he was also a bit of a playboy, and had a confidence bordering on conceit, having changed his name from Reginald to Rex, the Latin for king.

Patrick McGoohan If Niven was Fleming's first choice, *Danger Man* star Patrick McGoohan was EON's. McGoohan, however, viewing Bond as sexist, demeaning to women and not something he wanted his daughters to see, wasn't interested.

They could have been 007

Lord Lucan When Connery decided to hang up his tux for the first time, Broccoli was convinced Lucan was perfect for the role, 'He had it all – the looks, the breeding, the pride.' He also thought he had a licence to kill, so maybe Cubby was right.

Michael Billington Always the bridesmaid never the bride, Michael Billington, star of cult TV show *UFO*, screen-tested for Bond five times, more than any other actor.

James Brolin The current Mr Streisand wasn't just a contender, in 1982 he was Bond, for about 24 hours anyway. Following the release of *For Your Eyes Only*, Cubby Broccoli prepared himself for Roger Moore's customary plea for a pay rise by hiring Brolin as his replacement. As Brolin was getting ready to begin filming *Octopussy*, Moore came round to the idea of reprising his role and Brolin got the boot.

John Gavin A former US naval intelligence officer and one-time ambassador, John Gavin had enough real-life experience to play Bond standing on his head. Like Brolin, he came very close, before United Artists managed to lure Connery back.

Michael Gambon In 1970, when Broccoli was casting *Diamonds Are Forever*, Broccoli suggested Gambon, a relatively unknown stage actor, as the next Bond. After Lazenby, United Artists were unwilling to take on another unknown, though Gambon had already pointed out why he wasn't suitable during his audition: 'But Cubby, I'm in terrible shape. I've got tits like a woman!' 'Doesn't matter, so had Sean. We wrapped him in ice packs before every love scene.'

Adam West As filming was due to start on *On Her Majesty's Secret Service*, EON was still searching for a star. Broccoli asked his friend West, at the time riding high as the caped crusader. West turned him down, believing only a British star should play Bond. So EON hired Aussie Lazenby.

Stewart Granger Despite being 49 in 1962 when the casting call went out for *Dr. No*, Ian Fleming added aging Hollywood idol Granger to his shortlist of potential Bonds.

Peter Snow Yes, chiefly known to British viewers for his General Election night swing-o-meter, Snow auditioned for *On Her Majesty's Secret Service*, but at six foot, five inches EON producers felt he was too tall. Mind you, as host of popular BBC science show *Tomorrow's World*, he could have made a cracking Q.

Anthony Hamilton In 1985 former ballet dancer Hamilton was in negotiations to star in *A View To A Kill*. In the end Moore resolved his fee issues and Broccoli, who wasn't happy with a homosexual actor playing his very heterosexual hero, sighed with relief.

Mentioned in dispatches: George Baker (Inspector Wexford in the Ruth Rendell crime series), Ian Ogilvy (who succeeded Moore as Simon Templar), Liam Neeson, Sam Neill and Hugh Grant have all been cited, with varying degrees of seriousness, as potential Bonds at some time or other.

THE 007 FILES

Five men who have only one
thing in common: Bondage

007

'Bond is what every man would like to be...'

Raymond Chandler

The creator of Philip Marlowe went on to add 'and what every woman would like to have between her sheets', which might be a slightly more dubious proposition. But he's at least half-right: every man has imagined himself as Bond at one time or another (and many still do after a few beers) but only five can really lay claim to 'being' Bond. **Sean Connery**, **George Lazenby**, **Roger Moore**, **Timothy Dalton** and **Pierce Brosnan** are the ones who have entered stage right, turned and shot that cameraman in the eye at the start of a James Bond film. All have brought something to the role and all (yes, that includes George) are worthy of our respect.

Truly a man of both Britain and her Empire, James Bond has been played by an Englishman, an Irishman, a Welshman, a Scotsman and an Australian. Indeed, deciding who's the best Bond might just as easily be confirmed by a rugby tournament, but we'll just run our eye over them and let you decide.

Of course, being Bond is not just the responsibility of the actor involved. It's the directors and scriptwriters who shape the character and give them the words to speak, and the producers who raise the money for the stunts and special effects, which can turn a good film into a great one. But if a man is to be judged at all, let it be on his portrayal of Commander James Bond, the secret agent whose identity is the spy world's worst kept secret.

Sean Connery

Age at first performance 32
Total appearances 7
Pros The original.
Cons *Never Say Never Again.*
Trivia Connery, ambivalent about whether he wanted the part of Bond at all, refused to screen test.
Fashion The dinner jacket, the grey suits, the trilby, the casual wardrobe, even the ludicrous all-in-one blue towelling thing with the very short shorts he wore in *Goldfinger* – all classic style statements. The blot on the copybook is *Never Say Never Again*, where Connery shared top billing with a load of ridiculous wigs.
Best vehicle The Aston Martin DB5, of course, with the moon buggy from *Diamonds Are Forever* a close second.
Style As the first to play the role on film, Connery's Bond, with the right mix of cool, charisma, violence and arrogance, is the Bond against which all others are judged. He could get a woman to undress two minutes after meeting her, and 30 seconds after she had tried to assassinate him.

> Sean Connery is the Bond by whom all others are judged

Combat Always had his trusty Walther PPK automatic, but liked a fist fight too. Connery's Bond could handle himself and didn't mind knocking the hell out of anybody who got in his way. Being a former sailor, he also made it look like he could do it in real life.
Sex on a stick? Connery still tops polls of the 'World's Sexiest Man' variety despite his advancing years. As Bond, he naturally slept with every woman to cross his path. Some needed a bit of roughing up before they complied, which isn't the greatest

Water was always something of an aphrodisiac for Bond – and for the Bond girls ▶

seduction technique, but these were different times.

Faux pas On location in Japan for *You Only Live Twice*, Connery was asked his opinion of Japanese women. 'Japanese women are not sexy,' volunteered Connery, 'especially when they hide their figures in kimonos'. The furore which greeted this remark was one of the reasons Connery quit.

Connery on 007 'I never disliked Bond, as some have thought. Creating a character like that does take a certain craft. It's simply natural to seek other roles.'

Verdict Subsequent actors may have had films with bigger budgets and more special effects, and he may have come back once too often with *Never Say Never Again*, but Connery, to those for whom he was the first 007 (and many others since), just is Bond. Ironically, the dissenter, initially, was Ian Fleming who (even more ironically given his Scottish roots) doubted if a working class Scot like Connery could play his English hero. He suggested David Niven. It took the Marquess of Milford Haven's wife to convince Fleming that Connery 'had it' as 007.

Lazenby takes a drag. His Bond might have been more fun in drag ▲

George Lazenby

Age at first appearance 30
Total appearances 1
Pros Tough guy attitude, physical grace in the action scenes.
Cons He wasn't Sean Connery. He wasn't even Neil Connery.
Trivia Even though it's the middle of the night, George dons anti-glare goggles before the first big ski chase.
Fashion The perfectly trimmed hair said 'Dress me in something dull', and the black outfit for the skiing did the trick, but for the rest of the movie the wardrobe department said 'frills, beige cravats, jodhpurs and orange shirts. And full Highland dress'. Poor George looked ill at ease enough in the pinstripe, but the dress shirt was the biggest fashion disaster in Bond movies until Roger Moore's safari suits.

Nifty on skis, but not so hot in a kilt or a dress shirt

Best vehicle Not much of a driver, George always looked much more at home on skis.
Style As a former male model, Lazenby may have looked like a Bond, but his acting style came from the same mail order catalogue school. The dialogue didn't help. On the plus side he worked his way through the female population at a respectable rate, but then there's that ending when he's cradling his dead bride and saying, without a single hint of emotion: 'She's alright, really. We have all the time in the world.' He didn't, and Connery came back for the next film (*Diamonds Are Forever*).
Combat Not so bothered with guns, George was a hand-to-hand fighter who punched and kicked his way through opponents. Also very handy with a knife.
Sex on a stick? Well, he was a male model, and had the chiselled look of the time. And despite the film taking place over

Roger Moore gives the eyebrows a minor work out, auditioning for 007 ▲

a matter of weeks, he sleeps with three women before declaring his undying devotion and marrying one of them.

Faux pas Letting his ego run away on set so much that his co-star Diana Rigg decided to eat garlic paté before a love scene.

Lazenby on 007 'Producer Cubby Broccoli will tell you that I was a failure and difficult to work with. Unfortunately, he told a lot of people that and it meant that it was impossible to get employment. I was too immature for it.'

Verdict Lazenby had a tough job following Connery, and may just have been out of his depth. His director Peter Hunt's policy of isolating him during filming to create the feel that Bond was a loner probably didn't help. His only film is still a good watch, and is actually liked by many who don't like other Bond films.

Roger Moore

Age at first appearance 45

Total appearances 7

Pros The only Englishman to play Bond, and he was once actually in military intelligence.

Cons One quip too many, and at least one movie too many; he looked too old for all the action, indoors or outdoors, by the time he made *A View To A Kill*.

Trivia Moore never ordered 'a vodka martini, shaken, not stirred,' to stop him appearing to copy **Sean Connery**'s portrayal.

Roger Moore was and is the king of the blazer

Fashion It was the 1970s after all, but the safari suit, while reasonably louche, was never going to be a lasting symbol of MI6 cool. Lots of powder blue and light beige in evidence, and double-breasted jackets which rather than having lapels had a wingspan. Moore was, and remains to this day, the king of the blazer. Still, it was the best Saville Row had to offer at the time.

Best vehicle The amphibious Lotus Esprit, followed by the powerboat from the *Live And Let Die* Everglades chase.

Style Master of the arch comment, and even more arched eyebrow, Moore played the character with tongue planted firmly in cheek. Super-suave Roger, rather than acting in character, was himself on screen. He was superior, never got that angry and would rather leg it than get his nose bloodied or his shirt ruffled.

Combat In physical situations Moore tried more often than not to let his brains do the fighting rather than simply trying to punch his way out. A crack shot, but not a great physical fighter.

Sex on a stick? He slept his way through the movies, but the humour (and the ageing process) meant he was never a sex god.

Faux pas Only real gaffe was playing 007 when he was 57. And letting his perma tan turn orange might have gone down well in Holland but played very badly in the rest of the world.

Moore on 007 'This man is supposed to be a spy and yet, everybody knows he's a spy. Every bartender in the world offers him martinis that are shaken, not stirred. What kind of serious spy is recognised everywhere he goes?'

Verdict Moore was a great Bond who just outstayed his welcome and descended towards parody (as did the movies). Screenwriter **Tom Mankiewicz** probably put it best when he said that Moore was 'much more the Etonian dropout Fleming had envisaged and he was a good comedian, but Sean could be nasty, he had that lorry driver in him and the audience loved him for it'. Less would have been more – for Moore.

Timothy Dalton

Age at first appearance 40
Total appearances 2
Pros Intense, brooding.

Cons Slight lack of cool.

Trivia His favourite Bond novel is *Casino Royale*.

Fashion As befits the era, Bond's clothes are classic but rather bland. He looks more comfortable in 'smart casual' than the more formal suits and tuxedos usually associated with the character. His hair is somewhat informal too, and always looks like it needs a slight trim. Deducted several points too for exposing a bit too much chest.

Best vehicle Bond's back in the Aston, but is also rather good at controlling a cello case down a mountainside.

Style Probably the most different of all the Bonds, Dalton's was certainly the least relaxed and the most prone to moods. As a Shakespearean actor of the type loved by Americans (think Patrick Stewart with hair), Dalton's was a serious, emotional and dark Bond, looking for character motivation and fighting with inner turmoil. On his two outings, and in a reaction against the excesses of the latter Moore films, the camp and humour are reduced to a minimum. He once said that he liked *Casino Royale* so much 'because Bond says clearly that he's in a state of moral and ethical confusion'.

Dalton was liable to bare his chest for no good reason

Combat Dalton's Bond got beaten up rather a lot, but was always up for a sweaty scrap. Guns, fists, chairs, whatever he had at hand would do. As befits a more serious, demon-driven Bond, a lot of the violence was tinged with more realism than most 007 scraps.

Sex on a stick? Timothy Dalton's Bond didn't let the side down in the sack. His was an appeal based on darkness rather than wit, tenderness and suave gentlemanly conduct.

Faux pas Making Bond too serious. In Fleming's novels he's often on the edge, but there's always a certain sardonic distance. Besides, there's always a serious danger that as a Welsh actor playing 007 as a moody bugger, you're just going to end up reinforcing prevailing racial stereotypes.

Dalton on 007 'One day I saw Pierce holding that gun, I felt a weight falling away from my body. Only then I realised I'm back to being myself again, free.'

Verdict Dalton, if not perfect, was the right man for the job. But he struggled with some of the series' weakest plots. And in an era of huge budget Hollywood action blockbusters like the Indiana Jones movies and the Terminator series, the Bond films just seemed tired and not that distinctive.

Pierce Brosnan

Age at first appearance 42
Total appearances 4 (including *Die Another Day*)
Pros Cool, good-looking.
Cons No sense of any vulnerability, there's a danger of a certain smarminess creeping in.
Trivia Brosnan's late wife Cassandra Harris played the mistress of Milos Columbo (Topol) in *For Your Eyes Only*.
Fashion Undeniably cool and eschewing fashion while going for high style. Brosnan doesn't really 'do' casual, and is usually seen in either very expensive-looking suits or hi-tech action man fatigues. He's prevented, by contract, from wearing a tuxedo in any non-Bond movie. Slightly slimmer and less 'chunky' than other Bonds, Brosnan carries off the immaculately tailored clothes with huge amounts of style. A return to well-cut and finely-detailed glory.
Best vehicle The powerboat in the opening of *The World Is Not Enough*, but this may be eclipsed by a return to Newport Pagnell's best with the Aston Martin Vanquish in *Die Another Day*.
Style Brosnan's Bond is a return to the original mix of action and danger threaded through with the right amount of wit and humour. Like Moore he had played a similar character before

For his first 007 film, Brosnan didn't get a dressing room, just a chair and some straw ▲

(Remington Steele). Less violent towards women (unless, of course, they are being violent towards him), he's full of twinkling charm and oozing confidence in the role.

Combat As the first Bond for the videogame generation, Brosnan can't just go round beating and kicking people. He does all that of course, usually without either breaking sweat or loosening his tie, but there are also weapons aplenty. Yes, the trusty Walther makes an appearance, but so do lots of sub-machine guns and assault rifles too, along with the odd rocket launcher.

Sex on a stick? Brosnan is another perennial winner of magazine polls and, with this Bond, foreplay doesn't always contain a slap round the face – he's onto a winner.

Faux pas Not put a foot wrong. Yet.

Brosnan on 007 'It's a role better suited to someone who is in his 40s, old enough to have the confidence and the sophistication and strength to be able to stand there and just let the moment sit.

Bond is a man with the greatest of confidence. In 1986, I think I was 33 or something like that, and I still looked like a baby. Finally, I'm growing into this face of mine. That takes time.'
Verdict For many the best Bond since Connery, he's been helped by history, big budgets and tight scripts.

The other 007s

Great though the five main cinematic Bonds are, they're not the only ones to have taken on the role of the world's most famous secret agent. It took a while before Cubby Broccoli brought Bond to the big screen but others tried their hand…

Bob Holness Yes, that Bob Holness, as in 'I'll have a Q please, Bob' from the British TV quiz show *Blockbusters*. Holness played Bond on South African radio in the 1950s.

Barry Nelson played 007 in *Casino Royale* in 1954, on the 50-minute CBS Climax Mystery Theatre, the first ever on-screen appearance of the superspy (even if he was Americanised). After that the highlight of Nelson's career was a role as George the gas man in one of Alfred Hitchcock's TV shows.

David Niven was Bond in *Casino Royale*. Niven was the quintessential upper class Englishman and Fleming's very first suggestion for the role. He played it strictly for laughs (a wise move given the script), but were it not for his age could have made a great 'real' Bond.

'The name's Holness, Bob Holness…' ▲

Woody Allen, in *Casino Royale*, was Bond's nephew Jimmy Bond. Woody has always lived out his sexual fantasies on film, and what could be greater than playing Bond?

144

005
THE GIRLS

The quasi-definitive guide to the
finest eye candy in the movies

007

'For the first time in my life I feel like a complete woman'

Solitaire, Live and Let Die

Bond girls are a homogeneous breed: gorgeous, pathetically grateful (for the most part) when 007 notices them, big-haired (for the most part) and the object of endless double entendres.

In Fleming's novels, the Bond girls are described as if they're disguised boys. **Honeychile Ryder** and **Tatiana Romanova** both have their derrieres described in very male terms: Ryder's is temptingly boyish while Romanova's has 'lost the smooth downward feminine sweep'. Descriptions like this prompted Fleming's friend **Noel Coward** to reprove him in a letter: 'I know we are all becoming progressively more broadminded nowadays but really, old chap, what could you have been thinking of?'

In the movies, the Bond girls, as **Alexander Cockburn** pointed out in his excellent essay *The Secret Agent*, aren't boys but fish. Ryder emerges from the sea in *Dr. No* like a rare and beautiful species of marine life; **Halle Berry** seems set to emulate that arrival in *Die Another Day*. In *Thunderball*, Bond meets Dominique Derval underwater; in *Licence To Kill*, the first tryst between Bond and the CIA's Pam Bouvier is on a motor boat, one of ten such trysts involving boats, yachts and ocean liners in Bond movies. If the sea's too far away, Bond is always ready for action in a swimming pool (a climactic embrace with Bouvier), a bathtub (with Pola Ivanova in *A View To A Kill*), a waterbed (Tiffany Case in *Diamonds Are Forever*), the shower (with Stacey Sutton in *A View To A Kill*), saunas, steam rooms... Sigmund Freud would probably have a word for this.

Ursula Andress
Honey Ryder

Born 19 March 1936, Bern, Switzerland

Film Dr. No (1962)

More than just a pretty face? Course. Honey was as resourceful as a scout, even carrying a knife when she wore a bikini.

Skills Dispelling would-be rapists with black widow spiders.

Likes Collecting shells.

Dislikes Being bound and almost drowned by a sluice.

Post-007 After frightening Elvis with her outsize shoulders in *Fun In Acapulco*, brightening up *Playboy* in 1965, and a turn in *Casino Royale* (where she ices Giovana Goodthighs), Andress' career sank into 1970s erotica before she appeared in *Clash Of The Titans* as (what else?) a goddess.

Remembered for That bikini.

Lois Maxwell
Miss Moneypenny

Born 14 February 1927, Toronto, Canada

Film All, until A View To A Kill in 1985

More than just a pretty face? A hint of come-hither when she crossed her stockinged legs. Had the potential to be a bit of a saucepot, as she showed when she took her glasses off.

> 'You're late as usual, even from your own funeral'

Skills Incredible loyalty, spurred on in the hope that she might, one day, get off with her boss.

Likes Baking angel cake.

Dislikes Bond's women.

Post-007 Pops up at Bond conventions, but relatively unheard of. Lives in Fort Erie in her native Canada.

Remembered for Taking her hair down and glasses off.

149

Multi-tasking Moneypenny can simultaneously take letters from M and pine for 007 ▲

Ian Fleming and the women

'Women were like pets, like dogs, men were the only real human beings, the only ones I could be friends with', Ian Fleming once told an American friend during World War II. Certainly the names he gave his female characters in his novels (Pussy Galore, Plenty O'Toole, Irma Bunt... enough said, he would probably have approved, secretly, of Austin Powers' Ivana Humpalot) seemed to underline that contempt. And just in case there were any lingering doubts, he has the heroine of The Spy Who Loved Me pay for the privilege of having a sensible name (Vivienne Michel) by proposing, 'All women love semi-rape'. You can find similarly patronising lines about women in most of his Bond novels.

Given this evidence, it seems impossible to deny the charge that Fleming was sexist and misogynist. Certainly, at times, he treated women as casually and as cynically as Bond does (in the movies at least). Yet there may be more truth in the observation by a friend Mary Pakenham who said Fleming looked on women like a schoolboy, 'they were remote mysterious beings who you will never hope to understand but, if you're clever, you can occasionally shoot one down.'

Fleming's relations with women were complicated, essentially, by his uneasy relationship with his mother. He would sometimes insult a woman he fancied, a tactic which charmed ingénues while others were often repelled by his vanity.

The picture is further muddied by Fleming's own sado-masochism. British novelist Anthony Powell notes in his journals rumours that Fleming whipped his wife Ann Rothermere – a taste he may have shared with critic Kenneth Tynan.

His novels, he famously boasted, were aimed somewhere between the solar plexus and, well, the upper thigh' and some of Fleming's tastes are reflected in the books, notably the beating of Bond's genitals. Yet the girls in the books are not the ciphers they sometimes appear in the films, as Emily Jenkins noted in her article The Sensitive Bond for Salon, 'Fleming is an equal opportunity voyeur... his sensual catalogs of men's bodies easily equal those of women's'. Most of all, as Jenkins notes, his weakness for the ladies seems like pure libido in the films, in the books, he seems afflicted by an urge to give it all up for love. He is, as Jenkins says, almost the epitome of a hard-soft hero of a romantic novel.

And the girls are usually integral to the plot, often saving Bond's life. Beautiful as they are, they usually have a flaw or a wound which arouses his sympathy. He often treats them gallantly knowing, perhaps, that he's usually the first or last real man in their lives. On the evidence of the books, Fleming's comparison of women to dogs seems, in part, just the kind of posing and pontificating for effect which makes him so very hard to analyse.

Daniela Bianchi
Tatiana Romanova

Born 31 January 1942, Rome, Italy

Film From Russia With Love (1963)

More than just a pretty face? In classic Bond style, Tatiana was blessed with a good measure of innocence and naïvety, despite being an Army Intelligence corporal.

Skills Not many, to be honest. She does, however, fire a bullet into evil Rosa Klebb with the toad-faced baddie's own pistol.

Likes Wearing nothing in bed but a black choker.

Dislikes Guns. 'Guns upset me,' she purrs to James.

Post-007 A Miss Universe runner-up (1960), Daniela starred in 007 spoof Operation Kid Brother and wed a millionaire. Go girl!

Remembered for The choker scene, as it were.

Honor Blackman
Pussy Galore

Born 22 July 1926, London, England (which made her, at 37, the oldest Bond 'girl').

Film Goldfinger (1964)

More than just a pretty face? A firecracker and no mistake. Goldfinger's personal pilot, she flies small aircraft, can parachute and employs a bunch of girls to cavort at her feet. Big hints that Pussy leans towards the ladies when it comes to horizontal action, but of course, Bond puts her quite literally on the straight and narrow. Wears winklepickers. She is first seen above Bond, purring 'My name is Pussy Galore' which must make her a kind of opposite to Plenty O' Toole.

Skills Stunt pilot. Wearing a gold waistcoat and looking good.

Likes Ladies, first and foremost.

Dislikes Men, until Bond finally wears her down.

Post-007 Nothing particularly noteworthy, which is a shame.

Remembered for That name. The producers did think about 151 changing it to Kitty Galore. Having her own Flying Circus (her troupe of female acrobats) years before Monty Python.

Shirley Eaton
Jill Masterson

Born 12 January 1937, London, England
Film Goldfinger (1964)

More than just a pretty face? A bit mumsy, and very easily led. Had a sister, Tilly, who was a bit better looking. Sorry.

Skills In real life is pretty brave, being covered in gold paint which, if worn for more than an hour, could have blocked her pores and suffocated her – just as happens in the film. Spooky.

Likes Humiliating Goldfinger. Who wouldn't?

Dislikes Gold paint.

Post-007 Became one of the most photographed actresses of the 1960s after appearing on the cover of *Life* magazine in gold paint. A stint in sci-fi followed, including a part as Su-Mura, the leader of the all-female kingdom of Femina who wants, get this,

Shirley Eaton's only smiling because there's a six-inch square on her midriff which isn't painted gold – doctor's orders you understand, to stop her suffocating ▲

to take over the world. (The film was called *Future Women* in the US). She then wrote a book about being painted gold, amongst other things.

Remembered for Suffocating under a coat of gold paint.

Claudine Auger
Domino Derval

Born 26 April 1942, Paris, France
Film Thunderball (1965)

More than just a pretty face? A pretty miserable face actually.

Skills Discovers bombs, fires harpoons, assasinates bad guys. Look up 'multi-talented' in the dictionary and you'll find Domino Derval.

Likes Life's luxuries.

Dislikes Being kept a prisoner by SPECTRE Agent Largo.

Post-007 Having won Miss France at 15 and subsequently beaten Raquel Welch to the part of Domino, big things might have been expected for Auger, but she went straight to video-movies and married a British businessman.

Remembered for Looking sad.

Molly Peters
Patricia Fearing

Born 1942, Walsham-Lee-Willow, England
Film Thunderball (1965)

More than just a pretty face? Forget the face, this one couldn't stop showing her body. She was a trained physiotherapist, too.

Skills Nursing, and being nursed.

Likes Being rubbed with a mink glove (currently unavailable on Medicare or the National Health Service).

Dislikes Being dumped by Bond.

Post-007 Made a rubbish film called *Target For Killing* in 1966, co-starred with Jerry Lewis, Terry-Thomas and a woman called Nike in an even worse film *Don't Raise The Bridge, Lower The*

River. Nobody seems to know where she went after that. Perhaps to the supermarket for some tea.

Remembered for Being the first Bond nude – although she was only shown in silhouette. Still, naked's naked.

Diana Rigg
Tracy Di Vicenzo

Born 20 July 1938, Doncaster, England
Film On Her Majesty's Secret Service (1969)

More than just a pretty face? Intelligent, complicated, suicidal and up for a bit of adventure.

Skills Avoiding Bond's affection and driving bare-footed. Also survives a night in a barn during a snowstorm, being crushed under an avalanche. Finishes off two baddies all on her own, too.

Likes Wedding outfits made from old doilies.

Dislikes Being shot in the car whilst on honeymoon.

Post-007 *Moll Flanders*, some theatre, *Victoria & Albert*, became a Dame (the female equivalent of a knighthood) and edited a book of the worst ever theatre reviews, *No Stone Unturned*.

Remembered for Being the only Mrs Bond. Congratulations, girl, you cracked it! And being the only Bond girl to have more on-screen presence than 007. No wonder she had to die.

Jill St John
Tiffany Case

Born 19 July 1940, Los Angeles, USA
Film Diamonds Are Forever (1971)

More than just a pretty face? Not the smartest – starts off as a professional smuggler but ends up easily manipulated.

Skills Has a nice fake fur armchair to contemplate life upon.

Likes Diamonds, funnily enough.

154 **Dislikes** Plenty O' Toole (Lana Wood), a more striking and altogether sexier Bond girl who appears briefly in the same film.

Post-007 The first American Bond girl, St John went on to star as Eva Peron in *An Intimate Portrait*, and appeared in Robert Altman's *The Player*. She also had her own cookery programme for a while. A decent skier, she now owns a boutique in Aspen and is married to Robert Wagner. She was once married to a chap called Lance Reventlow which made her heiress-in-law to the FW Woolworth millions. Henry Kissinger was among her many admirers.

> Jill St John is the only Bond girl to be lusted after by Kissinger

Remembered for Being naked with Bond, (save for a white mink blanket) on top of a round waterbed with real fish in it. That's the 1970s for you.

Jane Seymour
Solitaire

Born 15 February 1951, Middlesex, England
Film Live And Let Die (1973)

More than just a pretty face? She's also psychic.

Skills Uses tarot to predict the future but can't have sex or her powers will be wiped out. Bummer!

Likes To wear her hair like an ice-cream cone on top of her head and complement the style with too much gold eyeshadow. Sex – with 007.

Dislikes Not being able to have a fumble. Having the producers threaten to redub all her dialogue unless she started sounding 'less Shakespearean'.

Post-007 What hasn't she done? *Dr Quinn Medicine Woman, Dr Quinn Medicine Woman: The Movie, Dr Quinn Medicine Woman: The Heart Within*. Not bad considering the Solitaire role was originally written for a black actress and Catherine Deneuve was offered the part before the medicine woman.

155

Remembered for *Playboy* – it's not often Hef's pages are graced with such an innocent woman…

Britt Ekland
Mary Goodnight

Born 6 October 1942, Stockholm, Sweden

Film The Man With The Golden Gun (1974)

More than just a pretty face? Not really, even though she has been assigned to staff intelligence for two years.

Mary's main skill is getting locked in Scaramanga's trunk

Skills Getting herself locked in the trunk of Scaramanga's car, watching helplessly as the Walther PKK and the golden gun slug it out. In other words, none to speak of.

Likes Sleeping in closets while Andrea Anders (Maud Adams, the future *Octopussy*) and Bond do the horizontal shuffle.

Dislikes The fact that she spends less time making out with 007 than Andrea does.

Post-007 The ex-Mrs Peter Sellers has starred in films with titles like *Love Scenes*, *Erotic Images* and, worse, *Marbella*.

Remembered for Having a name which isn't as good as Holly Goodhead.

Barbara Bach
Anya Amasova

Born 27 July 1947, New York, USA

Film The Spy Who Loved Me (1977)

More than just a pretty face? She matches Bond for intelligence, courage and, well, looking good in a suit.

Skills All a good KGB agent could ask for: points guns at seven-foot-tall men with gold teeth, destroys women with missiles.

Likes Saluting.

Dislikes The fact that she had a rubbish Russian accent.

Post-007 Did a few films in Italy, the cheesiest being *Screamers*

Barbara Bach, no relation to Johann Sebastian but she is related to Ringo Starr ◄

aka *The Fish Men*, *The Island Of The Fish Men* and *The Island Of The Mutations*, publicly described James Bond as a 'male chauvinist pig', married Ringo Starr.

Remembered for Looking fantastic in uniform. Being the first 'liberated' Bond girl. Kinda.

Lois Chiles
Dr Holly Goodhead

Born 15 April 1947, Texas, USA
Film *Moonraker* (1979)

More than just a pretty face? This one's an astronaut, so she knows how to knock up a decent meal with powdered food. And she even matches Bond with one-liners, telling him off for a crude gag: 'The face is familiar. As is the manner.'

Skills Indifference – she brings Bond down a peg or two. Oh, and she's trained to kill in unarmed combat.

Likes Her own space.

Dislikes Bond, until he makes her all giddy.

Post-007 Chiles was supposed to play Amasova in *The Spy Who Loved Me*, played Holly Harwood in *Dallas* and starred in *Speed 2: Cruise Control*.

Holly knows how to cook a meal with powdered food

Remembered for Floating around in space with Bond at the end, naked but for a sheet. Helping 007 achieve re-entry.

Carole Bouquet
Melina Havelock

Born 18 July 1957, Neuilly-sur-Seine, France
Film *For Your Eyes Only* (1981)

158 **More than just a pretty face?** Melina is certainly that – she has a PHD in marine archaeology, she's determined, courageous, and plays down her beauty by wearing terrible clothes.

Skills A dab hand at the crossbow.

Likes Keeping Bond waiting.

Dislikes Men who order her parents to be killed.

Post-007 Carole went through a spell of modelling, and succeeded Catherine Deneuve as the face of Chanel for a while. All gone a bit quiet for her since she stopped being Gerard Depardieu's squeeze.

Remembered for Those eyes… That hair… A hideous leather/suede blouson with woolly hood.

Maud Adams
Octopussy

Born 12 February 1945, Lulea, Sweden

Film Octopussy (1983)

More than just a pretty face? Runs her own business – a circus – which is actually a front for a gem-smuggling caper.

Skills Not many, so she employs gymnasts to look after her.

Likes Doing the splits and forward rolls. Having a bed shaped like a giant octopus. Smuggling diamonds. Running a circus.

Dislikes Not being able to keep the gold Fabergé egg.

Post-007 *Angel 3: The Final Chapter*, a movie encompassing prostitution, kidnap and action. Hmm… Appearing in the background of the fisherman's wharf bit in *A View To A Kill*.

Remembered for Looking better in a leotard than Olga Korbett. And in Maud's case, being the only leading lady to play two major Bond characters, appearing in this opus and also *The Man With The Golden Gun*.

Tanya Roberts
Stacey Sutton

Born 15 October 1954, New York, USA

Film A View To A Kill (1985)

More than just a pretty face? She's a geologist yet she needs help with everything from telling the time to boiling an egg.

Skills She can't do a thing for herself except look lovely. The straps on her dress fall down a lot and she squeals like a stuck pig throughout the film.
Likes Being saved.
Dislikes Cliff edges and bridges.
Post-007 Teen-flick *Almost Pregnant*. That's about it.
Remembered for A terrible performance.

Girls! Girls! Girls!

In *From Russia With Love*, Bond watches a purrfect cat fight between Vida and Zora (Martine Beswick, who also appears in *Thunderball*, and Aliza Gur), two gypsy women fighting over a very lucky man. Bond is rooted to the spot, and who wouldn't be? It's all a mush of long black hair, red lipstick, the vivid greens and yellows of split skirts and torn peasant tops exposing just the right amount of ample bosom. Saucy, and quite marvellous.

Margaret Nolan, Dink in *Goldfinger*, was also the girl on the main title sequence and poster. Nolan looks resplendent in gold, eyes shut, bikini sparing her golden blushes.

Lana Wood played Plenty O' Toole in *Diamonds Are Forever*. She got the part after producers saw her in *Playboy*. You mean film producers sit around all day reading *Playboy*? What a great job! Natalie Wood's little sis, Plenty drowns, but looks great dead.

Grace Jones scared the hell out of us in *A View To A Kill* as baddie May Day. Scarier than her character was her wardrobe – all snoods and jumpsuits. A whiz at martial arts, she beds Bond – but naturally goes on top. Don't suppose he had much choice. Some consolation, perhaps, for her best line being 'Wow, what a view!'

The Cigar Girl in *The World Is Not Enough*, Maria Grazia Cucinotta, is the sultry Italian beauty who offers Bond a cigar before assassinating a banker, as you do. She meets her death in a spectacular high-speed boat chase. She wasn't smoking at the time.

Caroline Cossey was a Bond girl with a difference. The difference being that the bikini-clad lass lounging around Hector Gonzales' swimming pool started life as Barry Cossey. The transexual now lives in Atlanta. Caroline/Barry is one Bond girl who has never starred as a *Playboy* centrefold.

Fiona Fullerton
Pola Ivanova

Born 10 October 1956, Nigeria
Film A View To A Kill (1985)

More than just a pretty face? A KGB agent, so she's not daft.
Skills Talking dirty while getting clean, in a hot tub with Bond.
Likes Bathrooms.
Dislikes Not being the leading lady, probably.
Post-007 Starred in British TV series *The Charmer*, with Nigel Havers. Also appeared in *The Secret Life Of Ian Fleming*, a TV movie in which Jason Connery appears as Fleming (and after you've seen it Fleming's secret life will still be a secret).
Remembered for Being less scary than Grace Jones.

Maryam D'Abo
Kara Milvoy

Born 27 December 1960,
Film The Living Daylights (1987)

More than just a pretty face? Sure. Kara's a Czech cellist. Try saying that after a couple of martinis (shaken not stirred).
Skills Grabs sticks, sits back and flies a cargo plane if necessary.
Likes Big instruments. Beautiful evening gowns, especially if Bond's buying. Vienna, obviously unhealthily influenced by Ultravox and Billy Joel.
Dislikes Having to carry a cello around.
Post-007 *Leon The Pig Farmer*, *Playboy*.
Remembered for Being one of the few women Bond cared for.

Carey Lowell
Pam Bouvier

Born 11 February 1962, New York, USA
Film Licence To Kill (1989)

More than just a pretty face? A pretty face with short hair.
Skills She's a freelance pilot who pops in to work for the CIA

when she's bored or needs some extra cash. Handles herself alright in a scrap.

Likes Heavy-duty weaponry.

Dislikes Being stuck in practical gear while co-star Talisa Soto swans around in some pretty fancy gowns.

Carey Lowell is chiefly notable for not having big hair

Post-007 *Fierce Creatures*. Has a daughter by the actor Griffin Dunne and a son (Homer Jame Jigme Gere) with Hollywood's most famous buddhist. 'Jigme' is Tibetan for fearless, which poor old Homer will need to be if school chums ever discover his middle name.

Remembered for Playing a leading lady without big hair.

Talisa Soto
Lupe Lamora

Born 27 March 1967, Brooklyn, USA

Film Licence To Kill (1989)

More than just a pretty face? Lupe doesn't say much, she's too busy being held a virtual captive in her lover's palatial home.

Skills With the ability to watch her secret lover's heart get ripped out and not throw up, she's got a stomach stronger than Jaws.

Likes Wearing sultry outfits and pouting.

Dislikes Welts. After a few too many, she pleads with 007 to take her away from all that.

Post-007 *Mortal Kombat*. Calm down!

Remembered for Taking a beating.

Famke Janssen
Xenia Onatopp

Born 1 January 1964, Amsterdam, Holland

162   Film Goldeneye (1995)

More than just a pretty face? Yep, she's also a brain which conjures up all sorts of fancy sadomasochistic adventures.

Skills Machine gun massacres and crushing lovers' spines in her thighs. Well if you've got to go…
Likes Killing people when they're at their happiest.
Dislikes Non-smoking establishments.
Post-007 *X-Men*.
Remembered for Being filthy and smoking cigars.

Teri Hatcher
Paris Carver

Born 8 December 1964, Sunnyvale, USA
Film Tomorrow Never Dies (1997)

More than just a pretty face? Well, she's an old flame too.
Skills Standing still without falling over while Bond takes an age

How to spot a villainess

Spotting a villain in a Bond movie is easy – he'll be huge with gold teeth, small with a bald head or thin with spectacularly coiffured hair. Spotting a villainess, on the other hand, isn't quite as simple. They are stunningly attractive, but so are the good girls. A villainess will usually be highly skilled in one-armed combat, martial arts or heavy weaponry and work for the CIA or KGB, then get changed after work and slip into something more uncomfortable, like a nightie made of diamonds. They will normally have a bad Russian accent, even if they are Russian.

Fur coats, bullet-proof handbags and guns hidden in stocking tops are a good give away when spotting a villainess. They generally wear a lot of red lipstick and have big hair for good measure. Naturally, they also look equally at home in a bikini, especially if it's topped off with a bullet belt draped around the waist.

Villainesses usually smoke and they have their own lighters, usually made from the ear of a former lover who betrayed them, but there is never any need to use them unless they need to fire minuscule bullets at the enemy without being seen, before slipping on the mink and strutting away in six-inch stilettos.

Villainesses are always sexier than the good girls but you wouldn't want to marry one. They're too scary. That's where Miss Moneypenny comes in. After all, most men would rather have a slice of angel cake and a cup of tea than be tortured all night. Then again…

to undress her just because he can. Hopefully, he was considerate enough to leave the heating on.

Likes Supermen.

Dislikes The fact that she winds up dead thanks to Bond.

Post-007 *Spy Kids*, described as *GoldenEye* meets *Willy Wonka...*

Remembered for Having most of her scenes cut.

Michelle Yeoh
Wai Lin

Born 6 July 1962

Film Tomorrow Never Dies (1997)

More than just a pretty face? Oh yes. A pistol-packing, leather-catsuited Red Chinese agent. Ouch! Definitely not the kind of woman you'd want to mess with.

Skills Independent, resourceful, packs a good punch.

Likes Performing her own cunning stunts and putting her work first – she doesn't fall for Bond until their mission is over.

Dislikes Nuclear war, so she stops it.

Post-007 Oscar-winning *Crouching Tiger, Hidden Dragon* where she got to show off her jumping, flipping, high-kicking skills and screeching skills.

Remembered for That leather catsuit.

Denise Richards
Dr Christmas Jones

Born 17 February 1972, Illinois, USA

Film The World Is Not Enough (1999)

More than just a pretty face? Dr Jones is an expert in atomic physics, so she knows a nuclear weapon when she sees one.

Skills Dismantling plutonium.

Likes Science. Bunsen burners, safety glasses and white coats.

164 **Dislikes** Having a ridiculous name.

Post-007 *Valentine*, a marginally above average horror flick about a spurned geek. And *Undercover Brother*, a funny comedy

about American politics in which she plays a white she-devil.
Remembered for Prompting the line: 'And I thought Christmas only came once a year!'

Bond girls fight it out!

While most men go on about women being rubbish at driving and even worse at fighting, Bond would beg to differ. He's had to deal with some really stroppy ladies, usually trained in unarmed combat or martial arts, and most of them practice their skills on him. Sometimes the ladies fight each other, pulling pistols from garters or throwing their buxom enemy to the ground in a cat fight. But who's the hardest?

The Contenders

Honey Ryder (Ursula Andress)
Known for her speedy recovery from drugged black coffee, Honey's very resilient and she's not scared of spiders either. She's up against Pussy Galore. Ladies, when you're ready…

Pussy Galore (Honor Blackman)
Most women are scared of spiders, so Honey need only throw one at Pussy to make her scream. And Honey's got that knife strapped to her knickers, so unless Pussy's leotard-clad gymnasts are on hand she'll probably come a crop-per. Pussy's pushing 40 as

well, so she'll probably get tired. Honey takes it and takes on…

Tracy Di Vincenzo (Diana Rigg)
Complicated, very intelligent women who attempt to commit suicide are a handful. She's finished off Blofeld's henchmen too – one with a champagne bottle over the head, the other impaled on spike – so she'd take Honey on no problem. Has little sideburns, making her macho. Tracy wins and meets…

Anya Amasova (Barbara Bach)
A top KGB agent who points guns at Jaws and destroys other women with missiles. Her sensible uniform proves a winner when Tracy trips over her dress during a spat in the living room, but Tracy soon gets one over on Anya by pulling her hat down over her eyes, rendering Anya temporarily unsighted. She clouts her with a bottle. Bingo! Tracy wins again to take on…

Dr Holly Goodhead (Lois Chiles)
She's an astronaut who's trained in unarmed combat and she's really, really

Bond girls fight it out!

pretty. Tracy isn't as easy on the eye so jealousy fuels this fight. Holly single-handedly killed two of Drax's guards, so she's not worried about Tracy. With a flick of the hair and the right leg, she flips Tracy onto her back. Tracy leaps up to attack but Holly, used to floating about in space, levitates into the air and sits on the ceiling. Tracy can't reach her, so Holly picks bits of Artex off and flicks them at Tracy, hitting her fatally in the eye. Holly's next contestant...

Xenia Onatopp (Famke Janssen)

An ex-Soviet fighter pilot, she massacres staff with a machine gun in the time it takes other Bond girls to slip out of a bikini. Holly is smoked down from the ceiling by Xenia's cigar, and takes a swipe at Xenia with her elbow, but the cigar gets in the way and burns her arm. As she cries in pain, Xenia throws her onto the couch, wraps her legs around Holly's head and crushes her skull between her thighs. Evil! Xenia must now fight:

Zora (Martine Beswick)

Zora lives in a caravan, so she's tough. Her breasts jump about in her gypsy top, distracting Xenia. As Zora grabs Xenia's hair, Xenia gets a finger through Zora's hoop earring and gives it a good tug. Her ear comes clean off. Xenia wins and up steps:

May Day (Grace Jones)

As evil girlfriend to Christopher Walken's Max Zorin, May Day is a whiz at martial arts. However, Xenia oils herself up so that May Day's leather gloves give her the slip. Xenia takes the opportunity to wrap May Day's yellow snood around her head. Xenia wins!

And the overall winner is...

Xenia Onatopp. She's beautiful and really good at fighting. Top Bond girl! She fully deserves her sought after prize: the 007 of her choice. Or her favourite Bond villain.

006
THE VILLAINS

'If we destroy Kansas the world may
not hear about it for years'

007

'Choose your next witticism carefully, Mr Bond, it may be your last'

Auric Goldfinger

The nearest thing cinema has to the pantomime villain, Bond's bad guys are as integral a part of the series as 007 himself. Bond without Blofeld, or the countless variations on the same old villainous riff, would be like fish without chips, Laurel without Hardy, or Siegfried without Roy. Hands up who hasn't murmured a murderous 'I've been expecting you, Mr Bond,' when stroking a cat? Next you'll be telling us you've never pranced about in front of a mirror with a hairbrush, thinking you could easily be mistaken for the vintage David Bowie.

It's a full 40 years since **Dr No** hatched his plans for world domination on Crab Key Island. And, like 007's vodka martini, the ingredients of the Bond villain have been shaken, but never stirred. The cold war metaphors of the earlier movies may have given way to techno-terrorism, but the masterplan remains constant: yep, it's world domination time.

All Bond bad guys – whether they sport an eyepatch, have mechanical hands or a bullet lodged in their brain – offer a glimpse of a world ruled by a dastardly dictator and, let's face it, the chance for a good old boo and hiss. Order is always restored by the time the credits roll, the villain of the piece meeting his doom at the sharp end of a modified Biro. And, rather than becoming outdated, the Bond villain is part of the zeitgeist. **Ian Fleming** would have felt vindicated by the emergence of such a demonic figure as Osama Bin Laden. One of the many reasons September 11, 2001 was so horrific to watch was the feeling in the back of your mind, that it was too perfectly evil, too much like a plotline from a Bond novel or script.

Christopher Hitchens described Bond villains as a 'metastasized subspecies of monsters in human form', but Fleming was careful to give them some depth. Hugo Drax, the villain in *Moonraker*, was originally called 'drache' which is German for dragon. The villains-as-dragons motif is explicit in Fleming's **On Her Majesty's Secret Service** where 007 muses, 'It would be amusing to reverse the old fable – first to rescue the girl, then to slay the monster'. In **For Your Eyes Only**, Tiger Tanaka remarks, 'You are to enter this castle of death and slay the dragon within'. **Rosa Klebb**, the ogress in *From Russia With Love* was inspired by Emma Wolff, a large, NKVD agent with red-dyed hair in Vienna whose mum would have glossed over her off-putting appearance by insisting she had a lovely personality.

So, fetch a fluffy white cat, pull up a leather-backed chair, practise your evil sneer and revel in our roll-call of Bond's nemeses. But spare a thought for the poor old megalomaniac. It can't be easy when you've got a pool of hungry sharks to feed and nothing in the freezer except deadly nerve gas.

Ernst Stavro Blofeld

Anthony Dawson/Eric Pohlman, From Russia With Love, 1963

Masterplan Something of a rarity in Bond movies, the aim here is good old-fashioned revenge. After the death of his old mucker Dr No, SPECTRE's founder Blofeld tries to lure Bond to his end using Lektor, a Russian decoding device, as bait.

What's he like? The faceless Blofeld is surprisingly quiet, but sadistic with it. After having one of his own agents poisoned, he says disapprovingly: 'Twelve seconds, one day we must invent a faster-working venom.'

Natural habitat SPECTRE Island (location unknown).

Accessories Fluffy white cat, a stash of Bob Martin's worming tablets, Siamese fighting fish.

Sidekicks Rosa Klebb (Lotte Lenya), kick-ass defector to SPECTRE from Russian organisation SMERSH. Klebb's most memorable weapon is her poison-tipped shoes. **Donald Grant** (Robert Shaw), psycho killer and Dartmoor escapee, recruited by Klebb as Bond's 'protector'. Smart, but not smart enough in his Orient Express showdown with Bond. **Kronsteen** (Vladek Sheybal), chess master who hatches the plan to kill Bond.

How does he die? You'll have to wait and see…

Superbad rating 🔫🔫🔫🔫🔫

Blofeld, as played by Donald Pleasance, You Only Live Twice, 1967

Masterplan This time it's war. World War III, to be precise. Those evil SPECTRE-types plan to steal American and Russian space capsules, bringing the superpowers to the brink of conflict.

What's he like? Blofeld's third appearance and he reveals himself at last – and boy, is it a let-down. Small, bald, and a whopping scar down his face. Bring back his midriff and the cat.

Natural habitat Indoors. (Too plain ugly to venture far.)

Accessories Own private railway.

Sidekicks Mr Osato (Teru Shimada), avuncular-looking white-haired oriental chap who runs Osato Enterprises, which supplies SPECTRE with whizzo technological innovations.

Helga Brandt, Osato's secretary who, thanks to one cock-up too many, is introduced to a shoal of piranhas.

How does he die? Blofeld makes a habit of cheating death. This time he blows up a volcano, yet somehow manages to 171 scarper, thanks to a secret passageway. Nice work, Ernst.

Superbad rating 🔫🔫🔫🔫

As played by Telly Savalas, On Her Majesty's Secret Service, 1969

Masterplan SPECTRE scales down its operations with a plan to infect Britain with a crop and livestock pest. If only they had just waited 32 years for foot-and-mouth.

What's he like? Savalas' Blofeld is calmness and smoothness personified, handling his affairs in an almost jocular manner.

Natural habitat Piz Gloria, an Alpine 'research institute'.

Accessories Speeding bobsleighs.

Sidekick Irma Bunt (Ilse Steppat), matronly madam, so mean that she guns down Bond's wife, Tracy Draco (Diana Rigg), just moments after the pair are hitched. What a bitch.

How does he die? Once more Blofeld escapes, despite crashing into a tree during some bobsleigh shenanigans.

Superbad rating 🔫🔫🔫🔫🔫🔫🔫

Blofeld, as played by Charles Gray, Diamond Are Forever, 1971

Masterplan The clue's in the title, with large shipments of uncut diamonds disappearing in transit. Blofeld and SPECTRE are again the brains behind this plan to make a diamond-powered laser satellite with which to take over the world.

What's he like? Gray's Blofeld is as different from Savalas' as Telly's was from Pleasence's. But it's a step back. His limp-wristed villain lacks menace.

Natural habitat Nevada and Las Vegas. And underwater.

Accessories His submarine, hair.

Sidekicks Willard Whyte (Jimmy Dean), not really a henchman, but a key figure, this reclusive Howard Hughes-style character likes to play nuclear blackmail games. **Mr Kidd** (Putter Smith) and **Mr Wint** (Bruce Glover), described by one reviewer as 'a pair of fey, but villainous homosexuals'. The most bizarre pairing in the Bond canon.

172 **How does he die?** Apparently seen off in his submarine after a skirmish with Bond. Is this really the last of him, though?

Superbad rating 🔫🔫🔫🔫🔫🔫🔫

Elliot Carver
Jonathan Pryce, Tomorrow Never Dies, 1997

Masterplan In a bid to get broadcasting rights in China, media mogul Carver tries to engineer a war between China and Britain by sinking British warship, 'HMS Devonshire', in Chinese waters.

What's he like? Carver has an impressive single-mindedness. 'There's no news like bad news' is his mantra.

Natural habitat Brent Cross Shopping Centre, New College, Oxford and Portsmouth Naval Base.

Accessories Seriously big drill, bad blonde hairpiece.

Sidekicks Dr Kaufman (Vincent Schiavelli), forensic scientist with a sideline in torture. **Mr Stamper** (Götz Otto), a calculating killer with striking looks and his own torture set. Stamper apparently feels no pain, a theme later developed with Renard in *The World Is Not Enough*. **Henry Gupta** (Ricky Jay) Another rare outing for facial hair, this techno-terrorist and surveillance expert, only has a small part.

How does he die? A real ratings-grabber, this one. Carver is killed by the huge drill used earlier to sink HMS Devonshire.

Superbad rating 𝓕𝓕𝓕𝓕𝓕

Hugo Drax
Michael Lonsdale, Moonraker, 1979

Masterplan To destroy Earth and start a master race in space.

What's he like? A dead ringer for the young Orson Welles, Drax broke new ground in becoming the first bearded Bond villain. Superficial good manners mask a nasty temper.

Natural habitat California, Venice and space stations.

Accessories Space shuttles (following the success of *Star Wars*).

Sidekicks Chang (Toshiro Suga) says nothing, aside from a couple of grunts, but certainly looks the part. An early exit opens the door for the return of Jaws, and audiences cheer wildly.

Jaws (Richard Kiel), the seven-foot two-inch legend, returns,

Auric's the name, world domination's the game – the cap is his most sinister feature ▲

with added speech. 'Well, here's to us', he says, and that's it.
How does he die? Eventually gets his lot in a climactic last
half-hour on a space station orbiting Earth.
Superbad rating 🔫🔫

Auric Goldfinger
Gert Frobe, Goldfinger, 1964

Masterplan The international bullion dealer aims to stockpile
vast quantities of gold and reduce the west to economic chaos.
What's he like? Not one for chit-chat (Bond: 'Do you expect
me to talk?' Goldfinger: 'No Mr Bond, I expect you to die!'), he's
no stranger to the dinner table. Likes golf, but is very likely to
move your ball when you're not looking.
Natural habitat Miami, London, Switzerland and Kentucky.
This is a villain with places to go, people to kill.
Accessories Gold spray paint, atomic timers, laser beams.
Sidekick Oddjob (Harold Sakata), mute Korean manservant,
arguably Bond's toughest foe, a dab hand with his steel-rimmed
bowler hat, but not the most natural golf caddy.
How does he die? Sucked out of a plane.
Superbad rating 🔫🔫🔫🔫🔫🔫

Kananga/Mr Big
Yaphet Kotto, Live And Let Die, 1973

Masterplan Kananga's out on his own to corner the world drug
market. Obviously, no one's warned him that certain Italian
families might have beaten him to it. And the villain has two
faces: Kananga, the heroin grower, and Mr Big, the supplier. The
cunning plan? Kananga grows and gives the heroin away. Once
the US is hooked and suppliers are out of business, Mr Big steps
in to charge what he likes. Clever.
What's he like? Cool crime syndicate boss with a devilish grin.

In the book, Fleming suggests that Mr Big was not born evil, but became evil, as the modestly named villain tells 007 'Mister Bond, I suffer from boredom. I am prey to what the early Christians call "accidie", the deadly lethargy that envelopes those who are sated, those who have no more desires... I take pleasure now only in artistry.' You have to admit as pleas of extenuating circumstances-cum-diminished responsibility go, it is pretty darned original, even today. In 1954, when the novel was published, Mr Big was clearly a villain way ahead of his time.

Natural habitat The mean streets of Harlem, and a small Caribbean island where he grows his opium.

Accessories Powerboat, sharks, alligators.

Sidekicks Teehee (Julius Harris), so nicknamed because of his fiendish laugh. Favoured weapon? A steel hook with pincers, a replacement for the hand he lost to a peckish alligator. Voodoo high priest **Baron Samedi** (Geoffrey Holder), proud owner of a great baritone laugh, uses his ceremonies to bump off the unsuspecting, **Whisper** (Earl Jolly Brown) Barry White looka-like who gets trapped behind an inflating settee.

How does he die? Expands and pops after Bond shoots him with a compressed air pellet, allowing our hero the cheesy classic line: 'He always did have an inflated opinion of himself.'

Superbad rating 𝔉𝔉𝔉𝔉𝔉𝔉𝔉

Kamal Khan and General Orlov
Louis Jourdan and Steven Berkoff, Octopussy, 1983

Masterplan International smuggling, though Khan, working alongside barmy Russian General Orlov, can't resist attempting to detonate an atomic bomb to start World War III.

What are they like? Two villains sharing equal billing is
176 a first. Jourdan is cool – check out his pronunciation of Bond – and calculating, while Berkoff is so hammy you could string him up in a butcher's. Why would any self-suspecting Russian gener-

al keen to invade Europe team up with an Indian jewel thief?

Natural habitat India, Cuba and Germany.

Accessories Planes, trains and heat-seeker missiles.

Sidekicks Gobinda (Kabir Bedi) is, like all the best baddies, virtually monosyllabic, and has a frightening stare. **Mishka and Grishka** (David and Anthony Meyer), real-life twins, extremely handy at knife-throwing.

How do they die? Kamal is killed when 007 forces Kamal's plane to crash. Orlov is shot by German border guards.

Superbad rating 🔫🔫🔫

Aristotle Kristatos
Julian Glover, For Your Eyes Only, 1981

Masterplan It's the Cold War revisited, with the Russians acting as pay-masters for Kristatos. Not content with selling NATO's top tracking system to the Soviets, he also wants Bond to kill his long-term adversary, and 007's pal, Columbo.

What's he like? Devious. A tea leaf who'd sell his granny's kidneys to get ahead. It's true, never trust a man with a beard.

Natural habitat Greece, Italy, the Bahamas…

Accessories More sharks. Next idea please!

Sidekicks Emile Locque (Michael Gothard) is a skinny nutter in a silly hat. Not a patch on Jaws, sadly. **Erik Kriegler** (John Wyman), an athlete working for the Russians.

How does he die? A knife in the back from Columbo.

Superbad rating 🔫🔫🔫

Emilio Largo
Adolfo Celi, Thunderball, 1964

Masterplan SPECTRE bounces back with its most audacious plot yet – holding NATO to ransom by hijacking a Vulcan bomber armed with a pair of atomic missiles. If it doesn't get its

$100m, it will detonate the bombs in the UK and the US.
What's he like? One of the nastiest villains, indulges in sadistic whims with gay abandon and likes feeding people to sharks.
Natural habitat Nassau, largely on his yacht, the Disco Volante.
Accessories Eyepatch, cigars.
Sidekicks Fiona Volpe (Luciana Paluzzi) SPECTRE's agent, killed by one of her own when Bond uses her as a human shield.
Vargas (Philip Locke) Largo's unpleasant bodyguard who keeps an eye on the inevitable relationship between Bond and Domino.
How does he die? Killing his mistress' brother was Largo's fatal mistake. Domino shoots him in the back with a spear gun.
Superbad rating *FFFFFF1*

Emilio Largo's surname means 'play slowly and broadly' – no wonder he hates mankind ▼

Max Largo

Klaus Maria Brandauer, Never Say Never Again, 1983

Masterplan The spectre of, yup, SPECTRE's Ernst Blofeld rears its head again. Yes, he was killed off in *For Your Eyes Only*, but that was made by Cubby Broccoli. *Never Say Never Again*, jointly scripted by *Thunderball* producer Kevin McClory, resuscitated Blofeld and a Largo from SPECTRE (this time Max, rather than Emilio), and waved a reputed $5m cheque to lure Connery back as Bond. The deadly plan, if you're still with us, was to steal Tomahawk cruise missiles from a US airforce base in the UK, leaving NATO at SPECTRE's mercy. Yes, it is almost identical to *Thunderball*. Just nowhere near as good.

What's he like? Mean – ties Bond up and leaves him for the vultures – and insanely jealous, too. Reacts violently to Bond's flirtations with his mistress, Domino, and even turns down 007's offer of $200,000 for a dance. That's with her, not with him, in case you were wondering.

Natural habitat The Bahamas, France, Spain and the UK.

Accessories Scaled down – even the eyepatch has gone.

Sidekicks Fatima Blush (Barbara Carrera) Despite bedding her, Bond blows her up with a fountain pen – if only they made such pens when we were writing to our pen pals! **Blofeld** (Max Von Sydow) Hurrah! A decent cameo from Von Sydow and the return of the fluffy cat.

How does he die? Shot by Domino while pursuing Bond.

Superbad rating 𝐅𝐅𝐅

Dr Julius No

Joseph Wiseman, Dr. No, 1962

Masterplan First villain out of the blocks for Bond's long-term foe, SPECTRE. His scientific overtures turned down by governments east and west, Dr No vows to exact his terrible revenge. His plan for world domination – financed by

$10m pilfered from the Chinese mafia – revolves around a nuclear-powered beaming device to control US missiles.

What's he like? Well-spoken with good manners, juxtaposed with a ruthless, calculating streak – 'I never fail, Mr Bond.' An unwanted child, the product of a Chinese and German sexual liaison, he obviously has issues to address.

Natural habitat Underground in Crab Key Island, Jamaica.

Accessories Black mechanical hands, Nehru collar, Brylcreem.

Sidekicks Professor Dent (Anthony Dawson), oily-haired geologist whose failure to kill Bond costs him dearly in the end.

Miss Taro (Zena Marshall), secretary and SPECTRE agent – 007 turns her and her silly beehive hairstyle over to the law.

How does he die? Meets his end in the vat of boiling water containing his nuclear reactor, establishing the kind of justice that runs through Bond movies like the stripe in a stick of rock.

Superbad rating 𝓕𝓕𝓕𝓕𝓕𝓕𝓕

Dr Noah/Jimmy Bond
Woody Allen, Casino Royale, 1967

Masterplan In this spoof from producer Charles Feldman (*Dr. No, From Russia With Love, Goldfinger*), SMERSH, headed by Dr Noah, is busy disposing of agents across the globe. The retired Bond is persuaded to return after M's death. Horrified by the activities of the new 007, he's back to fight the good fight. This involves battling against a nuclear threat, germ warfare and legions of Bond clones.

What's he like? Neurotic, sex-obsessed cat-fancier in a Chairman Mao suit.

Natural habitat Berlin and in the casino, silly.

Accessories Rubbish gadgets which don't work.

Sidekick Le Chiffre (Orson Welles), head of SMERSH and a real card sharp.

How does he die? Goes down in flames at the climax, as does the film. Five directors were involved – four too many, judging by the chaotic mess that sprawls across two hours 11 minutes. Great cast though – David Niven, Orson Welles, William Holden, Peter Sellers, Woody Allen and original Bond girl, Ursula Andress.

Superbad rating 𝐅𝐅𝐅𝐅𝐅𝐅𝐅

'The name's Bond, Jimmy Bond' ▲

Franz Sanchez
Robert Davi, Licence To Kill, 1989

Masterplan Drug baron Sanchez has no burning desire for world domination, he just wants to amass as much cash from his South American operation as he can. Unfortunately, he messes with Bond's CIA pal, Felix Leiter.

What's he like? Imagine an uglier Tom Hanks with pock-marked skin and you won't be too far away. Uses TV evangelism to help sell his wares.

Natural habitat Florida and South America.

Accessories Pressurised airlocks.

Sidekicks Lupe Lamora (Talisa Soto) falls for Bond after he offers her an escape route from Sanchez's clutches. **Milton Krest** (Anthony Zerbe) uses his own research company as a cover for his work for the evil genius Sanchez, who kills him in a pressurised airlock. **Ed Killifer** (Everett McGill), a bent cop, eaten by sharks. **Dario** (Benicio del Toro), a sadistic young man with a gold-toothed grin who takes voyeuristic pleasure in watching death.

How does he die? When Sanchez feeds Bond's old mucker Felix Leiter to the sharks and kills his wife, his cards are marked. 181 Bond douses him in petrol and then offers him a light. Stylish.

Superbad rating 𝐅𝐅𝐅𝐅𝐅𝐅𝐅

Francisco Scaramanga

Christopher Lee, The Man With The Golden Gun, 1974

Masterplan Working for the Chinese, Scaramanga aims to monopolise solar power – remember, there was an energy crisis on at the time – by wresting control of a solar-power converter.

What's he like? Suave and sophisticated, a cold-blooded assassin. Commands a million dollar fee per hit – and never misses. You wonder how Fleming's school mate at Eton, who also gloried in the name Scaramanga, felt about this oblique tribute.

Natural habitat Island funhouse.

Accessories Golden gun (naturally), flying car, third nipple.

Sidekick Nick Nack (Hervé Villechaize), diminutive peanut-chomping assistant who likes to flirt with the rules. As he knows he'll inherit Scaramanga's worldly goods should his master die, he isn't averse to giving Bond a sporting chance. Besides, he's anxious to start his next job: as the diminutive co-host of *Fantasy Island*, a place even stranger than Scaramanga's funhouse.

How does he die? Sadly, he's not the golden shot that he first imagined.

Superbad rating *FFFFF*

Karl Stromberg

Curt Jurgens, The Spy Who Loved Me, 1977

Masterplan It's that World War III riff again, as aquatic-obsessed megalomaniac billionaire Stromberg hatches his plan to capture British and Russian submarines, destroy New York and Moscow in a nuclear holocaust and build a new world under the sea. Let's just hope he's got planning permission.

What's he like? Not nice. Blows co-conspirators up without a second thought and drops a two-timing accomplice into a shark-infested pool. Mostly gets Jaws to do his 'chores' for him.

Natural habitat On his tanker, the 'Liparus', or in his undersea home, called, naturally enough, 'Atlantis'.

Accessories A fleet of vessels, a big gun with exploding bullets, motorbikes with exploding fibreglass sidecar.

Sidekick Jaws (Richard Kiel) replaces Stromberg's assassin Sandor and goes on to cement legendary status. His remit is to kill anyone who goes within an inch of Stromberg's microfilm, which contains all his work. Steel teeth make this task more straightforward. Escapes the sharks to resurface in *Moonraker* after thousands of letters clamoured for his return.

How does he die? Killed with his own gun.

Superbad rating 𝓕𝓕𝓕𝓕

Alec Trevelyan

Sean Bean, Goldeneye, 1995

Masterplan Janus, an arm of the Russian mafia, aims to train Goldeneye, a satellite-based weapons system, on the UK, causing a meltdown of military and commercial operations. Trevelyan also has his sights trained on the Bank of England.

What's he like? Trevelyan defected to the Russians from the British intelligence service, where he worked alongside Bond as 006. He still holds a grudge against Bond for the scars he won in an earlier mission. Some people just can't achieve closure.

Natural habitat Trains.

Accessories Tranquiliser darts, fireworks.

Sidekicks Xenia Onatopp (Famke Janssen) likes squeezing men to death with her thighs. 'She always enjoyed a tight squeeze,' Bond says, after she is poetically crushed against a tree.

Boris Grishenko (Alan Cumming), computer boffin and the brains behind Trevelyan's plan, who sports some horrible shorts.

General Ourumov (Gottfried Born), KGB defector with a speciality in code-cracking. Likes his vodka, which can make his work a bit hit-and-miss. Is killed by Bond in a fight on a train.

How does he die? Fittingly flattened by his satellite tower.

Superbad rating 𝓕𝓕𝓕𝓕𝓕

Brad Whitaker

Joe Don Baker, The Living Daylights, 1987

Masterplan Maverick arms and drugs dealer Whitaker, smarting at a failed military career, uses 'borrowed' Soviet money to buy opium to flood the US market. In tandem he tries to have 007 kill Pushkin, the Russian head of secret operations, who rightly suspects Whitaker of trying to implicate him in a plot to kill British agents. Sounds intriguing? It's not especially complex or gripping – possibly the least edifying movie of the lot.

What's he like? Paunchy. Not a lot of screen time, thankfully.

Natural habitat Morocco, Gibraltar, Austria and Afghanistan.

Accessories Plenty of snacks.

Sidekicks General Georgi Koskov (Jeroen Krabbé), a smart and untrustworthy KGB defector, is ultimately returned to his motherland where the Gulag no doubt awaits. **Necros** (Andreas Wisniewski) is a real cold fish. Poses as a milkman with a nice line in exploding gold tops. Gets his comeuppance when Bond cuts the laces of his shoes during their skirmish on the wing of a cargo plane. Fluent in a host of languages and his name translates as 'You kill'. You wonder what his parents could have been thinking of.

How does he die? Crushed by a statue. Novel.

Superbad rating 🔫🔫🔫🔫🔫🔫🔫

Viktor 'Renard' Zokas

Robert Carlyle, The World Is Not Enough, 1999

Masterplan International terrorist aiming to monopolise new oil resources in Azerbaijan. To effect his plan, he kidnaps oil baron's daughter Elektra King (Sophie Marceau), demanding a $5m ransom. The twist is, kids, the pair are actually lovers.

What's he like? Dangerous – he feels no pain. A bullet lodged in his head from a failed assassination attempt has destroyed his central nervous system, but is also killing him slowly.

Natural habitat Oil pipelines and submarines.
Accessories Nuclear bombs.
Sidekicks Elektra King (Sophie Marceau), working with Renard on the quiet, uses Bond as a pawn to get what she wants, not believing he will kill her if he has to. She eventually finds out the hard way she's got that last bit wrong. Seems to have a thing about ice – she's always messing about with it. **Sashenka 'Cigar Girl' Firo** (Maria Grazia Cucinotta) is gorgeous, but deadly and is known as the Cigar Girl because she offers one to Bond at the start of the movie. Commits suicide early on by blowing up her hot air balloon.
How does he die? Takes a plutonium rod in the chest at high speed from point-blank range in a finale with Bond on a submarine. Ouch. He felt that, right enough.
Superbad rating 🔫🔫🔫

Max Zorin
Christopher Walken, A View To A Kill, 1985

Masterplan Zorin aims to rule the world's computer market. A kind of forerunner of Bill Gates. Only joking Bill.
What's he like? A brilliant but truly unhinged mind, genetically engineered from World War II experiments. A serious adversary, especially when teamed with May Day (Grace Jones).
Natural habitat Florida, Latin America, France, Switzerland, Iceland and er, the Amberley Chalk Pits Museum, England.
Accessories An airship.
Sidekick May Day (Grace Jones), Zorin's 'problem eliminator', who can skydive off the Eiffel Tower. The scariest female Bond villain after Rosa Klebb. Switches allegiances to fight the good fight and sacrifices her life to stop an earthquake.
How does he die? In a scrap with Bond on the Golden Gate Bridge in San Francisco – Zorin plummets to a watery grave.
Superbad rating 🔫🔫🔫🔫🔫

The real Bond villains...

Benito Mussolini was the ultimate Bond villain even if he met his maker years before 007 had been nauseated by the smell of a casino at 3am. His ambitions for **world domination** were far in excess of the resources at his disposal. Like Ernst Blofeld (as played by Donald Pleasance), he was a pioneer slaphead whose skull looked, as **Alexander Walker** said of Blofeld's, 'like an egg cracked on the boil'. Also like Blofeld (as played by Charles Gray), he had a fondness for cats. The difference being that unlike Blofeld/Gray, Benito didn't pussyfoot around with plump cats; when he rode through the streets of Italy in his open top charabanc he sometimes did so with a lion cub on his lap. Il Duce also fancied himself as a swordsman in the bedroom (his definition of foreplay being the time it took him to push his conquest to the floor) and on a fencing court. Mussolini was about as trustworthy as **Auric Goldfinger** was on the greens and like Le Chiffre, the villain in Casino Royale, the whites of his eyes were completely visible around the iris.

Il Duce wasn't the only world leader with the credentials to be a Bond villain. Kim Jong-il, the current ruler of North Korea, heads the only state to successfully(ish) reconcile Communism and nepotism: Kim's dad (**Kim il-Sung**) founded Communist North Korea, with a little help from Joe Stalin. But Kim senior was too busy being a revolutionary to be a true Bond villain, so he left that to his son who is famous for his permed hair, platform shoes, $20,000 a year brandy habit and his alleged tendency to kidnap beautiful women and have them transported to his mountain lair for his nefarious ends. Almost as diminutive as Pleasance's Blofeld, Kim Jong-il is suspected of driving his country's development of nuclear weapons. For all his flaws, he is not a complete egomaniac, admitting to one couple he kidnapped to help him make a film, 'I'm a little turd, aren't I?' He has learnt English watching Star Trek reruns. A villain so bizarre even Fleming wouldn't have dared to make him up.

The tycoons who measure up as potential villains include the late great (in sheer physical proportions) Robert Maxwell, Rupert Murdoch (obviously a partial inspiration for **Elliot Carver**) and Sir James Goldsmith, the British takeover king who counts as a potential Bond villain if only for the global spread and lavishness of his homes: a hacienda in Mexico, a château in France, and a mansion and town house in London. Not forgetting his private Boeing 757 jet with two bedrooms, a kitchen and an office. Goldsmith, who died after being diagnosed with pancreatic cancer in 1997 when he was 64, was an associate of **Lord Lucan**, the British peer who vanished after his children's nanny was beaten to death with a pipe in November 1974 (and whom

187

Il Duce, dictator, fencer, lion tamer, modelling an Oddjob hat ▲

The real Bond villains...

Cubby Broccoli once asked to screentest for the 007 role). Goldsmith was even rumoured to have helped Lucan escape, a charge Lady Lucan vehemently denied. And in 1981, Goldsmith borrowed a mere $660m to buy a diamond company, thus taking Shirley Bassey far too literally. His last hurrah was financing his own anti–European political party which racked up 800,000 votes (and no seats) in the UK in the 1997 general election. With several families, ambitions to become a media baron, and a ready line in quips, Goldsmith would have made the perfect Bond villain. Next to him, poor old Ross Perot seems sadly normal.

But Goldsmith's a lightweight compared to America's most reclusive billionaire Howard Hughes and the Hunt oil family in Texas. In 1979 the brothers **Nelson and Bunker Hunt** decided they'd try to monopolise the world's silver. It sounds mad but the silver-fingers controlled half the world supply, driving the price from $10 an ounce to $50 before they ran out of funds. Their dad, Haroldson Lafayette Hunt, was one of the world's richest men (he won his fortune in a poker game), bigamist and a financier of **Senator Joseph McCarthy**. He hated President Kennedy for threatening to scrap tax breaks for oilmen and expressed concern that Jim Garrison (the New Orleans district attorney played by **Kevin Costner** in JFK) might try to implicate him in the JFK assassination.

Howard Hughes, a model for Blofeld, combined the oddness of Kim Jong-il with a personal fortune even the Hunts envied. A one-time Hollywood producer, procurer of beautiful women (who were often kept for his convenience in luxury which failed to disguise their status as virtual sex slaves), and record-breaking aviator, Hughes let his empire be used as a front for a CIA spyship, tried to buy Las Vegas (as well as several presidents) and may have inadvertently triggered Watergate (it may have been the files on his loan to Nixon's brother that the burglars were mistakenly looking for in that Washington hotel). He died a skinny, drugged-out recluse in 1976, possibly murdered by some of his own henchmen fearing their misdeeds were about to be exposed.

007
THE GADGETS

'If it hadn't been for Q Branch,
you'd have been dead long ago'

007

'I like a girl in a bikini. No concealed weapons'

Francisco Scaramanga

That moment Bond visits Q to be briefed on the gadgets that are going to a) save his own life and b) save the world, is always one to be savoured, as keenly awaited as the first cunning stunt or seduction. And let's face it, without the gadgetry, the stunts would be a lot less cunning and have a very different – and far less acceptable – outcome for Bond.

Much of the outlandish technology used over the years has migrated down to the consumer and 007 gadgets can be a licence to make money as well as save the world. When Brosnan steered his BMW with a nifty Ericsson mobile phone in **Tomorrow Never Dies**, every gadget lover in the land squealed 'I want one,' while in **The World Is Not Enough**, Dr Christmas' PDA (portable digital assistant) did for palmtop computers what Ursula Andress's bikini did for Jamaican tourism in 1962.

So in case you one day find yourself being lowered into a vat of sharks, or stuck on the moon with no obvious means of transport, here's a reminder of Q's finest, along with some villainous counter-gadgetry. Cars (with and without ejector seats and saw blades), exploding cigarettes, decapitating tea trays... they're all here including, of course, the daddy of them all, the trick briefcase, after which a tin of talc was never the same.

Now pay attention: In each genre of gadgets, the gizmos are listed in the chronological order of their appearance in the movies so you can get the full flavour of the escalating ludicrousness of the equipment 007 and his enemies get to use as they go about their deadly business.

Guns

Walther PPK

Dr No until Tomorrow Never Dies

Just before 007's mission to Jamaica, **M** summons Major Boothroyd the armourer and orders Bond to hand over his .25 Beretta. Bond is miffed, 'I've used the Beretta for 10 years, I've never missed with it yet.' 'Maybe not,' M replies curtly, 'but it jammed on your last job and you spent six months in hospital. If you carry a double-O number it's a licence to kill – not be killed.' Boothroyd extols the virtues of 'the Walther PPK – 7.65mm with a delivery like a brick through a plate glass window. The American CIA swear by it' – that's opposed, presumably, to any other country's CIA. Bond used the 21-ounce, six-round hand-gun until the **Walther P99** supplanted it in the 19th mission.

Rocket guns

You Only Live Twice

Used to great effect by Tiger Tanaka's Ninja commandoes to zap **SPECTRE** baddies at the assault on Blofeld's volcano HQ, these pistols fire gas-propelled rocket bullets (complete with four-port mini-exhausts) that explode upon impact.

Piton gun

Diamonds Are Forever, GoldenEye

Mark 1 is a basic bolt pistol loaded with mountain climbing-pitons attached to a rope which Bond uses to scale **Willard Whyte**'s penthouse pad. The high-tech Mark 2 comes with 40-foot high-tensile Kevlar cable, a three-pronged tempered-steel piton, auto cable feed-wind and – the icing on the cake – a com-

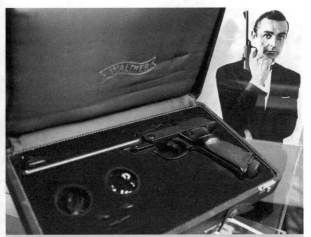

The Walther PPK, Bond's regulation issue since Dr. No – the CIA swears by 'em ▲

pact, steel-boring blue laser. In the **GoldenEye** teaser, our Milk Tray man does a gut-churning bungee jump off a Soviet dam, stops the rebound by firing the piton into the ground, reels himself down and cuts through a steel hatch with the laser before dropping straight into the toilets of the Arkangel nerve gas plant.

Shark gun
Live And Let Die
A pistol that carries compressed-air bullets which, on hitting their target, cause the victim's body to expand and explode. Bond uses it to further inflate Kananga's already sizeable ego.

The golden gun
The Man With The Golden Gun
Francisco Scaramanga's X-ray-defying killing tool is made

193

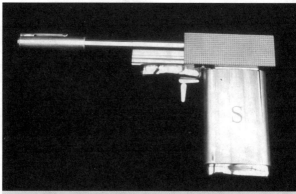

Take one lighter, cufflink and fountain pen and you too could make a golden gun ▲

from a gold cigarette lighter and case, gold fountain pen and cufflink. The 4.2 calibre takes a single, specially made gold bullet, usually inscribed with the victim's name. How very formal.

Ski-stick gun
The Spy Who Loved Me

Summoned by M, Bond zips into his banana-coloured jumpsuit and skis through the Alps. Waylaid by a posse of pesky Russians he fells them with his cunningly disguised ski-pole rifle (complete with retractable trigger).

Stromberg's table pistol
The Spy Who Loved Me

Under the antique dining table in **Stromberg**'s Atlantis HQ is a gun linked to a long acrylic tube – aimed at the stomach of the person sitting at the other end. In their last tête-à-tête, he pulls the trigger, Bond jumps to safety – then inserts his Walther PPK into his end of the tube, effectively reversing Stromberg's ploy.

Rayguns
Moonraker

Each *Moonraker* shuttle is equipped with a fixed on-board ray gun with radar lock-on and an automatic targeting device with an anti-jamming override. There are also portable versions, that are about the same size as the average assault rifle, and which pack roughly the same punch as **Goldfinger**'s humungous industrial laser.

Fountain pen gun
Never Say Never Again

Simply Q-tastic Union Jack fountain pen that fires an exploding nib. Used by 007 to dispose of painfully persistent SPECTRE Number 12 Fatima.

Signature gun
Licence To Kill

Bond plans to bump off drugs lord Sanchez with this camera which, with a few simple additions, transforms into a high-velocity sniper's rifle taking .22-calibre bullets loaded into the film spool. The handgrip has an optical scanner programmed by Q to recognise only 007's palm and fingerprints.

Walther P99
The World Is Not Enough

First glimpsed in *Tomorrow Never Dies*, Bond's latest weapon of choice is ultra-slim with a matte-black corrosion-resistant fin-ish and a grip – designed by Italian Olympic pistol makers Moroni – with interchangeable parts to fit any agent's grasp. Powerful but as discreet as a classy Italian suit, the P99 takes 16 rounds of 9mm ammo and has three independent automatic safeties: for the trigger, the decock and internal striker. It's also equipped with cocking and loaded chamber indicators. All of which makes it one very deadly phallic symbol.

Extraordinary explosives

Rocket-firing cigarette
You Only Live Twice
Inside this innocuous looking ciggie is a tiny, rocket-propelled explosive shell with a four-second delay fuse and a firing range of 30 yards. Integral in blasting apart Blofeld's dastardly plans for world domination.

Smoke-bomb lipstick
You Only Live Twice
Instead of grilling Bond, Osaka's nasty PA **Helga Brandt** pretends to fall for the secret agent's charms and 'escapes' with him in her Cessna. Brandt, who's piloting, touches up her lips – and then drops the lipstick on the floor where it explodes and fills the interior with smoke. Simultaneously, she pushes a button that glues Bond to his seat while allowing her to parachute out – leaving him sweating in the spiralling-out-of-control aircraft. Is our hero worried? What do you think?

Bombe surprise
Diamonds Are Forever
A revolting looking frosted cake served to Bond and Tiffany Case on board their luxury yacht by Blofeld fey assassins-cum-waiters Mr Wint and Mr Kidd. When their cunning cover is blown, there's a quick scuffle and Tiffany lobs the timebomb cake – which ends up in the ocean with Mr Wint.

Exploding sidecars
The Spy Who Loved Me
In pursuit of Anya and Bond in their Lotus Esprit, a Stromberg henchman rides a motorbike with sidecar that's released to become a contact bomb – with its very own heat-seeking guidance system and an explosive warhead.

Exploding milkbottles
The Living Daylights
Naff but effective diversion devices composed of nitroglycerine globules suspended in cream.

Dentonite toothpaste
Licence To Kill
Masquerading as a waiter at Sanchez's casino, 007 scales the roof, pulls a rapelling rope from his cummerbund and then abseils (completely unnoticed, of course) down to Sanchez's office window. There he applies the toothpaste (which is actually viscous Semtex mixed with paste and mint scent) to the frame, sticks in a detonator cap disguised as a cigarette, and blows a hole in the glass. The downside, of course, is that Dentonite is no use for protecting your teeth against plaque.

Pen grenade
GoldenEye
In the climatic scene in **Alex Trevelyan**'s Cuban HQ, Biro-twirling computer geek Boris is unaware that the pen he's frantically clicking is Bond's Q-Branch-issue Parker. Actually a class four grenade, the Semtex contained in its hollow core is armed via a four-second fuse – activated and de-activated by three clicks.

Exploding money
The World Is Not Enough
Elektra King's dad is drooling over his suitcase of loot – completely unaware that all the notes have been dipped in urea – in effect a highly compacted fertiliser bomb. In one banknote the metal anti-counterfeiting strip has been replaced with a magnesium detonator – activated by his lapel pin, which has been swapped for a copy containing a radio transmitter that triggers a humungous explosion ripping a hole out of the MI6 building.

Clever concealments

Surveillance

Tape recorder/box camera
From Russia With Love

Powered by a single, nine-volt battery, this reel-to-reel tape recorder is disguised as a box movie camera – used by Bond to take details of the Lektor decoder from Tatiana Romanov.

Odd-Job's steel-brimmed Derby
Goldfinger

Dapper **Odd-Job** wears a Derby hat with a razor sharp steel rim which lops the head off a statue at the golf course where Bond has just thrashed Goldfinger and fells the lovely Tilly Masterson.

Protective clothing
Casino Royale

007, aka Evelyn Tremble, is fitted with his latest 'work clothes' by Q's ever-so-slightly effeminate assistant. This bottle-green all-in-one that does up under the crutch ('also available in chocolate, oyster and calico grey') comes with, among other things, a poison capsule department, a switchblade and Geiger counter pocket and 'a cute little mini-gun in the gusset.'

Desktop X-ray
You Only Live Twice

Installed at waist level in the desk of baddie industrialist Mr Osato, and using electro-magnet radiation, this sees through the clothing of visitors to detect whether or not they are armed. That's his excuse anyway.

Spy shaving kit
Live And Let Die, A View To A Kill

This Q-kit includes a hairbrush with hidden Morse code

transmitter and a bug detector. An updated version of the bug detector is seen in Bond's 14th mission but here the micro-receiver is between the three rotating blades of an electric razor.

Cigarette-case microfilm reader
The Spy Who Loved Me
Bond always carries a silver cigarette case and lighter but this is the first Q-Branch issue model. A micro-film is inserted into the lighter, which in turn is slotted into the cigarette case, and the film image is then viewed on an attached fold-out screen.

X-Ray safe cracker
Moonraker
This speedy, micro-sized, safe-cracking device fits into Bond's sterling silver cigarette case which opens to reveal an LCD mini-monitor and three buttons: 'Activate' for power up, 'Engage' to start the integrated 'multi-tasking' computer's high-speed processing of possible combinations, and 'Open' to open the safe when the correct combination has been detected. A flat-plane X-ray scanner allows Bond to see the lock mechanism and watch the gadget 'cracking'. Also included are 10 'Class A' cigarettes.

X-ray glasses
The World Is Not Enough
Q-Branch specs used primarily for detecting concealed weapons or, inevitably in Bond's case, revealing women's underwear.

Weaponry
Poisonous shoes
From Russia With Love
SPECTRE standard issue, activated by a hidden catch in the sole. One click of the heels and a poison-coated knife pops out from the front. The poison on the blade tip is a liquid chemical compound similar in composition to phosgene gas.

Q-Branch's black leather briefcase
From Russia With Love
The first really high-tech Bond movie gadget, this battered brief-case contained 20 rounds of ammo hidden in the bottom of the case, a flat-bladed throwing knife that shoots out of the side, a .22 calibre AR7 folding sniper's rifle with infrared sights, 50 gold sovereigns in the case spine and a tin of talc (attached by a magnet) containing a cartridge of tear-gas which explodes if the locks are not turned horizontally. In Fleming's original story, 'the smart little bag' differed from the film's 'nasty little Christmas present', having a cyanide death-pill in the handle and a silencer for 007's Beretta in a tube of Palmolive shaving cream.

Homing device buttons
Casino Royale
Sewn into Sir James Bond's jacket by **SMERSH** lovelies at Castle McTarry, this homing button would direct exploding robot grouse at him, while he was out shooting on the highlands.

Two-way radio bagpipes
Casino Royale
Used by SMERSH agents to discuss Bond's whereabouts.

Stun gas cigarettes
The Spy Who Loved Me
Standard **KGB** issue fags which blow out a puff of stun gas. Q determines that it 'probably' contains chloral hydrate mixed with talcum powder, giving a knockout time of 12 hours.

Wrist dart gun
Moonraker
Hidden under the cuff, the dart gun, containing five 'depleted uranium' tips, five cyanide tips and a 10-shot charge of compressed propellant, is triggered by flexing the wrist.

Q, the PM and 'white heat'

Q (Desmond Llewellyn in the films) is often described as the archetypal, slightly eccentric British inventor, straight out of the same genre as boffins like Uncle Quentin in Enid Blyton's Famous Five children's books or, to return to the world of Ian Fleming, Caractacus Potts, inventor of a flying car and an automated breakfast maker in Chitty Chitty Bang Bang.

Yet in one disconcerting way, Q is deeply untypical of the post-war British inventor. After all, some of his inventions actually get used, albeit mostly by the Bonds of this world. Trevor Bayliss, creator of the wind-up radio and one of the few living British inventors to match Q's ingenuity in real life, says that 'it has been estimated that Britain has lost a total of £165 billion through inventions made here but exploited abroad'.

The first Bond films were made at a time of unprecedented optimism about science, technology and Britain's ability to use these tools to modernise itself. Labour Party leader Harold Wilson won the 1964 election, two years after Dr. No's cinematic debut, with a promise to transform Britain with 'the white heat of technology'. Six years later he was turfed out of office partly because Britain, to the people who lived there, still seemed in deep freeze. Q's gadgets were remarkable partly because, unlike so many other consumer goods in Britain at that time, they usually worked. As Kingsley Amis suggested, if Bond's mini-submarine had really been made in Britain it would probably have sunk. (Or have taken twice as long and twice as much money to develop as originally forecast.)

It is too facile to say that there was an inverse relationship between the amount of gizmos Q gave 007 and the real capacity of British industry. But by the time Octopussy, the most gadget-festooned Bond film, was released in 1983, Britain had become a net importer of industrial goods. The replacement of 007's Aston Martin with a BMW in Tomorrow Never Dies in 1997 seemed a metaphor for the fate of Britain's car manufacturing industry when BMW threatened, three years later, to close Rover, the prestigious British car maker it had acquired in 1994. (BMW later sold Rover to its management.) Perhaps the return of the Aston Martin in Die Another Day could signal a reversal in fortunes.

The country which gave the world railways, the Mini (car and skirt), and Concorde (with a little help from nos amis in France) has been so desperate to reaffirm its credentials as an inventive, technically driven nation that any place where two scientists are seen in public is immediately designated 'Silicon –'. And if it wasn't for Bayliss, James Dyson (inventor of the world's most efficacious vacuum) and Q, Britain would have seemed even less inventive of late. After all, Britain's most popular recent invention has been reality TV show Big Brother.

Holly's CIA issue
Moonraker
Bond, being an observant bloke with a fine eye for detail, clocks **Holly Goodhead**'s a CIA agent on discovering her dart-shooting diary, a two-way radio transmitter in her handbag, a perfume bottle that dispenses flames and a gold fountain pen with a needle in the nib (later employed by 007 in a near-miss with a giant boa constrictor in Drax's Mayan temple HQ).

Spinsaw yo-yo
Octopussy
Huge spinsaw attached to a length of bungee rope allowing the wielder to retract it quickly once his victim has been spliced.

Spectacle trigger
The World Is Not Enough
In the Swiss banker's office in Bilbao, 007 is held at gunpoint but bails out by flicking open his specs, pressing on the frame and remotely firing his Walther which is lying on a table.

For breaking in and out

Bodywrap breathing unit
You Only Live Twice
After being 'murdered' in Hong Kong and given a burial at sea, Bond's shroud is cut open to reveal the 'dead' secret agent enveloped in 'waterproof thermo-insulating polystyrene sheeting' and sucking on breathing apparatus. Naturally Bond emerges from the ordeal in immaculately pressed naval togs.

Whistle-activated keyring
The Living Daylights
This Philips model is calibrated for 007's whistle. One quick blast of 'Rule Britannia' and the keyring emits stun gas (chloral hydrate) rendering anyone within five feet out for the count for

30 seconds. A wolf-whistle activates 'micro-detonated' concentrated C4 explosive. Rather handily it also hides a skeleton key, able to open 90 per cent of the world's locks.

Leather rapelling belt
GoldenEye
Built into the silver buckle of 007's size 34 leather belt is a 75-foot high tensile steel wire (set to take only his weight).

Barclaycard
The World Is Not Enough
A credit card that slides apart to reveal a skeleton key. Probably the only time a credit card has ever been cool.

Wily wrist action

Geiger counter
Thunderball
007's steel wristwatch has a sweep-hand that rotates on detecting radioactivity – namely from atomic bombs.

TV wristwatch
Casino Royale
Evelyn Tremble's 1965 Rolex Oyster is switched for a special Q-Branch issue. When 'tuned to Channel Six', the watch face is instantly transformed into a television screen beaming the face of Vesper Lynd. 'It's a two-way television and radio wristwatch – an American idea, they got it from one of their comic strips,' says Q proudly.

Rolex
Live And Let Die
Equipped with a magnetic field powerful enough to 'deflect a bullet at long-range' (and unzip dresses), the watch's serrated face also rotates at high-speed to become a miniature buzz saw.

The Seiko
The Spy Who Loved Me, Moonraker, For Your Eyes Only, Octopussy

The star of four missions starts as a basic message receiver and evolves into an all-singing, all-dancing model complete with satellite uplink voice/data relay, digital LCD messager, radio transmitter/receiver and base-fitted speaker. For **Moonraker**, Q also fitted the watch with a secret compartment containing Semtex and an integrated TNT detonator.

Laser watch
Never Say Never Again

007 uses this to zap the manacles that are holding him in Largo's African castle before whizzing off to rescue poor old Domino from the slave traders.

Omega Seamaster professional diver laser watch
GoldenEye, Tomorrow Never Dies, The World Is Not Enough

In real life the Omega has an automatic chronometer and helium escape valve which releases air so it won't implode in the ocean depths. Bond's, of course, is a titanium issue to which, over three missions, Q has fitted ruby/diode lasers, a magnetic mine arm/disarm transmitter, and a small grappling hook with a 50-foot micro filament able to hold 800 pounds.

Villainous vehicles

Land
Exploding milk float
Casino Royale

SMERSH-issue, remote-controlled milk float with retractable spiked rods protruding from its headlights. Used to tail Bond on his way home, but he zips through his electronic gates, leaving the milk float to crash into them and promptly explode. It's a case of back to the drawing board for the men in white coats at SMERSH again.

Paraskis
The World Is Not Enough
Snow jet-ski type vehicles with parachutes, powered by a large propeller mounted on the rear. Not exactly speedy but very deadly, thanks to onboard machine guns and parachute mines.

Sea
Underwater bomb sleds and tows
Thunderball, Never Say Never Again
Bright orange/yellow with glass tops, powered by three propellers (rear centre and two smaller at either side) with recessed headlights. Employed by Largo's goons to transport two hijacked bombs to and from the secret underwater hatch on Largo's yacht, the 'Disco Volante'. Invariably flanked by one-man, battery-powered tows tugging SPECTRE baddies behind mounted spearguns.

Disco Volante
Thunderball, Never Say Never Again
The rear section of Largo's floating palace is actually a 50-foot cocoon – fitted with weapons and smoke makers – that separates from the rest of the boat. The forward section then transforms into a hydrofoil which can reach 95mph. There's also an under-water hatch to house two hijacked atomic bombs – hey, every hydrofoil will have one in a few years. In *Never Say Never Again*, the yacht is referred to by its literal translation – Flying Saucer – and also has a dance studio for Domino to strut her stuff.

The Liparus supertanker
The Spy Who Loved Me
The million-ton 'Liparus' swallows (well sort of) US, British and Soviet submarines via a mouth-like hull so enormous you could fit Cubby Broccoli's ego inside. Able to hold three nuclear subs side by side, which means the ship also has a monorail.

Stealth ship
Tomorrow Never Dies

Elliot Carver's radar-evading HQ, from whence he operates his dastardly Sea-Vac drilling machine, is based on the real-life US Navy's stealth vessel, jazzed up with bits of a stealth bomber.

Air

Spectre Bird 1
You Only Live Twice

Blofeld's 66-foot, rocket-eating space capsule with 'jaws', which open, 'swallowing' Soviet and US capsules. It's nonsense like this which gave someone the idea for the Star Wars defence system.

Flying matador
The Man With The Golden Gun

Scaramanga has a 1974, two-door bronze AMC Matador with detachable wing/jet section, fuel tanks for gasoline and aviation fuel and a retracting dashboard-cum-cockpit panel enabling him to convert it into an unconventional flying machine.

Helicopter with saws
The World Is Not Enough

Technically for keeping forests in check these helicopters – equipped with 17-feet of spinning, razor-tooth, circular saws – are employed by Electra King's outfit to cut Bond and colleagues down to size at Zukovsky's caviar factory.

Tasty technology

Baddies

The Lektor decoder
From Russia With Love

Property of the Russians, this typewriter-sized message decoder

One-man autogyro Little Nellie: conveniently packaged in four alligator leather cases ▲

(based on the German Enigma cipher machine, where data is fed in, decoded and printed out at the other end) is desperately sought by MI6, CIA and the other usual suspects.

Goldfinger's laser device
Goldfinger
This high-powered laser thingy, which looks a bit like a rocket launcher, emits a concentrated beam of 'extraordinary light not found in nature', can 'project a spot on the moon' and cut through solid metal. Not the sort of thing you want inching its way up between your legs, as Bond famously discovers.

SPECTRE voice synthesiser
Diamonds Are Forever
Electronic device resembling a dictation machine that can record and store up to 20 different vocal patterns on a standard cassette tape, allowing Blofeld to imitate **Willard Whyte**.

Digital photo identifier
A View To A Kill

Predecessor of the webcam employed by horse-dealing nutter **Max Zorin**. Visitors are filmed by a hidden camera and identified by a computer. When Bond poses as thoroughbred buyer James St John, Zorin sees right through his disguise.

The GoldenEye device
GoldenEye

An electronic pass card with an amber 'eye' at its centre. Once activated, the GoldenEye is slotted into a computer which sends encrypted codes to a Soviet satellite weapons system that uses controlled nuclear detonations to generate an electromagnetic pulse that paralyses and wipes out all electronic devices within 30 miles. Trevelyan steals it from a Siberian research centre so he can render all banks in the City of London helpless. That's the thing about Bond villains: if there's a hard way to do it… Couldn't he have just hired a few Nick Leesons?

GPS Encoder
Tomorrow Never Dies

'One of the closest-guarded secrets in the US military' is a little red box that was stolen from the CIA by Elliot Carver and which can re-code Global Positioning Satellites.

Bond
An underwater camera
Thunderball

Inspired by the **Mako Shark** underwater cameras popular in the 1950s and 1960s, this one uses infrared film and is capable of auto-shooting eight photos in total darkness. Question: how useful is that? Answer: Not very unless you happen to be James Bond and you need to snap the secret underwater hatch on Largo's Disco Volante.

Miniature re-breather
Thunderball
To avoid drowning in Largo's nasty, shark-infested pool, Bond uses a nifty cigar-sized breathing device with four minutes of oxygen. Every swimming instructor should have one.

Peel-off fingertips
Diamonds Are Forever
Q's press on/peel-off latex fingertips mean that Bond can drink martinis without having to worry about leaving any fingerprints.

3D visual identigraph
For Your Eyes Only
A bus-sized unit into which one inputs known details of suspected criminals and matches the info to the archives of the likes of MOSSAD and the CIA. Once a crim's been ID'd, a separate screen comes up displaying a computerised photo-fit graphic. Used by Bond and Q to identify Belgian psychopath **Emile Leopold Locque** – an employee of Greek heroin dealer Kristatos.

Goldenshower

It wasn't just the high-tech 007 gadgetry that Bond fans aspired to. The shower unit below, shown at the International Building Exhibition in the 1960s was deemed to be the very epitome of 007's luxury lifestyle. Well, the girl was anyway. Moneypenny's desk (see p220) was designed by Intra Design, a company within the Rank organisation. They didn't catch on.

Bond shower: girl not included ▲

Digital uplink camera
GoldenEye

A pocket-size, auto-focus, super zoom, night optics, digital camera used by Bond to snap **Xenia Onatopp** and Admiral Chuck Farrel. His pics are transmitted back to Moneypenny who faxes back the subjects' IDs to Bond's Aston Martin.

Key code over-ride
GoldenEye

Digital code-cracker for passcard-locking devices.

Ericsson mobile phone
Tomorrow Never Dies

Forget all about WAP or Bluetooth, this little beauty has a scanner that reads fingerprints, two retractable prongs that dish out 20,000-volt electric shocks and – a particular favourite of Q – a flip-up keypad under which lurks a touch-panel remote for the BMW. Sadly the commercial version doesn't offer the electric shock feature as standard. Or even optional.

Bond's beloved DB5: veteran of five movies and victim of one not-so-careful driver ▲

Bond's vehicles

Land

Aston Martin

Goldfinger, Thunderball, On Her Majesty's Secret Service, The Living Daylights, GoldenEye

In *Goldfinger*, Bond is initially reluctant to part with his beloved Bentley Mark IV, but M and Q have other ideas. His super-sleek replacement, the classic Aston Martin DB5, comes kitted with fairly standard 'refinements' – revolving licence plates, bullet-proof windshields, tyre shredders and high-pressure water cannons. It remains ahead of the field until *The Living Daylights* when Q introduces the gadget-tastic 1986 Aston Martin Volante. Here 'modifications' include outrigger ski rails, port and star-board missiles, rear-mounted rocket engine booster, hub cap-mounted laser beam, spiked gripping tyres, and an all-band scanner radio. Naturally Bond blows the whole shebang by running the car into a snowbank and activating the self-destruct system. The DB5 makes a brief reappearance in *GoldenEye*, this time with a refrigerated glove box for a bottle of Bolly.

Moonbuggy

Diamonds Are Forever

Developed by billionaire recluse **Willard Whyte** for future missions to the moon, this prototype is equipped with a remote-controlled robotic arm with claws. In it Bond makes a hasty, if slightly wonky, escape from Whyte's Nevada lab chased by scary security guys on three-wheeled, all-terrain dirt bikes.

The Lotus Esprit Special

The Spy Who Loved Me

Bond and Anya scoot off a pier to escape a machine-gun toting helicopter piloted by Stromberg's PA Naomi. Luckily their Lotus also doubles as a sub – complete with quad propellers and rear rudders, a dashboard-cum-submarine control panel, a nautical guidance system, and a host of wicked weaponry: oil slick camouflage, rear cement spray and harpoons. Apparently the underwater sequence took four months to plan and shoot – all for around three minutes of final footage.

Lotus Esprit Turbo
For Your Eyes Only

A brief but explosive appearance at Cuban hitman Hector Gonzales' pad in Spain. Typically ignoring the red 'Burglar protected' sign on the window, Gonzales' heavies try to smash their way in – unaware that the Turbo has vibration sensors on all windows, magnetic seal points on doors and boot and, crucially, four packs of C4 explosive in the front and rear. Lo and behold the car explodes in typically spectacular style. Again, sadly, this appealing alternative to the straightforward immobiliser is not available as an anti-car theft device.

BMW Z3 roadster
GoldenEye

'Now pay attention 007. First your new car. BMW. Agile, five forward gears, all-points radar, self-destruct system and, naturally, all the usual refinements. Now this I'm particularly proud of. Behind the headlights – stinger missiles.' The Z3 is also equipped with emergency rear parachute braking and an ejector seat, but for all its high-tech smarts sees very little action save a brief rendezvous with CIA man Jack Wade.

BMW 750il saloon
Tomorrow Never Dies

Star of one of the most Bond-tastic car chases ever, this Beemer is a techno-boffin's dream: voice-assisted navigation, tear-gas jets, rear-bumper metal spikes, a rack of rockets in the sunroof and a metal cutter behind the BMW badge. And – coolest of all – Bond drives it with his Ericsson mobile via remote control while he's lying on the back seat dodging bullets.

The Aston Martin V12 from *Die Another Day* – Bond's back with his old car marque ▲

BMW Z8
The World Is Not Enough
The irrepressible Q and his new assistant R packed the Z3's big brother with a multitude of goodies. The curvaceous supercar has titanium armour, a manoeuvrable ground-to-air missile launching pad, headlamp rockets, a needle thin sonic laser beam for eavesdropping on conversations and a remote handset. Oh, and let's not forget the six-beverage cup holders, although, hang on, what does 007 need with six cup holders? If he's in a gathering of more than three people, it's normally because the rest of them are trying to kill him. For all its accoutrements, the only action the Z8 sees is at Zukovsky's caviar factory, where it is sawn in half by a helicopter: 'Q's not going to like this,' Bond mumbles.

Sea
Underwater propulsion unit
Thunderball
Over-sized compressed air tank with propulsion device allowing

Bond to swim at 'lightning' speeds, equipped with twin explosive spear guns and, erm, a light. It also emits a scary neon green exhaust – originally designed to create a smoke screen, but used for no apparent reason in this mission.

'Modified' gondola
Moonraker

In Venice, 007 is attacked by a motorboat-full of machine-gun wielding goons – but wouldn't ya know it, his gondola happens to be a Q-Branch special, with dual hovercraft thrust turbines. Having careered around the canals he flips out the hovercraft skirt and glides smoothly onto St Mark's Square.

The Q-boat
The World Is Not Enough

Poor old Q is just putting the finishing touches to his whacky retirement 'hydroboat' when Bond nabs it for a chase down the Thames. Powered by a 350hp V8 Chevy 'jet' engine, which sucks water in, then pumps it out at high pressure, Bond can gun it to 70mph and then engage the dual rear rocket boosters to execute a gut-churning, 360-degree barrel roll over the Sunseeker boat.

Air
Bell Textron jet pack
Thunderball

Having throttled assassin Jacques Boitier, 007 straps into the conveniently hidden Bell Textron jet pack and zooms up into the air. 'No well-dressed man should be without one,' he quips to a doe-eyed mademoiselle on landing, before bundling the jet pack into the boot of his Aston Martin DB5 (in reality, of course, it would be red-hot to the touch). This device – which could reach a speed of 60mph in a matter of seconds and a height of some 600 feet – was originally developed by the **US Army** for their infantry before someone realised that it was perhaps just a tad too Buck Rogers – indeed it did make a brief appearance in *Lost In Space*.

Little Nellie
You Only Live Twice

Assembled from parts contained in four alligator leather cases, this lightweight, one-man autogyro, made from steel and fibreglass, is powered by a single engine and two rotor blades, and reaches a top speed of 130mph and a height of 18,000 feet. Luckily for Bond, Nellie is also equipped with an impressive arsenal – twin forward-firing machine guns, rocket launchers, heat-seeking air-to-air missiles, rear-firing flame throwers and aerial mines. (And she still manages to weigh in at a mere 250lbs.) Probably one of the most loved of Q's gizmos.

Acrostar mini-jet
Octopussy

An undercover Bond is sent to destroy a military installation in a mysterious banana republic and gets nabbed. His Brazilian babe contact pulls up in a car towing a horsebox and, while she uses her not inconsiderable assets to distract the guards, Bond jumps into the Acrostar that is concealed behind a false horse's rear in her trailer. The bum lifts up and Bond rolls off down the ramp and takes off. Trailed by heat-seeking missiles, he manages to shimmy through a hangar, leaving the missiles to blast the place to smithereens. If only there was a category at the Oscars for 'best horse's ass'.

XT-7Bs
Never Say Never Again

To access Largo's underwater weapons cave, Bond and Felix Leiter are shot out from a British sub in two rockets. The outer 215 casings fall away to reveal the agents each standing on what looks like the top half of a cherry-picker crossed with the Bell Textron jet pack. Pretty nifty but ultimately probably more *Thunderbirds* than *Thunderball*.

Dragon tank
Dr. No
Manned by two armed patrolmen, the Dragon tank boasts bullet-proof armour plating, flame-throwing cannons and, wait for it, high-powered search lights. Awesome.

Sewer-based periscope
From Russia With Love
With a periscope from a Royal Navy sub and installed in an Istanbul sewer directly below the Soviet embassy, Bond and Turkish ally Kerim Bey get a mouse-eye view of a conference room while high-level talks take place. Unfortunately there's no microphone so they have to guess what's being said. Not that 007 cares – he's too busy ogling Tatiana Romanov's legs.

Seagull snorkel/drysuit
Goldfinger
To blow up Ramierez's heroin plant, Bond dons a wetsuit with a replica seagull snorkel even Jacques Cousteau would have envied. Job done, he removes the wetsuit to reveal an immaculate white tuxedo, complete with a fresh carnation.

Electro-magnetic rpm controller
Diamonds Are Forever
One of Q's jolly japes, this joybuzzer ring controls the rpms of slot machine dials – and it pays off every time.

Finger clamp
Diamonds Are Forever
Each agent's holster is fitted with a metal clamp with razor teeth, to catch the fingers of anyone trying to disarm them.

Croc sub

Octopussy

Bond shimmies through the water around Octopussy's palace in a life-size replica of a crocodile – and no-one even notices.

Iceberg sub

A View To A Kill

A cunningly disguised mini-sub, designed to be indistinguishable from surrounding lumps in Siberia – except that it isn't.

Robot surveillance machine

A View To A Kill

Ancestor of the peskily popular Japanese electronic pets, the Snooper is another one of Q's hair-brained ideas that doesn't

The name's Bond, the game's...

Selling product of course.

001

Sales of Omega Seamaster watches doubled after starring in a Bond movie.

002

BMW was so keen for Bond to use its car it let the producers write off 17 brand new cars.

003

MGM probably earned $100m for The World Is Not Enough in product placements.

004

As Bond, Brosnan has only worn suits made by Italian company Brioni. The suits typically cost $6,500, but before you rush out and buy one, the bad news is that Brioni only makes 6500 a year.

005

The producers of the unofficial Bond film Never Say Never Again were paid to ensure that Connery smoked Camels on screen.

006

The product placement in Licence To Kill was so intense it inspired a website called Licence To Shill.

007

BMW was the first company to launch a car in a Bond film – the Z3 roadster had a cameo role in Tomorrow Never Dies.

serve any real purpose. Remote-controlled with high-powered audio pick-up mikes, Snooper raises its 360-degree rotating colour video head, beaming Bond and Stacey Sutton's shower antics to a television monitor in Q's Winnebago, parked outside in the street.

Metal-detecting garden rake
Living Daylights
When 007 arrives at MI6's Blaydon safe house, he is apparently unaware of the not-very-obvious garden rake planted in front of the entrance. The revolving rake turns out to be a metal detector alerting the security guard to his hidden Walther PPK.

Two-way radio broom
Licence To Kill
Bond has been captured by Sanchez. In the guise of a South American gardener, Q stands guard on the road side. As Sanchez's convoy passes, Q radios through to Pam Bouvier informing her of Bond's position. Then Q, rather ironically, carelessly chucks the broom on the roadside.

Held at Q Lab

Decapitating tea tray
The Spy Who Loved Me
One of Q's (and our) favourites, this deadly, razor-edged tea tray zooms along a magnetic rail until it reaches the victim and hoiks off their head.

Camel saddle
The Spy Who Loved Me
Also known as an impaling seat, this cloth-covered saddle hides a sword which shoots up between the rider's nether regions. The government should pass a law forcing Jilly Cooper to include this device in all her tedious riding novels.

Hookah
The Spy Who Loved Me
An Egyptian hookah with a trigger in the mouthpiece. When puffed it becomes a fully-operational machine gun.

Exploding bolas
Moonraker
Steel balls on thin rope that decapitate a victim, then explode.

Siesta machine gun
Moonraker
Life-size gaucho dummy that appears to be kipping under a sombrero, which splits in half to reveal a machine gun. Right.

Talon umbrella
For Your Eyes Only
On detecting water this brolly snaps down over the holder's head, stabbing its six-inch curved spikes into the neck.

Man-eating couch
The Living Daylights
A couch that revolves to envelope the sitter. Simple as that. Can't imagine why somebody didn't think of it before.

Ghetto blaster
The Living Daylights
A portable boom box concealing a mini-bazooka. 'Something we're making for the Americans. It's called a ghetto blaster,' announces Q wryly.

Laser Polaroid camera
Licence To Kill

Takes a photograph of someone while zapping them with a laser at the same time.

Making a debut in GoldenEye

Rocket-firing leg-cast

Q is sitting in a wheelchair with his leg up in a plaster cast.
An exploding missile shoots from the heel of the cast blasting
another dummy to smithereens. 'Hunting!' shouts Q gleefully.
Good bloke to have on your side, Q, but there were times when
you couldn't help wondering about his mental health.

Phone box airbag

In this phone box a giant airbag inflates crushing, in this case,
another hapless technician against the glass.

X-ray tea tray

A document scanner cunningly disguised as a silver tea tray.

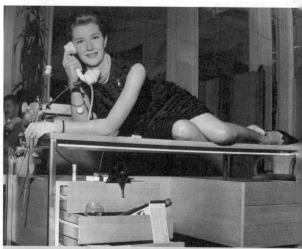

A reproduction Moneypenny – and we're talking about the desk ▲

008
THE MUSIC

The unmistakable sound of the
world's most famous secret agent

007

'Such a cold finger!'

Goldfinger lyric by Leslie Bricusse and Anthony Newley

Picture Roger Moore and Barbara Bach, coming over all tactile on a felucca as the suns sets on the Nile. Or Pierce Brosnan, scudding on a speedboat through the Thames in hot pursuit of an enemy operative. Chances are, your mental portrait is accompanied by a familiar soundtrack. Seductively romantic or heart-poundingly exciting, it's unmistakably the music of James Bond and as instantly recognisable as the themes from *Star Wars*, *Dr Zhivago* and *The Godfather*.

Series producer **Albert Broccoli** is rumoured to have boasted that half the world's population could tell a Bond tune when they heard one. Unlike our agent's dress sense (think polyester/ viscose safari suit with the kind of lapels that dogs bark at), but in keeping with his astounding gadgetry and hardware, they've generally stood the test of time and on four occasions have earned Oscar nominations.

So what makes a memorable Bond soundtrack? There are, fittingly, seven unwritten rules:

Rule One: Always pay homage to the franchise's musical heritage, particularly **John Barry**'s legacy. Even – in fact, more so – if you are John Barry. That means

◀ Jonathan Barry Prendergast, Bond music maestro

In For Your Eyes Only, the code for the 'Indentigraph' room is 'Nobody Does It Better' from The Spy Who Loved Me

subtle or (in the right hands) radical variations on the holy trinity: the 'James Bond Theme', '007' and 'On Her Majesty's Secret Service'.

Rule Two: Think location, action and love, and blend their respective orchestral arrangements with the movie's title and/or theme songs. It's all about continuity, see.

Rule Three: Commission one of contemporary music's most famous/hip names to perform the title and/or theme song. If they've just had a massive hit, you're laughing. Usually.

Rule Four: Make sure the vocals are female and sultry with it. When in doubt, call **Shirley Bassey**.

Rule Five: Write and compose the title song yourself. Or in collaboration with another lyricist and/or performer. Unless, that is, the performer happens to be **Paul McCartney**. And even then you should really proof-read the lyrics afterwards (see page 233). And whatever you do, steer clear of American AOR chicks and perma-shaded Irishmen named after hearing-aids (see page 237).

Rule Six: Change your mind and to hell with overblown egos. Leave the vocal versions of title songs until the end credits in one movie then stick them upfront with the opening sequence in another. Don't fret about abandoning your original choices for vocals, even if it's HRH Bassey, Dionne Warwick (see page 228) or Aretha Franklin (see page 231). And especially if it's Scott Walker (see page 238).

Rule Seven: Give French composers with synth fetishes a wide berth (see page 237). Nothing personal, but apart from those beautiful Parisian and Riviera locations, Bond and France just don't mix. It's a monsieur rosbif thing.

There. If you can observe all of these, you've got a smash hit on your hands. And you'll be a genius. Some Bond composers have hit pay-dirt (**George Martin, Marvin Hamlisch**). Others have fared admirably (Bill Conti, Michael Kamen). A few, perhaps

Den-dedder-den-den...

Vic Flick was the axeman behind the 'James Bond Theme', his famed guitar sound perfectly matching the trademark, opening gun-barrel sequence of the early movies. An original member of the John Barry Seven, he continued to work on the franchise's soundtracks as a session musician and spent most of the 1960s mixing in studios with the likes of Tom Jones, Shirley Bassey, Matt Munro, Lulu, Nancy Sinatra and Burt Bacharach (the creative force behind *Casino Royale*).

As a child, Vic studied piano until a friend bought him a Gibson guitar and he joined his first band. His first self-composed track for Barry was *Viva Zapata!* in 1952. For *Dr. No*, he was lead guitarist. 'Back then to us it was just another film session that we were perhaps more associated with than many others,' he recalls. 'It was probably 20 years later that I began to realise how significant the Bond movies were, and only recently that their amazing popularity has really hit me.' But he admits to 'an atmosphere of excitement'

when the 'James Bond Theme' was being laid down. 'It was very different to the majority of film themes. There was no film shown at the time of the recording so we could only imagine its content. When I saw *Dr. No* and heard how much the theme had been used throughout I thought how good it sounded.'

Vic also worked on the soundtrack albums of *From Russia With Love*, *Goldfinger* and *Diamonds Are Forever*. In 1989 he was approached by Eric Clapton to help compose a possible theme song for *License To Kill*, but the movie's producers showed little interest. After hearing David Arnold's *Shaken And Stirred* six years ago, however, he re-recorded key tracks for an album called *James Bond NOW*. Among the reworked themes is an acoustic version of *Diamonds Are Forever*. There are three of his own compositions too, including a Russian-Latin fusion called *Copacabinsky*.

He now lives in Santa Monica, California, with his wife Judy.

involuntarily, have missed the point entirely (**Michel Legrand**, **Eric Serra**). And one has recently struck gold: lethal trilbies off to **David Arnold**, the sovereign heir – at once faithful and innovative, scoring the last two movies, and single-handedly hauling the series into the 21st century. And owing everything to the man who counted it all off 40 years ago.

The name's Prendergast, actually. **Jonathan Barry Prender-** 225
gast. He's up there with Henry Mancini as arguably the most famous film composer in the world. He's scored over 80 movies,

including the Oscar-winning music for *Born Free, The Lion In Winter, Out Of Africa* and *Dances With Wolves*. Amazingly none of his 12 Bond films have been honoured with Academy awards. Ably-assisted by fellow writer **Monty Norman**, he gave us the tripwire stealth-and-subterfuge and swaggering brass crescendo of the original 'James Bond Theme'. Alone, he conceived the staccato trumpet and swirling strings of '007', followed by the cloak-and-dagger tempo of *On Her Majesty's Secret Service*.

Sharing the studio with session musicians hired by friend and

007 Bondian musical oddities

001
None of the tracks on David Arnold's *Shaken And Stirred* album appear in a Bond movie – but the Propellerheads have a track called *Backseat Driver* which appears on the *Tomorrow Never Dies* soundtrack.

002
Alice Cooper's 1974 *Muscle Of Love* album actually featured a song entitled The Man With The Golden Gun. His fans (and Cooper's camp) claim that this was commissioned for the movie but the producers backed out. It was written to attract Cubby Broccoli's interest. It failed.

003
Moby's 'James Bond Re-version' appears on the *Tomorrow Never Dies* soundtrack as well as his *I Like To Score* album and *James Bond Theme* maxi-CD. But it's not actually used in the film.

004
Punk band Gob recorded a cover of *A View To A Kill* on a Duran Duran tribute album, reducing it from three-and-a-half minutes to 58 seconds.

005
Pulp released their rejected theme for the film *Tomorrow Never Dies* under the title 'Tomorrow Never Lies' as the B-side of the single 'Help The Aged'.

006
It's more a sample than a cover, but John Barry's string arrangement 'Mountains And Sunsets' in *You Only Live Twice* was used by Robbie Williams on 'Millennium'.

007
Japanese combo The Surf Chamblers have performed a pretty faithful rendition of the 'James Bond Theme' that might drive your dog bonkers. It's a pitch thing.

The Bond hit machine

SONG/ARTIST	YEAR	UK POSITION	US
FROM RUSSIA WITH LOVE Matt Monro	1963	20	-
GOLDFINGER Shirley Bassey	1964	21	8
THUNDERBALL Tom Jones	1966	35	25
YOU ONLY LIVE TWICE Nancy Sinatra	1967	11	44
WE HAVE ALL THE TIME... Louis Armstrong	1994	3	-
DIAMONDS ARE FOREVER Shirley Bassey	1972	38	57
LIVE AND LET DIE Paul McCartney	1973	9	2
THE MAN WITH THE GOLDEN GUN Lulu	1974	6	-
NOBODY DOES IT BETTER Carly Simon	1977	7	2
MOONRAKER Shirley Bassey	1979	20	-
FOR YOUR EYES ONLY Sheena Easton	1981	8	4
ALL-TIME HIGH Rita Coolidge	1983	75	36
NEVER SAY NEVER AGAIN Lani Hall	1983	35	-
A VIEW TO A KILL Duran Duran	1985	2	1
THE LIVING DAYLIGHTS a-ha	1987	5	-
LICENCE TO KILL Gladys Knight	1989	6	-
GOLDENEYE Tina Turner	1995	10	71
TOMORROW NEVER DIES Sheryl Crow	1997	12	-
THE WORLD IS NOT ENOUGH Garbage	1999	11	-

fixer Sid Margo, Barry reworked his songs and arrangements throughout each Bond movie. Often he'd write and record right up to the final days of sound mixing to perfect a score that reflected the film's action and romance rather than just the hero, many of the soundtracks don't include these 'later' pieces.

Born in York in 1933, Barry had established himself by the late 1950s as the trumpet-playing leader of **The John Barry Seven**, a cutting-edge jazz instrumentalist group that created 'mood music' and had hits with 'Walk Don't Run' and 'Hit And Miss' (the theme for *Juke Box Jury*). Their distinctive sound came from Barry's brass and percussion orchestrations electrified by guitarist **Vic Flick**'s groundbreaking 'licks' (see p225 for more on Flick's licks). Barry also worked with rising pop star Adam Faith, composing the music for the 1959 hit 'What Do You Want?' and scoring his first film, *Beat Girl*.

In the summer of 1962, **Noel Rogers** of United Artists Music came calling. UA were making the first James Bond movie,

In Sean Connery's first scene in *From Russia With Love*, Matt Monro's title song is playing as background radio music

Dr. No, and Barry was assigned to rearrange a two-minute composition by **Monty Norman** without having seen the film. Despite this handicap, he brilliantly captured the mood of covert counter-intelligence. The credit for the 'James Bond Theme', which reached No.13 in the UK charts, remains a bone of contention: in 2001 Norman took legal action and a court ruled that Barry could no longer claim even co-writing the music.

There's no doubt, though, about the origins of the '007' tune, first introduced by Barry in 1963's *From Russia With Love* and later to reappear in further Bond adventures. He also arranged an instrumental version of **Matt Monro**'s title song (penned by Lionel Bart of *Oliver!* fame) around the movie's opening sequence, segueing into the 'James Bond Theme'.

The following year he was given full musical authority for *Goldfinger* and responded by composing the most memorable Bond song ever. At the time he'd also been working on *Zulu*. **Michael Caine**, then lodging in his flat, famously recalls how Barry kept him awake scoring the music for the Bond film. Originally performed by lyricist **Anthony Newley**, in an inspired decision *Goldfinger* was ultimately given to **Shirley Bassey**, whose uniquely powerful voice sustained its notes for breathless lengths. The single charted in both the UK and US and reached No.1 in Japan, and the soundtrack knocked *A Hard Day's Night* off the top of the American album charts, winning Barry a Grammy nomination and his first gold disc for over $1m in sales. 'The score really came together and everything culminated in this film,' he said later. 'Shirley was perfect casting, she brought such conviction.' Bassey, on the contrary, always claimed to loathe singing it in concert.

For *Thunderball* (1965), Barry wrote most of the score around **Dionne Warwick**'s 'Mr Kiss Kiss Bang Bang' (an earlier version by Bassey had failed to impress), a pseudonym for Bond in Japan

Matt Monro, billed as 'the singing bus conductor', crooned 007 into the UK charts ▲

and Italy and a theme song he'd written with **Leslie Bricusse**. At the last minute the producers opted instead for a title song sung by **Tom Jones** – who fainted during recording after completing the final top note - but Barry's original arrangements were still used to accompany the film's Bahamian setting.

John Barry is seen conducting an orchestra in *The Living Daylights*, but his appearance isn't credited

Within 12 months Barry became the first Englishman to win Academy awards for both Best Original Score and Best Song for 'Born Free' (performed by **Matt Monro**). A year later he was back with Bond, writing the music for Connery's last outing, *You Only Live Twice*. Over the opening credits, **Nancy Sinatra**, who'd recently charted with 'These Boots Are Made For Walking', sang a title track that had been first earmarked for Aretha Franklin.

In 1969, with George Lazenby in the Bond role for the first and last time, Barry scored *On Her Majesty's Secret Service*. The thrilling instrumental theme song accompanied the film's ski chases and would resurface in future movies. Equally outstanding was **Louis Armstrong**'s 'We Have All The Time In The World', written by Barry and Hal David for Bond's courtship with Tracy (Diana Rigg). It was Armstrong's last recording before his death. 'The pleasure of it was working with Louis, who was very ill,' recalled Barry. 'Having been laid up for over a year he had no energy left. He couldn't even play his trumpet and still he summoned the energy to sing our song.' The theme was a massive hit in the 1990s in the UK.

By now Barry had won an Oscar for *The Lion In Winter* and a Grammy for *Midnight Cowboy*. But the soundtrack to *Diamonds Are Forever*, Connery's resumption of the Bond role in 1971, earned a tepid reception despite another big Bassey title track.

Erstwhile Beatles producer **George Martin** was handed the reins for the next movie, *Live And Let Die*, starring Bond

Nancy Sinatra had to turn to knee-high socks after her boots went a-walking ◀

007 best Bond albums

001 Shaken And Stirred (David Arnold)
Tribute album with 11 tracks covering the best-known themes. Featuring Iggy Pop's bluesy rendition of 'We Have All The Time In the World', the Propellerheads cutting loose with 'On Her Majesty's Secret Service', and David McAlmont, it would seem, performing *Diamonds Are Forever* in distressingly tight underwear.

002 James Bond 30th Anniversary
The US limited edition double CD (released in 1992) has 31 digitally remastered recordings including both versions of 'Mr Kiss Kiss Bang Bang' by Shirley Bassey and Dionne Warwick, plus the original recording of 'You Only Live Twice' by Julie Rogers.

003 Bond: Back In Action (Prague Philharmonic Orchestra)
Released at the same time as Arnold's 'The World Is Not Enough', it's conducted by Nic Raine, a long-time collaborator with Barry, and features Vic Flick's nifty guitar work. Barry's original styles are captured in fuller suites from the first seven Bond films, spanning the string of Connery adventures and the one Lazenby experiment.

004 Licence To Chill: Spy vs Fly
A 'trip-hop tribute' by Washington/Bull released by Chromatic Records in 1999, featuring such gems as 'Diamonds R 4 Evah Medley', 'In The Hood Alone' and 'Martini Mix'. The album cover, replete with bulging ladies' buttocks in hot pants, is straight outta Staines. Respeck.

005 The James Bond Themes (e2)
No less than 18 tracks, including 'Casino Royale'. The themes are broken into two sections – action and love – and the orchestra is accompanied by singers trying to reproduce the sound of the originals. A bit like *Stars In Their Eyes*, and an album cover with quaint silhouettes of a man and woman. More Mr Bean than Mr Bond.

006 The Themes From All 15 Bond Films (Les Lowe)
From *Dr. No* all the way to *The Living Daylights*. Released in 1988, it features all the relevant tracks in strict chronological order. 'The only blemish,' says the wondrous 007 Bond Supplement website, 'is "Man With The Golden Gun" with the missing "The" which sounds nothing like the original.' You can't please all of the people…

007 13 Original Themes (Liberty)
Another stickler for the correct running order of the tracks, in this instance from the 'James Bond Theme' to *Octopussy*'s 'All Time High'. We just like the title. There's 13 of them, just in case you weren't sure.

At one point in *On Her Majesty's Secret Service*, George Lazenby's Bond walks past a cleaner who's whistling the *Goldfinger* theme

newcomer Roger Moore. It was a fabulous success, with Martin composing a new, improved 'James Bond Theme' and **Paul McCartney** and Wings performing only the second title track to appear as a real song within the main body of the film (the first was Monro's *From Russia With Love*). Written and recorded by Macca at his own expense, it earned Bond his first music-related Oscar nomination (Best Original Song) and reached No. 9 in the UK and No.2 in the US, the best American performance of a Bond theme at that time. This is despite the much-maligned line, 'But if this ever-changing world in which we live in' (**Chrissie Hynde** omitted the second 'in' on her version on David Arnold's covers album **Shaken And Stirred**).

Barry's return for *The Man With The Golden Gun* (1974) again failed to live up to his impeccably high standards. **Lulu**'s rendition of the frankly average title song didn't help. (Although to be fair to her, it would be hard to make a silk purse out of lines like 'His eye may be on you or me/Who will he bang? We shall see.') He took another break while **Marvin Hamlisch**, who'd written the music for *The Way We Were* and *The Sting*, was enlisted for *The Spy Who Loved Me* in 1977. It was a critically and publicly acclaimed Bond movie, earning Oscar nominations for Best Musical Scoring and Best Original Song and spawning a title song, 'Nobody Does It Better' by Carly Simon. 'It was time that Bond be pretentious enough and vain enough to have a song written about him,' remarked Hamlisch.

Two years later, Barry and Bassey were back for *Moonraker*, the former in top form and the latter seizing her chance after **Frank Sinatra** turned down the original theme, 'Think Of Me'. The theme ('Moon... raker!' could easily have been sung in homage to 'Gold... finger!') didn't real-

The opening four notes of Tina Turner's 'GoldenEye' can be heard in the background of one scene in *Tomorrow Never Dies*.

SHAKEN AND STIRRED

• • • The DAVID ARNOLD James Bond Project

Every Bond fan must have one ▲

ly gel though Shirl, as ever, tried her best.

It was followed in 1981 by the **Bill Conti** (of *Rocky* fame) score for *For Your Eyes Only*. Title singer and rising star **Sheena Easton** was the first to perform on-screen in a Bond film. It was nominated for Best Original Song at the Oscars but was beaten by *Arthur*. Today, in Britain, it's the stock-in-trade of female cross-channel ferry female singers.

Two years later Barry turned down the non-franchise *Never Say Never Again* (Connery reliving former glories to a very un-Bondlike soundtrack by **Michel Legrand**) to work on *Octopussy*, in which he elaborated upon many of his famous Bond motifs and wrote a magnificent romantic arrangement of 'All Time High', sung by **Rita Coolidge**. There was no title track for the first time in Bond history so, fortunately for lyricist Tim Rice, he didn't have to find a word that rhymed with Octopussy.

A View To A Kill (1985) saw Barry, fresh from Oscar success with *Out Of Africa*, collaborate with **Duran Duran**'s Simon Le Bon to pen the only Bond title song ever to top the charts in the US. The film also marked Barry's first significant use of the synthesiser in an energetic action score. The 'James Bond Theme' reappeared in revamped form, too.

In 1987, Barry worked on his 12th and Timothy Dalton's first Bond movie, *The Living Daylights*. As a swansong it was a vintage performance, bristling with catchy percussion and romantic interludes. Still innovative, Barry chose to end the film with a vocalised love theme ('If There Was A Man' by **The Pretenders,** a minor UK hit) rather than simply repeating the title song

007, Madonna and mousketeers

·The handover of the official 007 tux to Pierce Brosnan may have revived the Bond movie franchise but this hasn't coincided with renewed commercial success for the music of 007 – even if David Arnold seems, creatively, to be the best composer and all-round presiding genius of Bond music since Mr Prendergast moved on to celluloid pastures new.

For Die Another Day, the producers have therefore taken the extremely logical, if somewhat ironic, step of casting Madonna (as a fencing instructor) and asking Mrs Ritchie to sing the theme, Can't You See My Mind. Ironic, of course, because Madonna was called in by Mike Myers to lend her tonsils to Austin Powers The Spy Who Shagged Me, the title being an obvious spoof of you know what, to sing Beautiful Stranger, a top 20 hit in the US and a top five hit in the UK. The song generated more chart action than any Bond song since Duran Duran repeatedly danced into the fire with A View To A Kill over the credits to Roger Moore's final outing way back in 1985. In an obvious 007 homage, Myers also persuaded John Barry to act as composer for the second Powers film.

The Duran song, the first 007 single to be a US number 1, was also the last official Bond theme to grace the upper half of the Billboard singles charts. The singles have continued to be reasonably successful in the UK, although perversely the most successful Bond theme since then has been Louis Armstrong's We Have All The Time In The World, the theme to On Her Majesty's Secret Service, reissued and a No.3 hit after gracing Britain's small screens on a Guinness ad.

Bond's (and our) loss has, alas, been Walt Disney's gain with the likes of Phil Collins and Elton John both having top 20 US hits with singalong feelgood Disney themes which are ever present on the playlist of 'gold' (ie oldie) radio stations the world over.

Nothing against Disney (for whom Randy Newman did some fine work on Toy Story) but let's hope the Madonna move pays off since the average Bond theme is just more fun than mousketeer music. Bond themes are dramatic, often slightly preposterous, if not downright over-blown, but they do have certain crucial advantages over Disney's efforts.

They don't offer empresses of easy listening such as Vanessa Williams an opportunity to emote their way through ballads like Colors Of The Wind (a No. 4 hit in the US). They're normally sung by vocalists less monotonous than Phil Collins (a possible exception being a-ha). And they don't offer the listener a sugar-coated rose-tinted philosophy of life, as Disney have so often felt obliged to do since Elton John and Tim Rice collaborated on the monster that was the Circle Of Life, the grandiloquent, pseudo-profound theme to The Lion King. So come on 007, it's time you had the world humming again.

Shirl belts it out, her voice even louder than her outfit – but it's a close run thing ▲

(performed by subsequently miffed Norwegian group a-ha, who defiantly released their own remixed version on their third album, *Stay On These Roads*).

As Roger Moore's Bond glides past old acquaintance Sheriff Pepper on the river in *The Man With The Golden Gun*, we hear the five-note theme from *Live And Let Die*.

Barry was only 54, and three years later he'd win an Oscar for *Dances With Wolves*. But several sources quoted him as describing the modern Bond films as formulaic imitations – one reason he declined to work on *Licence To Kill* in 1989 and *GoldenEye* in 1995. Instead those honours went to Michael Kamen and Eric Serra respectively.

The former was the orchestral force behind Pink Floyd's *The Wall*, *Lethal Weapon*, *Die Hard* and *Robin Hood: Prince Of Thieves* (for which he was Oscar-nominated). **Gladys Knight** performed the memorable *Licence To Kill* title track, while **Patti Labelle** sang 'If You Asked Me To' over the end credits.

Frenchman Serra was an established movie composer with a penchant for synthetic percussion and Luc Besson's *La Femme Nikita* and *The Fifth Element* behind him. But in hindsight, scoring for Pierce Brosnan's debut was a mistake. Bond buffs accused him of being everything from amateurish to downright disrespectful. His crime? Neglecting Barry's original sound.

The title song, though ably performed by **Tina Turner**, was insipidly written by U2's Bono and The Edge, sounding almost like a bad pastiche of the archetypal Bassey/Bond theme song. **Minnie Driver**'s version of **Tammy Wynette**'s 'Stand By Your Man' didn't really help matters. Today any turkey of a soundtrack is now known in industry circles as 'a GoldenEye'.

Enter **David Arnold**. Thanks to him, 007 is hip and trendy. Thanks to his exotic instrumentation, sweeping orchestral love themes and mighty dance beats, Bond is cool again. When he was approached to work on *Tomorrow Never Dies* in 1997, he'd already made his name with *Stargate* and *Independence Day*. Admittedly, **Sheryl Crow**'s title song (self-penned with Mitchell

Froom) left a little to be desired, but Arnold had originally intended kd lang to perform the spectacular, Bassey-esque 'Surrender' over the opening credits. Either way, the rest of the high-octane soundtrack was stunning, regarded by many fans as not only a celebration of the franchise's true spirit – echoing Barry at his best – but also the start of an exciting new era. The movie ended, appropriately, with a cool club mix by Moby.

In 1999 Arnold's second Bond venture, *The World Is Not Enough*, enhanced his status as Barry's heir apparent, winning an Ivor Novello award (an English songwriter, Novello is now almost more famous for the eponymous award than for any of the songs he wrote in the 1930s and 1940s, such as *We'll Gather Lilacs*.) Again, the title song by Garbage's **Shirley Manson** just failed to seduce. 'The female vocals in Bond songs traditionally thrive on their sultry qualities,' claimed one Barry website. 'Garbage fail to capture the same enticing, raspy feel.' Another vocal by none other than **Scott Walker**, intended for the closing credits, was pulled after the previews and replaced with a house version of the 'James Bond Theme'. Otherwise, the 'Techno-Bond' score was a triumph.

Later that year, old and new were united when Arnold presented Barry with a Les Paul guitar specially made by Gibson at the Music Industry Trust's Man Of The Year awards. Also there was old-hand **Roger Moore** who told Barry, 'Any actor can only have his performance enhanced by your music behind him.' The same can be said of David Arnold today.

The James Bond sound returns with *Die Another Day*, **Madonna** singing 'Can't You See My Mind?' as the official theme, written by **Michel Colombier**, the French composer who has worked with everyone from Petula Clark to film director Jacques Demy. Colombier's score for Demy's film **A Room To Let**, in which every word was sung, helped make it such a critical smash that French movie reviewers paid for an ad in *Le Monde* urging the public to go and see the film. Don't bet on a similar ad appearing in *Variety* when *Die Another Day* breaks.

009

THE CONTEXT

Bond and beyond:
When fiction and reality collide

007

'History is moving pretty quickly these days'

James Bond, Casino Royale

Life is often held to be imitating art but nowhere are the distinctions between the two more blurred than in the strangely seductive genre that is spy fiction. **Ian Fleming** wasn't the first or the last novelist to trade on the the suspicion that submerged in his fiction are stories plucked from the secret history of the Cold War (**Len Deighton** and **John Le Carré** have since benefited from the same suggestion) but it remains an essential part of his mystique.

Given the exotic nature of Fleming's plots, the overlap between 007 and reality might seem slight. Yet he had the happy knack of anticipating events: his insistence on Bulgaria as the home of Russia's hitmen in **From Russia With Love** seemed prescient when, 24 years later, the Bulgarian secret service was accused of trying to kill the Pope. Fleming's knack has not always been maintained by his successors who, with one notable exception (in **John Gardner**'s work) often seem to follow the news. Fleming's riotous imagination as a novelist probably influenced the Cold War more than his riotous imagination influenced World War II as a commander in naval intelligence. What follows is a brief review of the occasions where Bond may have influenced reality. Truth can be stranger than fiction but, as Fleming's novels show, it can also be less conclusive and less entertaining. 241

◀ The 007 President: JFK, a Bond fan and a man of many Bondian traits

JFK, the 'assassin' and James Bond

When John F Kennedy listed From Russia With Love as his ninth favourite book (just above Stendhal's Scarlet And Black) in an article in *Life* magazine, the choice was widely (and wrongly) dismissed as a publicity stunt. Ian Fleming's biographer Andrew Lycett notes that some reports have Kennedy reading a Bond novel on **21 November 1963**, the night before his assassination while, elsewhere in Dallas that very night, JFK's alleged assassin **Lee Harvey Oswald** was also reading a Bond novel.

From JFK with love ▲

Kennedy was a voracious reader and, like 007 and (to a lesser extent) Fleming, a voracious womaniser. (Another similarity between Fleming and Kennedy was that both struggled with dominating father figures and grew up feeling overshadowed by an older brother – Joe in JFK's case and Peter in Ian's.) The author and the President met for dinner when Kennedy was still a Senator, introduced by Fleming's friend Marion Leiter, who had given JFK Casino Royale to read when he was seriously ill in 1955. It was at this dinner that Kennedy and Fleming famously discussed how to discredit Fidel Castro.

You could even argue Kennedy is the Bond President: charismatic, heroic (many have tried to discredit JFK's conduct when his PT-109 boat was sunk in the Pacific in World War II and he helped save the crew, but the balance of evidence and accounts from eyewitnesses is still in his favour), libidinous, self-contained and, ultimately, a lone wolf. Kennedy had half-expected to die young because of his many ailments, and Alan Seeger's *Rendezvous With Death*, which begins 'I have a rendezvous with death' was one of his favourite poems. In From Russia With Love, the British secret service man in Istanbul, Darko Kerim, tells 007, 'Life is full of death my friend',

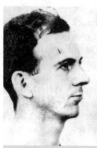

Lee Harvey Oswald, possibly a patsy, definitely a Bond fan ▲

a line which could almost have come from JFK's diary.

Jack Kennedy's sister Eunice had read almost all of Fleming's books and the President even read Cyril Connolly's spoof *Bond Strikes Camp*, presented to his wife by Randolph Churchill who found the

Kennedys' enthusiasm for 007 deeply disturbing, as did Graham Greene. JFK also had a private screening of Dr. No, the first Bond movie, at the White House. Not one to waste such a PR opportunity, Fleming had Vivienne Michel, the woman whose life story forms the heart of his 1962 novel *The Spy Who Loved Me*, say 'We need some more Jack Kennedys.' Her point, if she had one, being that too many decisions were being made by old people obsessed by memories of war. In the kind of irony even Fleming might have balked at, the world soon had one less Jack Kennedy, with another Bond aficionado Oswald charged with his murder .The assassin denied it – before he himself was shot – insisting to the press, 'I'm just a patsy', but there are more twists and turns in Oswald's own life than in the lives of most of Fleming's villains.

Fleming, the CIA and the sea shells that failed to kill Castro

Although Paul Johnson might have been overstating things when he dismissed the Bond novels as 'the crude snob-cravings of a suburban adult', Fleming was something of a social climber, taking care to ensure that he had friends and/or fans in the right places in society and in the intelligence community. CIA director Allen Dulles, who resigned after the 1961 Bay of Pigs invasion failed to topple Fidel Castro, was a Bond fan (he even made a rare trip to the cinema to see From Russia With Love), writing to Fleming to hope that 007 had not, after all, been killed at the shock conclusion to *On Her Majesty's Secret Service*. Fleming paid Dulles the ultimate compliment, having Bond read the CIA chief's book *The Craft Of Intelligence* (ghosted for him by Howard Hunt, Watergate conspirator and spy novelist) in *The Man With The Golden Gun*.

When Kennedy and Fleming met in March 1960, the novelist suggested the best way to deal with the Cuban leader was not to take him too seriously but to make him look ludicrous. His tongue-in-cheek suggestion was to drop leaflets over Cuba suggesting that beards were a natural receptacle for radioactivity, that the US had been spraying the islands with radioactivity and that beards would make their owners impotent. Kennedy thought this was hilarious but a CIA veteran at the dinner reported the ideas to Dulles who called Fleming to discuss these scenarios in detail.

Fleming's wheezes may have sounded like the kind of plots you would only find in a spoof spy novel but they were not inherently any more stupid than the CIA's own schemes. At their worst, they recruited the mob to help them run a Caribbean version of Murder Inc. Again, how influential the Kennedy brothers were in this is in dispute: critics say they were obsessed with killing Castro, yet the Cuban leader had begun to discuss peace with the US before Kennedy was shot.

The wilder CIA schemes, obviously inspired by Bond novels, included a plan to put powder in Castro's shoes to make his beard fall out. The CIA masterminds believed that the Communist leader would lose his charisma along with his beard. This plot misfired when the powder didn't work. Obviously on a roll, the agents then devised a drugged cigar which, when given to the leader before a vital speech, would make him seem disorientated. It might have worked, but as Castro's speeches were often very long-winded and slightly confusing, it's doubtful anyone would have noticed. A simpler plot, to give Castro an exploding cigar, brought no more success and finally the agency came up with the cleverest plot of all: to insert a bomb into a sea shell. Castro was rumoured to be a keen scuba diver and the, well, bomb-shell was designed to kill him while he was at his most relaxed. Sadly, one of the testers was injured developing a prototype (Q not being around at the time) and the shell was shelved.

Bond visited Cuba in the often-overlooked Fleming short story A Quantum Of Solace in which the dictator Fulgencio Batista is in power and Castro is leading the rebels in the hills. Although Bond is obliged officially to support the Batista regime, he does so reluctantly, and it's clear his sympathies lie with the rebels. Fleming even links Batista's regime to ex-Nazis and the same kind of gangsters who would later be hired by the CIA to try to kill Castro.

Moonraker, Star Wars and Ronald Reagan

In John Gardner's Bond novel For Special Services, the villain announces that the secret weapon 'the particle beam – once operational – will prevent any country from launching a conventional nuclear attack.' Published in hardback in 1982, the book looked even more timely in March 1983 when President Ronald Reagan proposed a space-based defence system, known as SDI (but quickly christened Star Wars by the press) which would use lasers and particle beams to protect the US and its allies from nuclear attack. Given the rather confused state American foreign policymaking was in at this time, it would be no great shock if Reagan had also hoped this initiative would stop Moonraker's Hugo Drax from firing his globes of poison into orbit to destroy humanity. (Or prevent some Blofeld clone from trying to send a laser into space as part of an evil plot to blackmail the world.) Despite the great communicator's best efforts, the rest of the world wasn't quite as enthused by Reagan's Star Wars as it had been by George Lucas' version.

It is only fair to note that American science-fiction writer Jerry Pournelle, who formed a group called the Citizens Advisory Council on National Space Policy (which reported to one of Reagan's national security advisers), must share some of the credit. But Pournelle foresaw the laser defence-in-space initiative as a means of protecting NASA's budget for manned space flight. Instead, $40billion later, NASA is further away from sending astronauts to Mars than ever but, much like the movie franchise, the Star Wars defence initiative seems to run and run. George W Bush is now pondering something called NMD (New Missile Defence) in which the missile repellents are based on land, sea and in space. As Reagan was known to confuse reel life with real life (he once claimed to have been a tail gunner

Che and Fidel get a round in after a CIA cigar fails to explode in Castro's mouth ▲

on a US bomber in World War II when he had actually only played a tail gunner in a movie) his liking for Star Wars is understandable, though the concept's appeal to Dubya is harder to explain.

The SPECTRE of nuclear-powered rogues

It's Emilio Largo's fault. Well, Fleming's. In his 1961 novel Thunderball, he raises the – oh, go on then – spectre of supervillains stealing nuclear weapons and threatening to destroy our cities unless we can rustle up $100million. In the film, SPECTRE agent Emilio Largo is responsible for implementing this nefarious scheme.

The fear of madmen armed with nuclear warheads has inflamed Western policymakers and tabloid headline writers ever since and, much like the Bond sagas, the plot (or the aim) remains almost the same, it's just the identity of the villain which changes. In the 1980s Mu'ammar Gaddafi was the man most likely to press the nuclear button, in the 1990s it was Saddam Hussein (or Boris Yeltsin – in the mistaken belief that he was ordering room service) and now, it's either North Korea's Kim-Jong-il, Saddam Hussein (as durable a bogey figure as Blofeld), or Osama Bin Laden.

When the Soviet Union collapsed in the 1990s, the media suggested that Soviet warheads (especially those in the non-Russian republics of the old USSR) would be sold as casually as tourist souvenirs on the streets of Moscow. Yet the Soviet Union's nuclear stockpile has, for all the alarmism, been reduced in a miraculously efficient fashion.

Only Russia, of the 15 republics which made up the USSR, still has a nuclear arsenal. The only real known conspiracy which compares for audacity with Largo's nuclear blackmail was a 1995 plot by Lithuanian traders to sell 40 shoulder-to-air tactical nuclear weapons to a man they thought belonged to a Colombian drugs cartel but who was actually an undercover US cop. The sting revealed that the arms had been signed off as for sale by a Lithuanian Defence Minister, and the transaction was being organised through a complex international corporate chain with links in Lithuania, Bulgaria and the Isle of Man.

This deal, although more spectacular than most, pretty much sums up the rather grimy reality of nuclear weapons smuggling. The testimony of experts like John Deutch, former director of the CIA, suggests that this trade isn't dominated by super-villains or a sophisticated criminal conspiracy like SPECTRE but by low-level spivs and black marketeers: a dodgy German businessman with a few ounces of plutonium 239 in his flat, an Eastern European entrepreneur with 11 cigarette packet-sized containers of strontium 90 or an Italian smuggler who threw a few ounces of fake plutonium in the river after shooting the buyer who didn't have the cash to pay for it or the sene to realise that his smuggled plutonium had actually come from a few smoke detectors.

There is, as politicians like to remind us, no room for complacency. The Russian mob is interested in the trade and police investigating one of the 1990s' biggest arms smuggling rings in Italy tried to interview a Spanish archbishop implicated in the conspiracy. Nobody except the dictators concerned know conclusively whether Iraq or North Korea could mount a Largo/SPECTRE-style plot. But *Thunderball* is, to date, more of a nightmare vision than a troubling reality.

From Bulgaria with love

In May 2002, Pope John Paul II, who has starred in more world tours than the Rolling Stones, arrived in Bulgaria and announced, to his hosts' evident relief, that he never believed the Bulgarians had anything to do with Turkish gunman's Mehmet Ali Agca's attempt to assassinate him. Bulgaria's old Communist leader, Todor Zhivkov, has vehemently denied any Bulgarian connection, famously insisting 'I'd have had to be out of my mind or on drugs to want to kill the Pope'. Indeed, it is fashionable to see the idea that the KGB conspired in some way with the Bulgarian secret service and Agca to kill the Pope as yet another right-wing fantasy typical of the Reagan 'evil empire' era. Fashionable but not necessarily right.

The idea that the Bulgarian secret service would do Russia's dirty work in the Cold War was floated by Fleming in *From Russia With Love*, where the crazed assassins who try to kill Bond, our man in Istanbul and a bunch of gypsies, are belligerent Bulgars, led by a Bulgarian gangster called Krilencu who behaves so inappropriately that he has to be shot. At the end of the novel, with Fleming uncertain about his character's future and book sales, Bond is left unconscious after being poisoned by villainess Rosa Klebb (repulsive, lesbian but not Bulgarian).

In 1978, 21 years after publication, Bulgarian dissident Georgi Markov was famously killed by a pellet containing ricin (three times as deadly as cobra venom with no known antidote) fired through the tip of an umbrella. KGB defector (and ex-major general) Oleg Kalugin has said 'Bulgarians, in the person of the party secretary, [Todor] Zhivkov, requested the Soviet KGB to help them get rid of Georgi Markov'. Yuri Andropov, then head of the KGB, initially refused but was persuaded to give the Bulgarian secret service, DS (Durzhavna Sigornost), the equipment to carry out the assassination. Markov died within four days of the attack. Initially, it was assumed he had suffered from blood poisoning but after an autopsy found a small hole in his right thigh, the authorities realised he had been a victim of a Klebb-style attack.

Zhivkov's alleged involvement in the Markov affair does, at least, cast some doubt on his protestations of innocence about the plot to kill the Pope. The difficulty for investigators is that the assassin, Ali Agca, is at best a serial fabricator (he claims to have been asked to kill Lech Walesa and Malta's leader Don Mintoff and announced, during the trial, that he was Jesus Christ) who belonged to a fascist terrorist group called the Grey Wolves, implicated in the deaths of thousands of 'leftists' in Turkey's equivalent of Argentina's dirty war. A year after he had been imprisoned for his attempt on the pontiff's life, Agca suggested he'd been put up to the act by the Bulgarian secret service and their pals and paymasters in the KGB.

This might seem like a desperate PR stunt by an assassin grown addicted to the oxygen of publicity but two separate investigations by American journalists concluded that Agca was picked up on the day of the assassination (13 May 1981) by Bulgarian airline official and intelligence officer **Sergei Antonov** who, with two Bulgarian diplomats, gave him a gun and drove him to St Peter's Square where the Pontiff was shot. These investigations also showed that Agca, who had escaped from a Turkish high-security prison in 1979 with the aid of persons unknown, had received considerable financial and practical aid from a group of Turkish arms smugglers with strong links to Bulgarian intelligence. There is also evidence in released communiques from the Russian Politburo that the KGB was encouraged to discredit the Pope, whose Polish nationality seemed a threat at a time when the Soviets were trying to regain control of Poland after the Solidarity strikes in the shipyards of Gdansk. Mikhail Gorbachev, though, denied that these efforts were meant to embrace anything as drastic as assassination.

As it is now a matter of national pride in Bulgaria that their agents had nothing to do with the plot against the Pope and the new head of Bulgarian intelligence admits that many files have been destroyed, the truth may never be known. The plot itself is as labyrinthine as any of Fleming's and the one man who might be able to shed some light on the whole murky business, Antonov, was freed by an Italian court for lack of evidence. He has since returned to Bulgaria and lives on a state pension – he is unable to work having suffered some kind of breakdown, allegedly because of drugs used in his interrogation.

Although journalist **Alexander Cockburn** blames **From Russia With Love** for 'the legend of the Bulgarian-KGB plot to kill the Pope' there's more than enough conflicting evidence to suggest that the story would have surfaced (and indeed still deserves investigation) even if a certain famous spy novelist hadn't already planted the seeds of suspicion.

010
LOCATIONS
The world according to 007,
a jetsetting hero for a jetset age

007

'What kind of work do you do anyway?'
'Oh I travel...'

Thunderball

The world is not enough for James Bond which may be why he traverses it so often. Usually the same old places mind: the Caribbean, Vegas, Monte Carlo. Never Grimsby, the Lincolnshire port of which neighbours say, 'Grimsby isn't the end of the world but you can see it from there,' and seldom New Jersey, the 'Garden' state where taxi drivers boast, 'There are two seasons in New Jersey: winter and construction.' The closest Bond got to seriously slumming was when he visited Harlem in *Live And Let Die* but he's soon whisked off to more traditionally exotic climes. When we first met Bond, we travelled vicariously through him so it made sense for Fleming and the filmmakers to give him the kind of backdrops which most of us, at the dawn of a jetset age, could only dream.

Locations were also one of the few cards Hollywood could play in its continual war with television. The 1950s had proved that 'bigger' or 'wider' pictures were not going to win audiences back and the low budgets of most TV shows didn't permit the cast to hop to the south of France (*To Catch A Thief*), north Africa (*Lawrence of Arabia*) or to Jamaica (**Dr. No**) with its backdrop of constant sun, white sands, blue skies and palm trees.

Since then, the settings for Bond's missions have become as key to the movies as the gadgets, the girls and the theme song. When *Dr. No* was released in 1962, the furthest most British families

◀ James Bond festival, Ocho Rios, Jamaica

James Bond and Johnny foreigner

'Sawed off cissies who eat snails and slugs and cheese that smells like people's feet... Utter cowards who force their own children to drink wine, they gibber like baboons even when you try to speak to them in their own wimply language.' This is actually PJ O'Rourke's jaundiced assessment of the racial characteristics of the French, as immortalised in *Foreigners Around The World* in *National Lampoon* magazine in 1976. While it may be longer than 007's view of them (in *Casino Royale*, he notes that 'all French people suffer from liver complaints'), it's just as dismissive.

Bond's view of the world in the novels is fundamentally that of his creator, and Fleming was not without his own moments of xenophobia, once noting, after a tiresome visit to Goldeneye by some garrulous Americans, that 'all foreigners are pestilential'.

In the Bond novels, foreigners often are pestilential. His villains are an international cast of Russians, Bulgars, Germans, Koreans, Mexicans, Corsicans, Chinese, Yugoslavs and even Americans – although moments of Yankee villainy are more than balanced by the virtuousness of Bond's good buddy from the CIA, Felix Leiter.

Just in case we are in any doubt that these Johnny and Joan foreigners are not to be trusted, Fleming often underlines their sexual perversity: Blofeld is asexual in *Thunderball*, possibly because his muscles are wasting away, while Emilio Largo, whose hands are twice as big as they ought to be for a man of his size, has a sexual appetite larger than 007's, Fleming's and JFK's combined. *Scaramanga*, apart from having the same number of nipples as Ann Boleyn, likes to have sex before a kill – some silly superstition about improving his eye – and may even have a crush on 007.

It's the casual dismissal that you find in most Bond novels which reinforces the Bondian world view. We are told that Albanians, as a race, are not noted for their beauty – although, to be fair, this opinion is offered in Kingsley Amis' Bond novel *Colonel Sun*. America's cuisine, we are informed in *Live And Let Die*, is of such a standard it's a pleasant surprise to find an edible dish. Bulgarians are just blunt, brutal, instruments of Soviet power, in *From Russia With Love*. The Japanese, in *You Only Live Twice*, are a separate human species. As for the Germans, well as Bond notes in *Moonraker*: 'Scratch a German and you will find precision.'

Given that almost every nation has been seriously dissed in the novels, it is a miracle that 007 ever managed to find a following outside certain gentleman's clubs in London. His motto, far from being the world is not enough, could almost have been 'Britain is more than enough, thanks all the same old chap.' Maybe it's true what they say, travel really does narrow the mind.

travelled for a holiday was a Butlins-esque holiday camp. Even those Brits who could afford Bond-style locations were hindered by rules which meant holidaymakers were only allowed to take £25 out of the country (the sum climbed to £50 by 1970). Ironically, in **Kingsley Amis**'s Bond novel *Colonel Sun*, 007 regrets the end of this era: 'There appeared ahead of him a B.E.A Trident newly taken off from London Airport, full of tourists bearing their fish-and-chip culture to the Spanish resorts, to Portugal's lovely Algarve province, and now, as the range of development schemes grew ever wider, as far as Morocco.'

We may travel more these days but with 20 screen missions under his belt, Bond has clocked up more air, sea and road miles than the greediest of television travel presenters and has had islands, beaches and lagoons named after him. And he still travels in a style to which so many of us would love to become accustomed, in fancy cars, helicopters, and private jets.

His flights are never delayed. He never frets away the hours queuing to check in for his flight. Even undercover he never travels in that class euphemistically referred to as thrift, economy or coach (why don't they just call it cheap and be done with it?). So join us – if you'd care to – on a whistlestop tour of the best Bond locations. For further info on these (and other) locations, you could do worse than try www.roughguides.com. There, that's our Bondian bit of product placement over and done with.

Caribbean

Ocho Rios, Jamaica
Dr. No

Where better to shoot the first cinematic incarnation of Fleming's hero than the place where his creator first put pen to paper: well, typewriter to paper. In 1962, when *Dr. No* was released, Jamaica was free from honeymooning couples on all-inclusive package holidays and Fleming had been living there since 1952. His neighbour, just along the coast, was **Noel Coward** (Goldeneye was named by Fleming after one of his military operations against the Germans, although Coward referred to it as the 'Golden eye, nose and throat clinic'). Because of his proximity, Fleming acted as a location scout on the film, which was shot around his home turf of Ocho Rios, an area of outstanding beauty and beaches, whose charm has just about survived its development as a mass tourist resort.

Fans can visit Goldeneye, now owned by Island Records founder Chris Blackwell, who became friends with Fleming while working as location manager on *Dr. No*. If your budget stretches to $4,000 a night, you can even rent the bedroom, with the very desk where Fleming wrote **Casino Royale**.

Live And Let Die returned to Jamaica, which posed as the fictional island of San Monique and hosted the chomping crocodile scene at the Charles Swaby Swamp Safari Park(www.roundhilljamaica.com/newsletter/V_seeJamaica.htm).

Highlights

Goldeneye Set in 17 acres within beautiful tropical forests, but when Fleming first moved in it was all but a concrete retreat. Since then visitors who stay here are asked to plant a tree to contribute to the growth of the area. The food has improved since Fleming's day: Noel Coward used to tell his host: 'Ian, it tastes like armpits.'

James Bond Beach Available only to customers of Goldeneye.

Dunn's River Falls The spectacular 600ft falls where Bond, Quarrel and Honey bathed and she asked if he'd ever seen scorpions sting themselves to death. You have to admire her natural curiosity.

Practicalities

Regular flights from Heathrow and Gatwick with Air Jamaica (www.airjamaica.com) and British Airways (www.britishairways.com); Regular flights are available from most US cities.

The house at Goldeneye sleeps six at $4,000 per day; villas on the cliffs set you back $1,000 per couple (all-inclusive). Contact Island Outpost (www.islandoutpost.com). If this is a bit steep,

Jake's at Treasure Beach, 'the chic-est shack in the Caribbean', offers a laid-back, rum-fuelled stay at $114 per day (room only). Cost of a vodka martini Included in the price of accommodation – well, you are already paying $4,000 a night to stay there.

USA

Las Vegas

Diamonds Are Forever

The book was deemed the weakest of Fleming's early Bond adventures due to the constant change in locale, yet the varying locations worked a lot better on film. Of all Bond's destinations in *Diamonds are Forever*, Las Vegas is undoubtedly the star. Since 1971, when the film was released, Vegas has changed radically but it's still worth hunting out Bond's old haunts.

The film's hallmark action sequence saw 007 careering through the streets of Vegas in a moon buggy, passing sights such as the **Golden Nugget Hotel** on Fremont Street and the Circus Hotel and Casino. **Howard Hughes**, on whom Willard Whyte (aka Blofeld) was very loosely based, allowed his Vegas hotels to be used in the film for the paltry fee of a 16mm print of the final cut.

Bond's hotel suite and Blofeld's apartment were actually studio sets created by production designer **Ken Adams**. Director Guy Hamilton had chosen a suite at **Caesars Palace** to double as Bond's room at the Whyte House Hotel, the ornate and vulgar suite with a sunken

Spy museum

Despite pleas by the Ian Fleming Foundation to create a James Bond museum, the best we can offer you for the moment is the International Spy Museum in Washington (that's DC, not the espionage hotspot that is Tyne & Wear). The museum opened in July 2002, and in addition to lectures, workshops and demonstrations on just what it's like to be a secret agent, the museum also holds the world's largest collection of Bond-style gadgetry. If you're a complete spy nut you can also attend one of their 'Come as Your Favourite Spy' evenings. Check out the not-so-secret website www.spymuseum.org for more info.

living room and mile-long bathroom just what they were look-ing for. But Adams reckoned he could create something far more vulgar on the Pinewood back lot – and he did exactly that.

You can visit the International Hotel, which doubled as Blofeld's HQ, or the **Las Vegas Hilton**, the exterior of which became the Whyte House Hotel. You can even take a quick peek at the luggage locker at the Las Vegas MacCarran International Airport where the diamonds were left for pick up.

For added authenticity, director Hamilton went so far as to recruit Vegas regular **Sammy Davis Jr** for a cameo role, although his scenes were cut on its theatrical release.

Highlights

Las Vegas Simply soak up the atmosphere wandering around.

Caesars Palace Although Hamilton and Adams out-vulgared the real thing, the OTT-style still has to be seen to be believed.

The Venetian Wasn't around when 007 was in town but we think Bond would appreciate the marble baths and walk-in showers – and M could keep in touch (to 007's chagrin) via the in-room fax. For those obliged, unlike Bond, to pay their own way, prices for rooms vary from $175 to $250.

Practicalities

As Vegas is plonked down in the middle of the desert, it's a good idea to rent a car. For a bit of style, Rente-a-Vette (www.exotic carrentalslasvegas.com) offers Corvettes, Porsche Boxsters and Maserati Spyders. Accommodation-wise, Vegas is also home to the **Casino Royale Hotel** (www.casinoroyalehotel.com). Famed for its James Bond connection, the Las Vegas Hilton offers reasonable rates with prices starting around $55 per night (depending on the season, see www.lvhilton.com). If you fancy yourself as a bit of a high-roller when it comes to gambling, head for Caesars Palace, where the slot machines accept $5,000 bets. Room prices are less heady, starting at $89 (www.caesars.com). Cost of a vodka martini at the Casino Royale Hotel – out of well $2.25, call brand $3.25, premium brand $4.25.

New Orleans
Live And Let Die

Knee-deep in 1970s culture and soaked in jazz, *Live and Let Die* marked a new era with **Roger Moore**'s debut. One of Fleming's most thrilling novels, Bond heads to New Orleans to foil the plans of voodoo-worshipping drugs baron Kananga/Mr Big. The French quarter, with its constant carnival atmosphere, is alive and kicking throughout (the Fillet of Soul bar and restaurant doubling as Kananga's lair), but images of voodoo and death are similarly all around. As the only American city below sea level, New Orleans' deceased cannot be buried underground and rest in stone crypts in the 'Cities of the Dead'. Funeral processions feature heavily, often used as devices for bumping off British secret service agents.

Highlights

French Quarter Visit Kananga and Tee Hee's haunts with blues and

A typically lively New Orleans street – before they bring out their dead ▼

jazz bars, and clubs aplenty – and a few too many strip clubs.

Cities of the Dead Four major burial sites, if headstones are your thing.

Practicalities

A limited number of airlines fly to New Orleans from the UK, with prices steeper than to many other US cities – US Airways flights come in close to £500. Check out www.expedia.com for flights from the UK and the US. Room rates in the French quarter vary from $100 to $1000 depending on whether you opt for Hotel Monte Leone (http://new. orleans.a-z-hotels.net) or the W New Orleans hotel (www.starwood.com/whotels). If, like Fleming, you're curious about voodoo, then **The Historic Voodoo Museum**, 724 Dumaine St, is worth a visit – some 15 per cent of the population still practise voodoo so show the appropriate respect.

England
London
Octopussy, GoldenEye, The World Is Not Enough

Few Bond films don't feature London – unsurprising really, considering the capital is the home of the MI6 headquarters. But it wasn't until *Octopussy* that specific areas of the city featured heavily (apart from St Paul's Cathedral starring briefly in *On Her Majesty's Secret Service* when Bond heads to the College of Arms to check out Blofeld's ancestry).

In *Octopussy,* the auction house Sotheby's is the setting for Bond's first encounter with villain Kamal Khan, with Bond switching a fake Fabergé egg for the real thing while ensuring Khan pays over the odds for the trinket. And in Pierce Brosnan's debut, *GoldenEye*, the real MI6 building is featured which, as we all know, is located on Vauxhall Bridge even though the Government does not admit it. You can't enter unless you're a genuine member of British Intelligence (or a double agent) but the building is still worth a look from the outside.

Two films later Brosnan returned to London in *The World Is*

Not Enough, and overseas fans were treated to a whistlestop tour of the city with a speedboat chase down the Thames. Bond even managed to find a use for the Millennium Dome, landing on it in the opening sequence.

Stoke Park Golf Club, Buckinghamshire

Goldfinger, For Your Eyes Only, Tomorrow Never Dies

Stoke Park Golf Club in Stoke Pogues, played host to the most famous golf game in movie history, and also made an appearance in two other Bond films. Bond does a round at the club with arch nemesis Auric Goldfinger (defeating him thanks to the 'strict' rules of the game), and the club's church was later used for the opening scenes of *For Your Eyes Only*. Bond also appears there to visit the grave of his dead wife Tracy in *On Her Majesty's Secret Service*. The club's interior is also briefly shown in *Tomorrow Never Dies*.

Highlights

Stoke Park Golf Club Complete with special *Goldfinger* themed bar, hosting Bond events (www.stokeparkclub.com).

The River Thames A river cruise will pass many of the London landmarks featured – and at a more leisurely pace than Bond.

Practicalities

Wherever you happen to be in the world, getting a flight to London sorted out shouldn't be a problem and once you're in the city, the London Tourist Board can point you to the places to visit (www.london touristboard.com). As far as accommodation goes, there are hotels and guest houses to suit all budgets but if you want to go for the total Bond experience, then the **Four Seasons Hotel** in

Stoke Park: Goldfinger is no longer a member ▲

Canary Wharf with its fantastic views of the Thames is where we think Bond would choose to stay in the capital (www.four seasons.com for rates).

Cost of a vodka martini at Stoke Park Golf Club: £7.50.

Iceland

A View To A Kill, Die Another Day

Bond's latest outing, *Die Another Day*, was set to be called *Beyond the Ice*, which probably explains why Iceland is a key location in the film with sequences shot on the 1000ft deep ice lagoon in Jökulsárlón. For an important chase sequence, 225 Norwegian spruce trees were brought in from eastern Iceland.

Iceland, heavily disguised as Siberia, also featured in Roger Moore's final curtain call as Bond, **A View To A Kill**. With some 11 per cent of the country under ice caps, the remote mountains of Breidarmerkurlon were perfect for the film's opening scene, the crew using the same handy lagoon which would later feature in *Die Another Day* (and which is now called the James Bond Lagoon). The land of geysers was also a horribly apt locale for Moore's Bond who was, by this time, looking like a bit of an old geezer himself.

Highlights

Vatnajokull lagoon Featured in not one but two Bond movies, and host to two different Bonds, Europe's largest glacier is a must-see.

Practicalities

Flights to Iceland are expensive so it's worth booking in advance. Once at the airport, the most economical route into the city is by Flybus (around 45 minutes). Head to www.icetourist.is for a wealth of info. We imagine Bond would stay at the Reykjavik Radisson (www.radisson.com/reykjavikic_saga): stylish, cosmopolitan and located in the grounds of the city's university with its ready supply of impressionable young girls. To make the most of your trip, take a guided glacial tour (www.vatnajokull.com).

Cost of a vodka martini at the Radisson: 11 euros.

Italy
Venice
From Russia With Love, Moonraker

In an electrifying Bond finale in *From Russia with Love*, 007 abandons the traditional Venetian gondola for a motorised hover version, speeding down the Grand Canal and out into the **Piazza San Marco** in pursuit of SMERSH agent Rosa Klebb. Once you've enjoyed a more sedate trip down the canal, you can head to *Moonraker* territory and the Venini Museum. Doubling up as an antique glass museum and Hugo Drax's nerve gas laboratory, it staged Bond's spectacular fight with Chang which destroyed the entire museum collection – tut tut.

Cortina D'Ampezzo
For Your Eyes Only

Just two hours away in the car from Venice, Cortina D'Ampezzo, in the Italian Alps, is the quintessential skiing village, which played host to the 1956 Winter Olympics before its Bond film potential was fulfilled in *For Your Eyes Only*.

The German ex-ski champion, **Willy Bognor**, who also worked on *The Spy Who Loved Me* and *On Her Majesty's Secret Service*, co-ordinated the spectacular stunt in which Bond is hotly pursued by Kriegler on skis and then attacked by ski-borne motorbikes on the bob-run.

If hitting the slopes isn't your thing, you could always stay at the **Miramonti Hotel**, the exterior of which was used in the film, or head to the nearby shopping centre, where filming was initially hampered by a distinct lack of snow. In the end, 25 truckloads of virgin snow was brought in and spread around.

Highlights

Cortina D'Ampezzo Fantastic scenery and great skiing even before you stalk out Bond's route.

Harry's Bar, Venice Featured in *From Russia With Love* – where better to try a vodka martini for only 11 euros?

Venini Museum But please don't re-enact the Bond/Chang clash.

Practicalities

Most airlines fly to Venice so you should be able to find well-priced flights. Once at the Marco Polo airport, travel the 13km to the city by bus, train, car or Vaporetto (water bus). To get to Cortina, many visitors opt to use the Dolomiti bus service (www.dolomitibus.it). Accommodation is as cheap or expensive as you want – check out www.hotelinvenice.com.

Monaco
Monte Carlo
GoldenEye

Designed for (and by) the rich and famous, Monaco, aka the jewel of the Cote d'Azur, with its capital **Monte Carlo**, is a Bond

SOUVENIR DE MONTE CARLO.

movie waiting to happen. Disappointingly though, the thrilling car chase doesn't actually take place in Monaco, it was actually shot 20 miles north-west of Monte Carlo.

If time is limited, the one place you must visit is the Casino de Monte Carlo, the largest and most famous gambling establishment in the world. Be warned, you won't be let in wearing a T-shirt or shorts. Alas, only the exterior of the building and that of the neighbouring **Hotel de Paris** were used in the film. Additional Bond locations worth visiting include the beautiful La Condamine harbour where Xenia Onatopp stole a helicop-

262

A casino fit for royalty ▲

ter from a moored battleship, and the Fort Antoine Theatre on the Avenue de la Quarantaine, where Bond is seen walking through the middle of a performance in order to spy on Xenia.

Highlights

Royal Palace Not in the film, but worth a look, as is the **Monte Carlo Golf Club** with its course 2600ft above sea level. ·

Fort Antoine Theatre Closed in 2002 for engineering work on the sea wall, but performances are due to resume.

Practicalities

A number of airlines operate frequent services to Nice and the Cote d'Azur International airport, which lies only 22km from Monaco. In Nice you can fly by helicopter, or use more mundane means (car, bus, train or sea services). On the hotel front it ain't cheap but Hotel Discounts at www.hoteldiscount.com is a good place to look for cheaper options. For general info head to www.conferencemonaco.com/touristboard.htm or www.monte-carlo.mc.

Switzerland

Swiss Alps
Goldfinger

Goldfinger marked the debut of the classic Bond car, the Aston Martin DB5, and Switzerland as a location. With snow-capped mountains, glamorous resorts and the kind of prices only an MI6 agent could afford, Switzerland feels like 007's natural habit on assignment. Your tour should first stop in the mountains near Andermatt where Bond girl Tilly Masterson tried to kill Goldfinger. From here, head to the Pilatus Factory at Stans, the exterior of which doubled as Goldfinger's Auric Enterprises where he uttered the line: 'No Mr Bond, I expect you to die!'

Bern, Piz Gloria, Schilthorn Mountains
On Her Majesty's Secret Service

Having soaked up the atmosphere from one of the best Bond films, head to Bern for sights from the most under-rated one.

Piz Gloria: snow, bigger cable cars than San Francisco and a revolving restaurant ▲

Once you've viewed the Heilligirst Church, next to the train station, the offices of Blofeld's attorney (Gumbold) is a suitable next port of call in the Schweizerhof Hotel. Most interior shots were filmed at Pinewood, but you can see where the safe was cracked. Saving the best till last, your final destination should be Blofeld's hideaway, 2,300m up at the very top of **Mount Schilthorn**. Called **Piz Gloria** in both the film and real life (the owners chose to name it after Blofeld's hideaway), it was a half-finished restaurant, albeit it complete with spectacular 360 degree views of the Alps and Switzerland, when it was discovered by production manager Hubert Frolich. But it was close to the description given by Fleming in the original novel and the owners agreed to allow filming to take place on the condition that EON Productions furnished the now revolving restaurant's interiors and also build a helicopter-landing pad (well, if you don't ask, you don't get). To complete the high old time offered to Bond fans visiting the area, there's a chance to make the longest, vertical cable car climb in the world.

As lavish as this may sound, the cost to transform a rather dull restaurant into a villain's secret lair was just £60,000 (compared to the £300,000 needed for Blofeld's rocket base in *You Only Live Twice*). Your final stop should be **Jungfraujoch** where the highest railroad station in Europe can be found.

Highlights

Piz Gloria Take a 360 degree perspective on the world.

Murren Located beneath the peak of Schilthorn, Murren became the home of the film's bobsled run. The town is also linked to Piz Gloria by the funicular railway, which still operates today.

Ticino Featured in *GoldenEye*, the **Verzasca Dam** in Ticino in the Italian region of Switzerland, doubled as the dam at the Arkangel Chemical Weapons Facility in Russia. Bond jumps from the edge of the dam, now famous as the world's longest bungee jump.

Practicalities

Switzerland is served by most of the bigger airlines, prices depend on the time of year. Once there, the cable car to Piz Gloria is open all year and takes 30 minutes to reach the peak from Interlaken. For more information on Schilthorn try www.schilthorn.ch; for general information go to www.rail europe.com/us/rail/passes/switzerland_index.htm. Moderately priced accommodation can be found at www.expedia.com.

China

Hong Kong

You Only Live Twice, The Man With The Golden Gun

China has featured in three Bond films so far, in *The Man With The Golden Gun*, briefly in *Diamonds Are Forever* (Tiffany Case is sent to collect the diamonds from 007 in China), and *You Only Live Twice*, although Japan was the principle location (see below). China was set to host *Licence to Kill*, EON Productions hoping it would be the first major Western production to be filmed there, but when Spielberg beat them to it with *Empire of the Sun*, China was ditched in favour of Mexico. Hong Kong was also set to feature in *Tomorrow Never Dies*, but Henry Kissinger (advisor to the studio's president, John Calley) deemed the original plot surrounding the Chinese takeover of Hong Kong too risky. In contrast, Fleming's original *The Man With The Golden Gun* was set in Jamaica but as some of Bond's previous outing in

Cardigan Bay: it's the new Korea

Strange as it may sound, it isn't always easy making Scotland look like Scotland, or Russia look how audiences think it looks. Thus location scouts need ingenuity, wit and the ability to see that, for example, a particular part of Cornwall could be Korea.

Quarzazate, Morocco
In deepest Morocco, Quarzazate was set to be the next Casablanca, but was too much of a ghost town. It may not have made it as Casablanca but producers felt it would make a good Afghanistan in *The Living Daylights*.

Chatham High Street, Kent
In *The World Is Not Enough*, Bond is seen racing down the Thames when his speedboat cuts out of the water. Miraculously, Bond is no longer in London during this split second episode, but has been transported to not-so-glam Chatham High Street in Kent. And no one noticed the join.

Nene Valley Railway, Northamptonshire
Remember Bond wrestling with two circus performers aboard a speeding train in *Octopussy*? Well Bond wasn't in East Germany but on the Nene Valley railway in Northamptonshire.

Penbryn Beach, Wales
Who'd have thought the green and sheep-infested Wales had any resemblance to Korea, yet location managers on *Die Another Day* deemed Cardigan Bay to be a perfect substitute for the rugged coastline of Korea. Newquay's Holywell Bay beach was also converted into a Korean battlefield for the movie.

Live And Let Die was filmed there, a new location was sought.

In terms of Bond sites to visit, there is the interior of the Queen Elizabeth I ocean liner, which sank in Hong Kong Harbour and was transformed into the British Secret Service's Far East HQ. The Hong Kong-Macao hydrofoil, in which Bond chases Scaramanga's girlfriend, is still in use.

Highlights

Hong Kong With few specific sites to see, it is a better idea to go to Hong Kong to experience the culture in general.

Getting there

Flights and accommodation can work out on the expensive side but Opodo (www.opodo.co.uk) is a good general place to start for UK tourists, with flights listed at under £500 as we went to

press. If you can afford it, head to the Hong Kong Conrad (www1.conrad.com.hk/eng) and live out your stay in style; for other places to stay, head for www.discoverhongkong.com.
Cost of a vodka martini at the Conrad – Hong Kong $72.50.

Japan
Kagoshima, Mount Shinmoe
You Only Live Twice

Bond was a God-like figure in Japan, and his comments about Japanese women not being sexy only heightened interest in him further. The furore which followed was cited as one of the reasons Connery quit as Bond (see page 136).

You Only Live Twice went on to be one of the most colourful Bond films, thanks partly to the Japanese influence. Begin your tour at **Kagoshima** – originally famed as the place where Christianity and guns were introduced to Japan – and wander around the seaport where the fight scene took place.

Although the **Sakurajima** volcano is the film location of Blofeld's secret lair, the volcano was too active to be used in key scenes and nearby Mount Shinmoe was used as a substitute. Only part of the filming took place on location, art director Ken Adams designing a replica model at Pinewood for the more complex shots. You should also take in the tiny fishing village of **Akime** (there are only 180 residents), referred to in the film as Ama (Kissy Suzuki's home), and where the six-foot two-inch Bond tried to blend in as the tallest Japanese fisherman in the country. The nearby **Rosaki Cave** was used for Bond and Kissy's cave scenes. Leaving the best till last, take a trip to the magnificent **Himeji Castle**, the largest wooden building in the world and home of the film's Ninja fighting school.

Highlights

Himeji Castle No Ninjas – not teenage nor mutant – but fine views.
Kagoshima No single location stands out from the film, but the town offers a good flavour of Japan and its influence on the film.

The Sakurajima volcano: a little too shaken and stirred at times for Bond and crew ▲

Practicalities

Like China, flights to Japan can be costly so it's worth looking at a number of vendors before you book (www.dialaflight.com, www.opodo.co.uk and www.cheapflights.co.uk are all worth a look). Once in Tokyo, the **Shinkansen bullet train** will take you to Himeji in about three hours, the castle is only a 15-minute walk from the station, and the Himeji Hotel and Inn Association has properties in the area with prices to suit all budgets. (www.city.himeji.hyogo.jp/english/himeji/node82.html). You can get a ferry to Sakurajima from Kagoshima – they run 24 hours a day, and there's a sightseeing bus when you land.

For more info **Best try** http://gojapan.about.com.

Thailand

James Bond Island, The Man With The Golden Gun

The Man With The Golden Gun was one of Fleming's weaker

novels and, as a movie, didn't live up to its backdrop. When location scouts arrived in 1974, they found a tiny chain of islands in the mangrove-lined bay of **Ao Phang Na**, and the boulder-shaped **Ko-Ping-Kan** became Scaramanga Island (now referred to as James Bond Island). Most of the high-octane action sequences and the finale occurred there, including the final duel between the two adversaries. Some 100 miles up the coast, the **Mergui Archipelago**, featured briefly in *Thunderball*.

Phuket

Tomorrow Never Dies

James Bond Island also pops up in *Tomorrow Never Dies*, when Bond and Wai Lin begin their search for the stealth boat, but most of the action occurs in the city of Phuket (pronounced 'Poo-ket'), the surrounding area doubling as Vietnam. Director **Roger Spottiswoode** and his 200-strong crew were at Heathrow ready to fly to Vietnam when they were told shooting had to be moved. EON Productions says it chose to switch locations, but the Vietnamese said they couldn't handle such a large production. There were rumours that Communist parties in Vietnam or China were unhappy with the decision to permit filming and the film's licence was revoked. So the island of **Phang Nga** became Along Bay in Vietnam, site of one of the movie's most spectacular scenes, the motorcycle leap across a hovering helicopter.

Highlights

Phang Nga Bay Great location with familiar sights.

James Bond Island The only way to see James Bond Island is by boat. The chance to pose like Scaramanga and 007 on the very strip of sand is so irresistible to many that the island can get pretty packed and the souvenirs are at international tourist prices. In the nearby town of Phang Na you can take James Bond Tours (the company has an office in the bus station).

Bangkok Featured in *The Man With The Golden Gun* and *Tomorrow Never Dies* – as if you needed an excuse to go there.

Practicalities

Increasingly popular (blame *The Beach*). Flights and accommodation prices are gradually becoming cheaper and thus more accessible. Check out the usual vendors for details. Phuket has its own international airport or you can fly to Bangkok and take an internal flight (www.thaiair.com). Alternatively, if you like scenic routes, catch a train from Hualomphong in Bangkok to Surathani and a bus to Phuket (www.phuket.com).

Pinewood Studios

The versatility of Pinewood Studios, tucked away in the quiet English county of Buckinghamshire, knows no bounds. A working laboratory in *Dr. No*? A pipeline in Caucasus in *The World Is Not Enough*? Ken and Cubby (see below) could replicate these on the backlot before you could say 'Live and let die'. And as a result Pinewood has starred in 19 of the 20 Bond films (the exception: *Moonraker*).

Goldfinger

Production manager Ken Adams was denied access to the real Fort Knox (spoilsports) so Cubby Broccoli asked Adams to create, 'A Cathedral of Gold' to double as the interior of the gold depository.

You Only Live Twice

Pinewood constructed a volcanic crater set to become the centrepiece of the film. Costing $1m (more than the entire *Dr. No* production) the crater was, at the time, the largest studio set ever made in Europe – so large it was visible from a motorway three miles from Pinewood.

Diamonds Are Forever

Las Vegas may be famed for its unique brand of OTT hotel accommodations, but the production crew felt they would have to use the Pinewood backlot as Bond's hotel suite at the Whyte House Hotel, producing a suite of such cheerful vulgarity it must have influenced designers in the city of lost wages.

The Spy Who Loved Me

Cubby Broccoli (by now sole producer of the Bond franchise) wanted to make this the most ambitious Bond production yet and once again employed Ken Adams to construct the studio sets. Broccoli's vision of the film's climax was so grandiose that an entire new sound stage had to be built at Pinewood, christened 'the 007 stage'. The area housed three nuclear subs, including supertanker 'Liparus'. The 007 stage was destroyed by fire in 1985, but has subsequently been rebuilt.

011
THE EPHEMERA

'Pay attention 007. I want you to take good care of this equipment'

007

'If you take the top off, you'll find a little red button. Whatever you do, don't touch it'

Q, Goldfinger

Contrary to popular belief, the history of movie merchandising does not start with **Star Wars**. A decade before Luke Skywalker, any self-respecting 007 fan would be woken by his James Bond alarm clock, lift his head from his James Bond pillowcase, get clean with his James Bond bubblebath and dry off with his James Bond towel. Survival rations for the school day would be cunningly concealed in a James Bond lunchbox and though the toy Walther PPK, silencer and handcuffs would probably get lifted by Headmaster No and his henchmen at the school gates, there would be some Q-supplied weaponry in reserve. In practised hands 007 rubber bands (Super Quality! Multicoloured!) were deadly up to five yards.

Those toys, games and knick-knacks from the early **Sean Connery** era were the launchpad for what has become a massive industry in James Bond memorabilia and collectables. An industry that ranges from rare first editions of **Ian Fleming**'s books to *Moonraker* bubblegum cards and Jaws masks.

In 1998 **Christie**'s hosted the UK's first major James Bond auction. The 272 lots that went under the hammer included props, clothing, posters and toys, mostly from private collections, like that of Graham Rye, president of the James Bond International Fan Club. Rye made £61,750 from one item alone: **Oddjob's bowler hat**. It went to an anonymous telephone buyer after a frantic eight-way bid.

More than £500,000 was raised in total, though it was the props that attracted the serious money. The **Rolex Oyster Perpetual** watch that Roger Moore wore in *Live And Let Die* went for £28,150. Seven gold bullets used in the advertising campaign for *The Man With The Golden Gun* sold for £1,500. Each. Q actor Desmond Llewellyn was an interested observer, especially when he realised he was dressed in the suit he'd worn in *The Living Daylights*. 'When I saw the prices that some things were getting, I was tempted to strip off and put it up for auction,' he said.

You don't have to be an anonymous squillionaire with a penchant for lethal bowlers to start a James Bond collection, though, clearly, it helps. The sheer breadth of the market, plus the

fact that some merchandising was made in very high numbers and very low quality, means there's plenty out there at affordable prices. With an incredible number of people wishing to sell and buy, you certainly won't be alone.

So what follows is a rough guide to the essential collectables of the world's least secret agent, with some estimations of price, a few indications of availability, and the occasional friendly reminder of what the compulsion to own a 12-inch figurine of **Ursula Andress** says about so many of us.

As worn by Urs, that £35,000 bikini ▲

Toys and games

007: The Aston Martin DB5 is the grandaddy of all Bond paraphernalia. Launched in 1964 by British die-cast manufacturer **Corgi**, it had all the features in miniature of the car Sean Connery drove in *Goldfinger*. Machine guns at the front, pop-up bulletproof shield at the rear, revolving number plates and, best of all, the ejector seat that at the flick of the switch sent the villain over the room, under the sofa and through the crack in the floorboards where he would never be seen again.

It's been re-issued over and over again in the intervening years – you could probably pick up a new one from Toys'R'Us tomorrow – but the real collector's piece is from the first issue. Plenty were made, but most were played with, which means few are in a condition of which Q would approve. Somebody who was sad enough to keep it in a box all these years would now expect to get no less than £300. A pristine boxed example, autographed by Desmond Llewellyn with the line 'I never joke about my work, 007', sold for £700 at the Christie's auction.

006: The James Bond attaché case was, in the words of one collector, 'the Holy Grail' of his childhood. This little box of lethal tricks was manufactured by **Gilbert**, maker of many Bond-related toys, and was first issued on the back of *From Russia With Love*, just in time for Christmas 1964. It contained everything the junior spy could possibly desire – a handgun with attachments to make a rifle with telescopic sights, red plastic bullets that popped out feebly, passport, foreign currency, confidential code book, even handy business cards stamped '007'. The only thing it lacked was the makings of a dry martini. An original set in good condition could change hands for around £1,200.

005: Of the many **James Bond board games** that were launched in the mid-1960s, one really stands out. This was

Triang's **Largo vs James Underwater Battle**, launched in 1965 to coincide with *Thunderball*. You could play by the rules if you wished, but the best bit was the beautifully detailed frogmen figures, to be used wherever and however your imagination dictated. The bath mainly. **Triang** was based in Hampshire and a number of games have surfaced there recently, often in mint condition, from former Triang employees. Expect to pay at least £250.

004: Gilbert's James Bond doll, complete with miniature cap-firing pistol, was first released in 1964. It was reissued a year later in *Thunderball* guise, Bond's black suit giving way to shorts, snorkel and flippers. An **Oddjob companion doll** came out at the same time, first in a butler suit, then in karate gear. The dolls alone now change hands for around £200, and a mint condition boxed example of the rarer Oddjob would cost twice that much.

003: Corgi's long-standing relationship with Bond produced a series of classic toys beyond the Aston Martin, many of which have been reissued and are widely available. Good condition first issues of the **1967 rocket-firing Toyota 2000GT** from *You Only Live Twice* are priced up to £200. The real rarity, though, is the **OHMSS set of Corgi Rocket miniature cars**, launched in small numbers in 1970 and never re-issued. Don't expect any change from £2,000 if you do stumble across a good set.

002: The Gilbert 007 road was the Scalextric alternative for James Bond fans. Launched in 1965, working examples now sell for £300 and a really good example can fetch twice that.

001: To the despair of dealers and the delight of collectors, Airfix has recently reissued **Little Nellie**. Unmade kits of the *You Only* *Live Twice* **autogyro** had been selling for up to £300 until then.

A cap-firing Bond is worth a bit (£200) but a rare Oddjob could net twice as much

The nerd who kept his DB5 in its box has the last laugh – it could fetch £300 now ▲

Books

It shouldn't cost you a fortune to build a complete James Bond library, but then again, it could. First editions of Fleming' novels are now highly prized collector items and change hands rarely, a eye-watering prices. But just so that you know what you're looking for when you browse through the boxes in boot sales and house clearances with a hopeful heart, here are seven tips.

007: The first edition of the first book, **Casino Royale**, with cover design by Fleming, is extremely rare. The original print run in April 1953 was only 4,750 copies and you can pa anything up to £10,000 for one in mint condition. Bu keep your eyes open for the first US paperback edition published by Perma. It was called **You Asked For It** and worth around £120.

006: Rarest of all 007 first editions is Fleming's last full-length (unfinished) work, **The Man With The Golden Gun**. It was published in April 1965 after his death and tweaked to completion by **Kingsley Amis**. The embossed golden gun stamped on the front boards oxidised and the book was recalled, though some copies did manage to get released abroad. Copies of the 'official' first edition change hands for up to £200.

005: A limited edition version of **On Her Majesty's Secret Service** was simultaneously released with the normal first edition. This special edition, however, featured an exclusive portrait of the author by his friend Amerst Villiers on the frontspiece, a clear plastic dust jacket, and all 250 copies were autographed by Fleming. Prices range up to £8,000.

004: From Russia With Love was the first Bond novel with dust-jacket artwork by Richard Chopping, who was responsible for many subsequent covers. The design – Fleming's idea – was a superbly detailed painting of a snubnose Smith & Wesson .38 revolver belonging to his friend **Geoffrey Boothroyd**, a firearms expert and the inspiration for Q. Look out, too, for the Book Club issues. Bond publishers **Jonathan Cape** rejected the first print run and sold the copies to the Club. They're not as valuable as the Jonathan Cape books (up to £1,200), but still highly collectable.

Also collectable, Bond the comic strip from the *Daily Express* (see page 21 & 282) ▲

003: The first 12,500 copies of **Diamonds Are Forever** were released in 1956 with an incorrectly numbered chapter listing. They are worth around £2,500 apiece today. The mistake was corrected in later reprints together with some minor text amendments by Fleming after a cousin of his wife objected to his name being used for one of the villains.

002: Moonraker, the third in the series, featured cover artwork by Kenneth Lewis from a Fleming design, and pristine first edition copies are now worth £5,000-plus. Later reprints with black covers and the title embossed in silver foil also fetch good prices. And you can get up to £200 for a copy of Perma's first US paperback edition, entitled **Too Hot To Handle**.

001: Something of an oddity – no Fleming words, no Chopping artwork – **Colonel Sun** was published to mixed reviews in 1968. **Kingsley Amis** wrote it (as Robert Markham) and the cover was the work of Tony Adams, with a generous nod towards Salvador Dali. All melting guns, protruding breasts and dragon-shaped clouds. Very surreal. Fifty quid should be enough for a good first edition. Keep your eyes peeled for another Amis effort, under the nom-de-plume of Lieut-Col William 'Bill' Tanner, **The Book Of Bond** or **Every Man His Own 007**. A mint condition first edition hardback is worth £75-plus.

Recordings

A James Bond collectors' website recently offered for sale a set of original vinyl Bond soundtrack albums, from **Dr. No** to **Licence To Kill**, plus the rare tenth anniversary double album and 12-inch singles of *The Living Daylights* by **a-ha** and *View To A Kill* by **Duran Duran**. All, apparently, in mint condition. The asking price? Just £150.

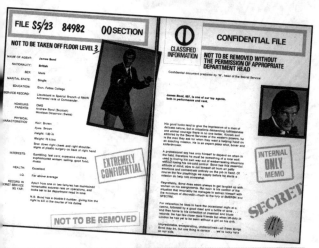

We paid a tenner for this 1979 *Moonraker Special* hardback – well, it is classified ▲

It shouldn't be too hard to track down most of the classic soundtracks on vinyl, and it shouldn't be hard at all to get them on CD. But there are one or two exceptions, and a number of oddities that can add that special flavour to your 007 music collection. Just about everybody strong enough to hold a guitar has recorded something from the 007 repertoire at one stage or another. The artists range from Count Basie to Moby, from the Prague Philharmonic to the Starlite Orchestra And Singers. But though it's one thing to own Lulu's version of the 'The Man With The ·Golden Gun', it's quite another to own Alice Cooper's and Liza Minnelli's rendition.

007 Never Say Never Again: No official soundtrack album for **Sean Connery**'s last – and unofficial – outing as Bond was produced at the time of the film's release in 1983. But there were

me Japanese bootleg issues and a more widely circulated pirate assette version a few years later, both of which are worth a few ob. It wasn't until 1992, though, that Silva Screen Records eleased a legitimate CD of **Michel Legrand**'s jazz score, with ome bonus tracks from the original recording sessions.

06 Casino Royale: The spoof James Bond featured a sound-rack composed by **Burt Bacharach** with **Herb Albert** and the ijuana Brass performing the title theme. It's as 1960s as, well, urt Bacharach, with the undoubted highlight being **Dusty pringfield**'s whispery, wistful version of 'The Look Of Love'.

05 Shaken And Stirred: The David Arnold James Bond roject CD was released in 1997 to rave reviews. Arnold, who ad written the *Tomorrow Never Dies* soundtrack, collaborated vith an eclectic group of artists – from Leftfield to Iggy Pop nd Pulp – to produce a compilation of reworked classic Bond hemes. 'I've heard hundreds of different versions and interp-etations of my music, but this is the only one to add anything to t,' said composer John Barry. The Propellerheads' 'On Her Majesty's Secret Service' is probably the pick of the tracks and vas also released as a single with three different mixes.

04 The Best Of James Bond 30th Anniversary Collection: Released in 1992 and still the best 007 compilation round, this has all the classic songs and great singers, plus 'For Your Eyes Only' by Sheena Easton. Best of all it has Dionne Warwick singing 'Mr Kiss Kiss Bang Bang', which was only used as an instrumental in the film. A limited edition version vith extra tracks, including the 'Laser Beam' music from *Goldfinger* and Shirley Bassey's take on 'Mr Kiss Kiss Bang Bang' s also worth looking out for.

007 by Yaroslav Horvak, one of Bond's comic strip creators (see page 21 & 279) ◄

003 From Russia With Love: John Barry composed 11 Bon' soundtracks but this was his first, although the title song wa actually written by **Lionel Bart** of *Oliver!* fame. It was sung b **Matt Monro**, aka 'the singing bus conductor' and the sing reached 20th spot in the UK charts in November 1963. A goo condition 45 from the first issue should cost around £5.

002 Dr. No: Introducing **Monty Norman**'s classic Jam Bond theme, one of the world's most instantly recognisab pieces of music and used to death on countless 007 fan website The highlight of this album is surely Sean Connery's rendition 'Underneath The Mango Tree'.

001 Octopussy: Reckoned something of a return to form fc Barry after *Moonraker*, the original A&M CD release from 198 is now almost impossible to find following a product recall an failure to re-release. Going rate now is £150-ish. Rather bette value for money is Rykodisc's 1997 reissue which has thre bonus tracks and dialogue from the film, one of which is Q explanation of the acid pen. The spin-off single, 'All Time High was sung by Rita Coolidge with lyrics provided by Tim Rice.

Top trumps: forget Pokemon, these have far more currency with Bond fans

Websites

With the number of web pages about James Bond now numbering into the millions, separating the wheat from the chaff can be a time-consuming exercise. So we've done the leg work for you. Here are the best, and in a few cases the weirdest, sites dedicated to everything 007.

General

The Art Of James Bond www.artofjamesbond.com

We particularly liked the Ken Adams section explaining the genius behind the early Bond film sets. But there are many, many, more gems here, including some fantastic illustrations of Bond novels serialised in Playboy.

Marciniak's Place www.marciniak.com/index.html

Hard to resist any site which offers such treasures as 'the On Her Majesty's Secret Service' tapestry contest. There's also a comprehensive list of Bond related literature, a must for the serious aficionado. This is, after all, one of the few places on the web you read about Israel's answer to 007.

James Bond Multimedia www.jamesbondmm.co.uk

The women, the cars, the gadgets and a few 'fascinating' facts; did you know that Richard Kiel could only wear his metal teeth for 30 seconds at a time as Jaws, otherwise he was in agony?

00 Heaven www.00heaven.org

Nothing flashy (or requiring you to update your version of Flash) just everything you need to know about the Bond author, stars, films, books and women.

007 Database www.007database.com

If the Bond phenomenon appeals to you because of the eye candy for both men and women, this comprehensive database isn't for you as it's all info and no pictures.

Make Mine A 007 http://home.earthlink.net/~atomic_rom/007/intro.htm

Perhaps taking the fascination with Bond just that bit too far, here you'll find an exhaustive examination of Bond's drinking habits on page and screen, although you'll doubtless head straight for the recipe section.

The Ultimate James Bond Website www.crosswinds.net/~jb007ohmss/

Includes another theory as to why Fleming chose 007 as Bond's code; this time it's because it was the number of the bus route which went past his home.

007 Forever www.007forever.com

Comprehensive resource and the place to go if you want to find out about up-and-coming Bond weekends (US-based), which offer a chance to meet Bond stars.

Kuroshin.org www.kuro5hin.org/story/2002/7/15/16126/6536
'Technology and culture from the trenches' is the motto. Well, from their trenches, the people behind this site have produced an entertaining essay on Bond which no fan can afford to miss.

Ian Fleming

Mr. Kiss Kiss Bang Bang www.ianfleming.org/index.shtml
The official site for the Ian Fleming Foundation, its aim being to preserve Fleming's legacy.
007 www.klast.net/bond/fleming.html
A selection of articles about Fleming, including his fascinating connection to Swindon.
Her Majesty's Secret Servant www.hmss.com
Despite a dubious mock-Bond homepage, the book section has a number of useful articles about Mr Fleming, including how he defeated writer's block when he first began *Casino Royale* and an essay on the semiotics of Bond which isn't as daft or as pretentious as you might expect from the title.
Red Flame www.redflame93.com/Fleming.html
Fleming, Rudolf Hess and Aleister Crowley. A strange site which suggests the eccentric sinister Crowley was the inspiration for Bond villains and may have offered to help Fleming interrogate Hitler's deputy Rudolf Hess. This is the kind of obscure gem of a site which makes the Internet such an intriguing cyberplace to travel.
Counterpunch www.counterpunch.org/bond1.html
Worth a visit just to read the essay on Fleming and Bond by Alexander Cockburn, the site's co-founder. Vanity Fair writer Christopher Hitchens' encomium to Bond is also worth reading. You can find it on http://books.guardian.co.uk/Print/0,3858,4375624,00.html.

The Bonds

Sean Connery http://seanconnery.com/index.cfm
Sir Sean's official site, yet he felt the need to dedicate an area to the paintings of his wife, Micheline. All very touching but not what Bond and Connery fans want. Instead try www.sean-connery.co.uk.
George Lazenby www.angelfire.com/nm/lazenbyland
With only one Bond film to his name it's hardly surprising there are only a limited number of Lazenby sites on the web. But Lazenbyland is the most comprehensive, despite the picture of Lazenby as an Evel Knievel figure on the homepage.
Roger Moore www.therisingeyebrow.com

The name alone makes this a must for Moore fans. There's also the official site www.rogermoore.com which comes complete with 'experimental chat room'.

Timothy Dalton www.klast.net/bond/dalton.html

This general 007 site has all the usual info and news on Dalton, before and after Bond.

Pierce Brosnan www.klast.net/bond/brosnan.html

Considering Pierce is the current 007, you'd expect a wealth of fan sites. No such luck, but check out this site to discover, amongst other things, how Pierce came to be Bond.

Bond No. 6 http://uk.geocities.com/thenext007uk/

Speculation mounts as to who will eventually take the Bond baton from Brosnan, with possibilities according to this site ranging from Clive Owen to Russell Crowe.

The books

The James Bond novels and stories www.klast.net/bond/novels.html

The books reviewed and rated, from Fleming to Amis, Gardner and Bond.

Bondian www.bondian.com

Bills itself as a 'field guide' to Ian Fleming's character but it's more fun than that. One of the few sites which can tell you about Bond's publishing history in the Czech republic.

The movies

James Bond www.jamesbond.com

High-tech to the point of being annoying (especially if you haven't got the right version of Flash) but also fairly detailed. The official 007 gateway, this now comes complete with Miss Moneypenny's rolodex and is a good place to find trailers and do a bit of Bond-related-shopping although when we paid a visit the Bond store was closed, presumably temporarily.

John Barry soundtracks www.filmtracks.com/composers/barry.shtml

Probably the best guide to the life and works of the musical maestro.

Bond & Beyond www.bondandbeyond.com/html/interviews/desmondllewelyn.htm

There can be no Bond book without direction to an interview with Desmond Llewelyn.

Richard Kiel www.richardkiel.com

Apart from the usual stuff (bios, interviews and a chance to buy his new book) there's also a 'testimony' from the actor about how God saved him from 'the bondage of alcoholism'.

So farewell then Mr Bond...

It seems appropriate, at this juncture, to allow 007 and his associates a few closing remarks

001 "The name's Bond, James Bond" JAMES BOND, DR. NO

002 "Names is for tombstones, baby!" MR BIG, LIVE AND LET DIE

003 "What, no small talk? No chit-chat? That's the trouble with the world today. No one takes the time to give a really sinister interrogation any more" JAMES BOND, GOLDENEYE

004 "It's just a hat, darling, belonging to a small man of limited means who lost a fight with a chicken" JAMES BOND, LIVE AND LET DIE

005 "My dear girl, don't flatter yourself. What I did this evening was strictly for Queen and Country! You don't think it gave me any pleasure do you?" JAMES BOND, THUNDERBALL

006 "If I want sarcasm, Mr Tanner, I'll talk to my children, thank you very much" M, GOLDENEYE

007 "Farewell Mr Bond. That word has, I must admit, a welcome ring of permanence about it" CARL STROMBERG, THE SPY WHO LOVED ME